MAVERICKS ON THE BORDER

MAVERICKS
ON THE
BORDER

THE EARLY SOUTHWEST
IN HISTORICAL FICTION AND FILM

J. DOUGLAS CANFIELD

THE UNIVERSITY PRESS OF KENTUCKY

Publication of this volume was made possible in part by
a grant from the National Endowment for the Humanities.

Scholarly publisher for the Commonwealth,
serving Bellarmine College, Berea College, Centre
College of Kentucky, Eastern Kentucky University,
The Filson Club Historical Society, Georgetown College,
Kentucky Historical Society, Kentucky State University,
Morehead State University, Transylvania University,
University of Kentucky, University of Louisville,
and Western Kentucky University.
All rights reserved.

Editorial and Sales Offices: The University Press of Kentucky
663 South Limestone Street, Lexington, Kentucky 40508–4008

01 02 03 04 05   5 4 3 2 1

Library of Congress Cataloging-in-Publication Data

Canfield, J. Douglas (John Douglas), 1941-
Mavericks on the border : the early Southwest in historical fiction
and film / J. Douglas Canfield.
p.   cm.
Includes bibliographical references (p.   ) and index.
ISBN 0-8131-2180-9 (cloth : alk. paper)
1. American fiction—Southwestern States—History and criticism.
2. Historical fiction, American—History and criticism. 3. Mexican-American
Border Region—In literature. 4. Western stories—History and criticism.
5. Western films—History and criticism. 6. Southwestern States in literature.
I. Title.

PS277 .C36 2000
813.009'3279—dc21   00-028310

FOR LINCOLN FALLER

Contents

Acknowledgments

My interest in Faulkner goes back to undergraduate days. I am especially grateful for encouragement received in graduate school from Cleanth Brooks and later from Maynard Mack, who invited me to compile *Twentieth Century Interpretations of Sanctuary.* Thanks also to Joe Blotner, Arthur Kinney, Jack Matthews, and Phil Weinstein for dialogue on Faulkner over the years. And thanks to Thadious Davis and Hortense Spillers for recent advice.

This book probably began in germ on a trip to Taos and the Kit Carson Museum. Guests of Lincoln Faller and his wife Kathleen, my family and I took several side trips into Carson country, and Lincoln encouraged me to pursue my interpretation of Carson as a multicultural polyglot who made a fatal decision to identify with John C. Frémont, Senator Thomas Hart Benton, and Manifest Destiny. The gist of that argument has been published separately. But it initiated my fascination with how twentieth-century authors and film-makers have repeatedly placed protagonists in these Southwest Borderlands facing existential crises of identity and ideology. For Lincoln's encouragement all along the way—for the time he generously gave me, often into the wee hours, discussing these ponderous things—this book is dedicated to him.

I am grateful to L.D. Clark, Jane Coleman, Montserrat Fontes, David Morrell, and Bob Houston—all of whom generously discussed their work with me when they must have felt like bridegrooms trapped by some mad mariner, growing more ancient and gray by the day.

I am grateful to my department head, Larry Evers, and my dean, Chuck Tatum, both of whom toil in these fields, for important leads and for support both moral and institutional.

I am grateful to Armando José Prats, whom I met over e-mail discussing his important work and who gave me extraordinarily generous and detailed and helpful readings of this manuscript. *Gracias, compadre.*

I am grateful to students in a graduate class at the University of Arizona at the beginning of this project and to students in an undergraduate class at its conclusion for grappling with its texts, its concepts, and its obsessed projector.

I am grateful to several research assistants—Keith Anderson, Amy Murphy, Elise Marrubio, Danika Brown, and especially Paul Burkhardt— for help tracking in the wilderness.

And finally, I am profoundly grateful to my family (not just immediate, but mediate in-laws as well), who were literally a captive audience, made not just to listen to my ravings but to watch Westerns until they vowed to eschew the genre for the rest of their lives. Some have already headed east.

INTRODUCTION

Life on the frontier is a way of imagining the self
in a boundary situation—a place that will put you
to some kind of ultimate test.

Jane Tompkins, *West of Everything*

It is not enough to stand on the opposite river bank,
shouting questions. . . . It is not a way of life. At
some point, on our way to a new consciousness,
we will have to leave the opposite bank . . . so that
we are on both shores at once and, at once, see
through serpent and eagle eyes.

Gloria Anzaldúa, *Borderlands/La Frontera*

The American hero in the early Southwest traditionally rides out of the
Southeast to wrest fame and fortune in the midst of violent contending
forces on the border between cultures: Indian, Hispanic, Anglo. I am interested in a series of figures, portrayed by twentieth-century artists in historical fiction and film, who on this border are, as Jane Tompkins puts it in the
first epigraph, exposed to "some kind of ultimate test," are faced with cultural dilemmas that compel them to make extraordinary existential choices.

Some explanation of terms is in order. By "historical" I mean fiction
and film that situate their stories in real historical situations and events. By
"early Southwest" I mean that period of which 1833 is the beginning, "the
year the stars fell," as Faulkner puts it—an event (the Leonid meteor shower)
remarked upon within a couple of these works and signifying an ominous
beginning at around the time Faulkner's patriarchs carved out of the wilderness their plantations and bequeathed to their heirs the sins contaminat-
ing them or the necessity of moving on to new wildernesses, especially in
the West. The terminal date is 1917, the year marking the end of the Mexican Revolution, the Wobbly strike in Bisbee, Arizona, and America's entry
into the war to end all wars—a year that might be said to mark the end of

the early Southwest and the era of the mountain men, the scalpers, the Apaches, the Buffalo Soldiers, the *villistas,* the gunfighters, and the two-gun sheriffs.

Several twentieth-century authors and filmmakers proffer protagonists faced with existential choices. They have bequeathed to our border culture a pantheon of mavericks, many historically based, all imaginatively conceived as straddling a cultural cusp representative of excruciating dilemma. I have called them existential heroes. In an unpedantic way, let me rehearse a few of the aspects of existentialism, a nonsystematic philosophy available to Western thinkers and writers at least since Nietzsche and Dostoyevsky and significantly availed in the twentieth century.

Instead of arriving on a planet with a clear ontology, humans have evolved shaping their own essence—a task, once conscious, faced with the *fear and trembling* Kierkegaard so well expressed. For they are confronted with the awesome task of deciding who and what they are, who and what they will be. In the typical midcentury cliché, then, *existence precedes essence.* Nor is there any universal set of principles—metaphysical or ethical—to guide them. In a radical sense, each individual confronts the choice of identity and the choice of morality *alone*—though some may paradoxically find their answers in a collectivity.

Following Kierkegaard, the Christian existentialist views this absence of absolute meaning to existence as an absurd gulf to be leapt by faith: *credo quia absurdum* ("I believe precisely because it is absurd.") Fideism, though not systematic philosophy or theology, provides an exit. For the secular existentialist, however, there is no exit from absurdity. No effort to philosophize—surely not this modest and cursory one—can redeem us from radical *freedom:* to choose what we will-to-be. Such freedom is a nightmare, causing nausea, perhaps. Or perhaps it is a glorious risk, gambit, gamble. Having no access to the *Ding an sich*—the Essential Thing or Being in Itself—the existential protagonist still may choose to roll Sisyphus's rock toward its summit, as Camus said so memorably, if only to be overwhelmed and have to start again. Few can face such freedom, can be *rebels* against convention, can venture into the void.

Later in the twentieth century, poststructuralist theorists continued the existentialist insight that reality is constructed. One of the most interesting for my purposes here is Julia Kristeva. In her *Powers of Horror* she developed a theory of the *abject,* of that liminal state between constructing consciousness and what Freud called *the reality principle,* the inescapable matter of our being that reasserts itself. Against the abject, one creates selves and systems that make life endurable. The abject manifests itself in the detritus of the body—its secretions and excretions—whose rejection, in the name of filth, constitutes the self, the ego with its attendant superego. As Kristeva puts it,

> [R]efuse and corpses *show me* what I permanently thrust aside in order to live. These body fluids, this defilement, this shit are what life withstands, hardly and with difficulty, on the part of death. There, I am at the border of my condition as a living being. My body extricates itself, as being alive, from that border. Such wastes drop so that I might live, until, from loss to loss, nothing remains in me and my entire body falls beyond the limit—*cadere,* cadaver. [. . .] How can I be without border? (3–4)

So the ultimate existential border defines the conscious, myth-making self against Sartre's *néant*—nothingness. Several of the works I treat reduce their protagonists to such states of abjection, and Kristeva's theory of the abject seems to me to have extraordinary explanatory power, especially as we try to understand Richard Slotkin's lifelong theory about the frontier's—and as I focus it, the border's—regeneration through violence.

Regeneration through suffering and sacrifice was another prominent theme of the mid-twentieth century, the time when the consciousness of most of these authors and filmmakers was forged. It was associated with the theory of tragedy, about which much profound was thought and said, from Hegel and Nietzsche in the nineteenth century to Unamuno and Jaspers and Santayana in the early twentieth to Northrop Frye and Richard Sewell at midcentury. Tragedy was a major topic in literature departments in the 1950s and early 1960s. Aristotle's theory of tragedy from *The Poetics* had become again so influential as to trickle down into American high schools, where a generation of students wrestled with the problem of whether *The Death of a Salesman* could be a real tragedy. According to Aristotle, a tragic protagonist must be neither wholly good nor wholly evil but essentially worthy. Aristotle never mentions a *tragic flaw* per se, but he does say that such a protagonist commits a mistake, a *hamartia,* that commits him to the circle of fate surrounding him or her. Such a mistake was often labeled *hubris* in midcentury discussions, an overweening pride that blinds a protagonist (like Oedipus) to the truth. A protagonist's mistakes may bring about disastrous loss, but all is not necessarily lost. One possible interpretation of the ending of *Oedipus Rex* is the lesson, "Through suffering alone does wisdom come." Most of us went on to read *Oedipus at Colonnus,* where the long-suffering protagonist is apotheosized, taken ito the company of the gods themselves.

What the existential philosophers and critics added to Aristotle was the very notion of "boundary-situation" Tompkins employs: protagonists of extraordinary consciousness come face to face with the void, with a cosmos without essence, without essential meaning, free from the sovereignty of mind. Tragic art is born from this shock and its attendant pain transformed into "the condition of suffering—which is the condition of pain and fear contemplated and spiritualized" (Sewell 6). Anthropological theory from Frazier to Frye added another dimension: such suffering is necessary for regeneration, just as autumn is necessary for spring. The king must die. From loss comes, paradoxically, gain. As Wallace Stevens phrased it inimitably, "Death is the mother of beauty," so the protagonist, cursed with consciousness, must accept the "sure obliteration" of the cycle of life and go "downward to darkness on extended wings" ("Sunday Morning").

Not all the works I treat are tragedies: some, like *Buffalo Soldiers* and *Dreams of the Centaur* and *Como agua para chocolate* and the two novels by Jane Coleman, are more a form of romance, in which protagonists triumph over circumstances, even near-total abjection, and prevail, sometimes in real time, sometimes in magical. Others, like *Go Down, Moses* and *Los de abajo,* seem bleakly to shade into satire, where the choices of the protagonists are not redemptive or transformative but either futile or degenerative. But tragedy is central to many, and suffering is endemic to all. And to all but McCarthy's kid, this suffering is not just that of body but that of mind, of consciousness, as they contemplate what Sewell calls "the first (and last) of all questions, the question of existence: What does it mean to be?" (4).

External borders are interesting kinds of voids, of liminal spaces between things that seem to be determined like states and cultures and ideologies. The Southwest border between the United States and Mexico has become a site for the investigation of clashes between force fields, of attempts to negotiate the space between, negotiations the *mestiza* writer and theorist Gloria Anzaldúa calls "crossings." She means crossings of consciousness: "Every increment of consciousness, every step forward is a *travesía,* a crossing. I am again an alien in new territory. [. . .] But if I escape conscious awareness, escape 'knowing,' I won't be moving. Knowledge makes me more aware, it makes me more conscious. 'Knowing' is painful because after 'it' happens I can't stay in the same place and be comfortable. I am no longer the same person I was before" (*Borderlands/La Frontera* 48). Obviously, the border, itself unstable, is always more metaphoric than literal, representing that mental state where worlds collide. But like Anzaldúa, I am especially interested in *this* geographical border, beginning as it does in the confrontation with and attempt to escape from slavery, as the Eastern wilderness dies and heroes move west. As in my second epigraph, Anzaldúa envisions crossings that are successful, like those of several of these mavericks, as they cross into new identities and perhaps bequeath them to others. Other crossings represent a complete going over "the border into a wholly new and separate territory" (79) and essentializing it, going native, if you will. Some pay for their crossings with tragic loss. Some fail to make them successfully, finally dying in an obliteration so sure it leaves a stunning void. Whatever their final dispositions, these mavericks most often represent, soon or late, figures of resistance to oppressors and oppressive histories and codes. Whether they discover adequate ideologies in which to thrive, even their voids are filled with the stuff of legend.

A word about genesis, inclusion, exclusion: after discerning a pattern of existential crossings in several novels and films, I began searching for others. Because as I found more the book began to feel unwieldy, I decided to limit it chronologically to the period of the early Southwest, though I gesture in my epilogue toward other works that continue my theme, including, of course, McCarthy's novel *The Crossing* (set between the World Wars). McCarthy has arguably become canonical in American literature. Canonical also (in literature of the Americas) are Faulkner, Azuela, Fuentes. And such films as *Broken Arrow* and *The Wild Bunch* are canonical in film studies. Several of the works I treat are uncanonical, however, and they may be unfamiliar to many of my readers. But like Blake Allmendinger, who titles his provocative recent book on the Western *Ten Most Wanted: The New Western Literature,* I think it is a good thing to bring fine new "Westerns"— a term whose meaning Allmendinger blessedly extends—to the attention of those interested in the genre. I think it is a good thing to cross the border and call attention to fine work done in Spanish. I think it is a good thing to juxtapose canonical with uncanonical (to sandwich L.D. Clark between Faulkner and McCarthy, Esquivel between Azuela and Fuentes), to juxtapose elite with popular (films with novels, recent films with classics). Why? Because these are well-crafted new works about important historical events and important themes of identity amid cultural cross-currents.

In the interest of multiculturalism and with an appreciation of the emerging field of border studies, particularly as it concerns Chicano culture, I searched for a fine historical novel or film created by a Chicano/Chicana featuring an existential crossing set in the early Southwest. My good friend (and dean), Charles (Chuck) Tatum, an expert in Chicano literature and culture, put me onto the wonderful new novel by Montserrat Fontes, *Dreams of the Centaur.* Born in Texas, Fontes, whose patronym is Portuguese but who also descends from the Sonoran Elías family, self-identifies as a "Chicana writer."[1] Aware of the importance of gender in the macho terrain of the Western (Tompkins opines that "the Western is [. . .] antifeminist; it [. . .] worships the phallus" [28]), I searched for works with women protagonists, preferably written by women and preferably offering a feminist tonic to the machismo. I knew about Esquivel, but Fontes and Jane Candia Coleman were great discoveries, both creating, like Esquivel, women protagonists whose consciousnesses were similarly agonized but differently conceived. Because she has created *two* such rare protagonists in two novels set in the period, Coleman has merited two chapters.

I searched too for works that exposed not just the mistreatment but the *enslavement* of Indians (the Yaquis in *Dreams of the Centaur*), for this unpleasant reality has been swept under the rug all too long; works that remind us too of atrocities committed not just against the "other" but against versions of the self (Texas Unionists in *A Bright Tragic Thing* and the Wobblies in *Bisbee 17*). I was lucky enough to find at least some of what I was after; I am sure I have missed some; others just did not fit the pattern I was writing about—either thematically or chronologically. For not every historical "Western" set in the Southwest Borderlands during this classic period focuses on an existential crossing, with the requisite consciousness, the requisite angst.[2]

What about protagonists portrayed by John Wayne—in, for example, *Red River* or *The Searchers*? I find the resolution of conflict in those films sentimental, frankly. But I have included David Morrell's *Last Reveille,* whose protagonist, Morrell says in the introduction to the reprint, was modeled on Wayne: it is as if Wayne were finally provided a decent script posthumously.

By common consent, Azuela and Faulkner are considered proto-existentialists. As with artists generally, they were there before the theorists conceptualized the movement. The rest of the works I treat all hail from the second half of the twentieth century, beginning with *Broken Arrow* in 1950. It is as if it took half a century before the Frederick Jackson Turner thesis about the frontier—that it formed the American character into a figure of self-reliance, a figure that confirmed our cultural strength and superiority—could be challenged in fiction and film. One might profitably contrast two 1949–1950 films about Apaches: *Ambush* and *Broken Arrow.* In the former, there is no questioning of the moral and cultural authority of the Anglo hero, and the Apache chief is named Diablito! In the latter, the Anglo hero's sense of self and of cultural superiority are radically destabilized; authority is at least shared between General Howard and Cochise, who break the arrow together. Even then, the audience knows that the peace did not last and that the Chiricahuas were eventually run off their land. It could perhaps be said that with *The Wild Bunch* in 1969 Sam Peckinpah took the next major step in problematizing the Turner thesis in film. The "Western" has never been the same, but not just because of slow-motion violence: In these works there is a new metaphysic afoot. God's not in his heaven (at least not apparently), and all's not right with the world. O cursed spite that ever these mavericks were born to set it right.

If most of the works I treat are from the 1980s and 1990s, then I say hooray for the New Western Literature! I hope I have contributed to Allmendinger's project of "animating and enlarging the field by finding new texts to read" (7). I am not so much interested in increasing the canon per se, however, as I am in the project, from the theorist Antonio Gramsci to the novelist Toni Morrison, of reconstituting history through popular memory at work in literature and film. I am profoundly moved by the way in which that project enables us to confront aspects of our historical selves that we forget at our peril. And in the works I treat, I am profoundly moved by the ways in which the very (comforting) concept of the self is problematized.

I am aware of critiques of Anzaldúa's treatment of the border by privileging the marginal, the liminal, essentializing them into a transcendent *mestizaje* (mixedness).[3] Unlike other recent books in border studies, however, this is not a book about the border as a liminal space for Chicanos (see José Saldívar's *Border Matters,* for example). Important as that work is, it does not tell the whole story of border crossings. I am trying to tell another part of that story, borrowing critical concepts from Anzaldúa and others. But mine is not a coherent narrative. It follows no archetype from oppression and exclusion to resistance and liberation. It analyzes many different stories. Its rationale is perhaps similar to Russ Castronovo's rationale for making an analogy between the Southwest border and the Mason-Dixon line: "Telling this story demands an ambivalent narrative, one that refuses a clear teleological narrative line in favor of a series of competing tales that compromise and undercut one another. Single stories cannot be told because stories do not exist in some sort of fixed isolation, but are instead always bordered by some other story" (216). Like Castronovo, I am wary of the self-serving nature of this kind of study: yet one more Anglo scholar appropriates contested ground as part of cultural imperialism. But I am finally warier of our *not* listening to these various artistic voices and ignoring the stories they still have to tell, tragic as well as romantic. For, however fictionalized and fragmentary, they are part of the vexed histories of the American peoples of the Southwest Borderlands. And like all historical artistic works, they tell us as much about our times as about the earlier times. Obviously, we would not keep writing about this classic period and about this classic setting if they were not profoundly attractive: the West, the wilderness; cowboys and Indians; outlaws and lawmen; Pancho Villa and his Revolution. Perhaps, like the spectacular yet harsh big woods and mountains and canyons and deserts, the figures and the passions with which these artists populate them seem monumental, elemental. Perhaps, as Fuentes and Anzaldúa both suggest in a stunning and memorable image, the border in the Southwest remains a *herida,* a *wound* between cultures, between past and present, that we are still attempting to heal, to cauterize. We are diminished by the grandeur of setting, of *agon,* of Titanic combatants. Ours seems a banal existence by comparison. Yet imagination acts as a whirlwind, wrenching us back to *those thrilling days of yesteryear,* as the Lone Ranger show announced. We watch in fascination and in awe as these protagonists negotiate their crossings—or not—and we realize that we are the ones who must cross cultural and temporal gaps lest they fester into wounds because we have forgotten, neglected them, failed to interpret them aright. We may never get it all right, may never heal all the wounds—between North and South, between Anglo and Indian and Mexican, between law and outlaw. But failure does not relieve us from the responsibility—and the vertiginous thrill—of crossing.

PART I

SOUTH TO WEST

In these first three novels, I begin in the postbellum South, that part of it that was called the West, at least until Anglo expansion moved into Mexican territory. It was the Reconstruction era, when African American southerners struggled with their new freedom and Anglo-American southerners struggled with their humiliation and their consciences at the same time.

I begin with Faulkner's Ike McCaslin in Mississippi, hunter par excellence chasing a dying wilderness and its ideals, choosing to live as a maverick on the margins of society alone and celibate rather than accept a heritage tainted with slavery but finally failing to transcend it. Following the typical migratory pattern of movement from the South to the Southwest and traveling backward in time to the Civil War itself, I move west to L.D. Clark's Todd Blair, son of a Texas Unionist who had migrated to the Cross Timbers country of north Texas to find land and elbow room—and to escape the same curse of slavery—only to be hanged by the Rebels. Todd must choose a course of action, a choice complicated by his falling in love with the daughter of the Rebel commander. Finally in this part, I travel even further back in time to follow Cormac McCarthy's "kid" west across the borderlands with a marauding troop of post–Mexican War Indian scalpers till he confronts choice and must wrestle with the judge who would not let him escape the code of the savage warrior.

While Faulkner's novel refers to actions both before and after the classic period of the Old Southwest, and while Clark's novel is narrated retrospectively from sometime in the 1930s in the New Southwest, the main action of all three novels occurs in that tempestuous, mythic era in American history of the second half of the nineteenth century—the cataclysmic time of the Civil War, the Mexican-American War, the Indian Wars.

1

IKE McCASLIN'S FAILED CROSSING

GO DOWN, MOSES

> Epic song and tragic disclosure have traditionally
> had as their purpose a restoration of a lost unity.
> Through their intervention, we are guaranteed to
> regain it. The Faulknerian intervention accepts the
> possibility of a return to equilibrium. . . . This
> intervention extends into multiplicity, into what we
> would call the suspension of identity. Into the
> inextricable, which is its boundless home.
>
> Edouard Glissant, *Faulkner, Mississippi*

In *Go Down, Moses* (1942) William Faulkner creates Ike McCaslin as a
maverick on the border between two heritages, one white, the other mixed.
Ike attempts to cross over from the former into the latter. In doing so he
attempts not just a repudiation of his Anglo heritage but a restitution to
those black members of his family cursed by his grandfather—and by the
system of slavery itself. Ike ultimately fails to cross over, and he fails to
return the world to "equilibrium," as Glissant puts it in the above epigraph.
Ike cannot escape his contamination.

Then he was sixteen. It was December and Ben, Lion, and Sam were
dead. So Ike had to read those ledgers instead of waiting till "some idle day
when he was old" (*Go Down, Moses* 256). Because he was caught between
cultures and had to decide which legacy he was going to accept. For like
Sam Fathers, Ike "Had-Two-Fathers" (160)—at least two: his natural father, Theophilus ("Uncle Buck") McCaslin, son of the founder of the
McCaslin plantation, old Carothers himself; and his spiritual father, Sam,
who raised him to be a great hunter and heir to the Chickasaws and their
respect for the land. From each father, Ike receives a legacy. Because of its
contamination, Ike repudiates one heritage and chooses another, ostensibly

more pure. Ironically, however, Ike's choice is absurd, for every legacy, even the Indian, is empty, as signified in images of empty vessels.[1]

Ike understands the legacy bequeathed him by Sam, "his spirit's father" (311). He has been "consecrated" to it for years now (159). But he does not yet understand the McCaslin patrimony. What horrifies him most Faulkner stresses in italics: that his grandfather Carothers refused to acknowledge a bastard mulatto son and that he committed incest with Tomey, "*[h]is own daughter*" (259). What saddens Ike most is the absence of love, or at least the acknowledgment of love: "*But there must have been love* he thought. *Some sort of love. Even what he would have called love: not just an afternoon's or a night's spittoon*" (258). He reflects now on Tomey's mother Eunice's suicide: "he seemed to see her actually walking into the icy creek on that Christmas day six months before her daughter's and her lover's (*Her first lover's* he thought. *Her first*) child was born, solitary, inflexible, griefless, ceremonial" (259). The clue to the crime revealed in the ledgers is that Eunice was bought in New Orleans for $650. As Ike speculates, the truth strikes him, and the pages of their own accord flip "back to that one where the white man (not even a widower then) who never went anywhere anymore than his sons in their time ever did and who did not need another slave, had gone all the way to New Orleans and bought one" (259). And he must also wonder why Carothers would have paid so much just for a wife for the slave Thucydus, whom she did not marry for two years. In typical fashion, Faulkner burdens the reader with co-creation of the narrative. Maybe Carothers went down to New Orleans to buy himself a concubine. But why would a married man, and one who never traveled, who did not need another slave girl but could have taken anyone he wanted, go to all that trouble and in broad daylight, so to speak? It must have been some kind of status symbol to have a concubine of incredible beauty. Perhaps it was also the white man's attraction to the exotic, erotic other who supplants the proper but passionless southern matron. Ike is incapable of acknowledging, much less articulating such desire. It remains the South's dark secret. He cannot even imagine a relationship that is strictly subject-object. Ike projects love to cover shame: just as Carothers was Eunice's first lover, he must have loved her too.

But being white (and perhaps still "unwidowered"), Carothers could not acknowledge any subject-to-subject relationship (Ike seems to think) and married Eunice off to a black as soon as she was pregnant with Tomey. Whatever his motivation, however, Carothers callously displaces one concubine only to supplant her with her and his own daughter. Following Uncle Buddy, Ike sees Eunice's response to the incest as a repudiation, a repudiation he must emulate. For he has discovered that his paternal legacy is empty.

The mystified ideology of Southern aristocracy is symbolized by Carothers's great House: an edifice that is a monument to the white man's vanity and rapacity and fanatical myth of racial purity. It is a House that Carothers contaminates not so much with incest as with denial of subjecthood to humans he uses and discards. The image of the spittoon is apt. McCaslin's is a House that Carothers's twin sons, Buck and Buddy, out of their own shame at their father, abandon to the blacks, a gesture that Ike's mother's seduction of his father into reinhabiting (having evicted the blacks) makes meaningless. It is a House in which Zack Edmonds, Carothers's grandson through a female line and inheritor of the plantation through Ike's eventual default, repeats Carothers's original act of summoning a black woman and keeping her, in which Zack and his black cousin Lucas Beauchamp, descendent of Tomey, contend over that woman, who is Lucas's wife Molly, and finally into which Zack's son Carothers ("Roth") Edmonds refuses to bring his even quite "light-colored" black kin-mistress (321), thus recapitulating not only his namesake's miscegenation and incest but his denial. In other words, the McCaslin House is never a home in which even lovers and kin can live together because of a senseless, meaningless, empty racial myth. Throughout *Go Down, Moses,* Faulkner stresses this point by juxtaposing the House against the homes of the blacks, because these homes have fire in the hearth, what Faulkner calls in the story that gives the novel its title, "the ancient symbol of human coherence and solidarity" (361). The McCaslin House, on the contrary, is empty of the purity it promises.[2]

Ike has another heritage from the whites, a maternal legacy, given to him by another of his many fathers, his mother's brother and his "godfather" (287), Hubert Fitz-Hubert Beauchamp. The name itself reflects the vain pretensions of the southern aristocracy, as does the name of the Beauchamp house, which Ike's mother Sophonisba (Sibbey) "still insisted that people call Warwick because her brother was if truth but triumphed and justice but prevailed the rightful earl of it" (288). But this house too is empty of the nobility it pretends to enclose, that the family genealogy promises. For despite his self-righteousness in refusing to allow "on his place" Tomey's Turl, Carothers McCaslin's son-grandson, "that damn white half-McCaslin" (6), when Sibbey leaves to marry Buck, Uncle Hubert takes into his house, in Sibbey's own dress, a black lover—but not as a wife, even though he hypocritically protests, "They're free now! They're folks too just like we are!"; even though Faulkner emphasizes that the woman is "lighter in color" than Turl himself (289). And she too is evicted, a victim of Sibbey's wrath and the white man's racial myth. The emptiness of "Warwick," "the very citadel of respectability," is symbolized by "the cold unswept hearth" (290) and by its actual, physical emptiness: Uncle Hubert is forced to sell off the "fine furnishings" (288) as his whole way of life decays—even while he continues to foxhunt—until the "almost completely empty house" (291) burns down so fast that Faulkner again seems to stress its lack of substance.

Of course, Ike inherits a more specific bequest from Uncle Hubert: "a Legacy, a Thing, possessing weight to the hand and bulk to the eye and even audible: a silver cup filled with gold pieces and wrapped in burlap and sealed with his godfather's ring in the hot wax, which (intact still) even before his Uncle Hubert's death and long before his own majority, when it would be his, had become not only a legend but one of the family lares" (287). In other words, this is a legacy that has also been mystified, that pretends to hold a Divine Presence, a Promise of Worth. It is a Silver Chalice, a Holy Grail. But there is no Divine Presence, no indwelling spirit in either of these houses, and Faulkner underlines its absence in the slow melting away of the substance within the cup and finally of the cup itself into not a Chalice of Promise but a practical coffeepot filled with Worthless coppers and eternally unredeemable IOUs (at 20 percent per annum), written in all the amazed self-deception of "what dreamed splendid recoup" and signed "as the old proud earl himself might have scrawled Nevile" (293).

Thus the legacies Ike receives from his white progenitors are empty myths of aristocratic purity, of noble lineage, of inherent worth. And thus in his no-man's-land between possible identities, Ike rejects the text of the ledgers into which he was born and chooses instead Sam's seemingly rich, full, meaningful patrimony. He becomes the priest of the wilderness, for which role Sam had trained him, "had marked him forever" (171). He becomes the heir to the barren remnant of the Old People, just as Sam had become Jobaker's heir. This legacy seems to promise Divine Presence. Sam's voice is characterized as "the mouthpiece of the host" of the wilderness (165), the spirit that is manifested in the three theophanies Ike is vouchsafed: the phantom buck, whose spirit travels in the same tracks with the yearling so that none but the worthy can see him; the Bear, who first watches Ike unseen then reveals himself when Ike is untainted even as he leads him back into space and time, symbolized by the compass and watch Ike had left behind; and finally by the snake, whom Ike salutes in the ancient "tongue of the old fathers" (234). And of course the wilderness is spoken of throughout *Go Down, Moses* as animate with Divine Presence, "musing, inattentive, myriad, eternal, green" (307)—and most important, timeless and deathless. This wilderness was both "mother and father" to Sam and is now Ike's "mother who had shaped him if any had toward the man he almost was" (311).

He becomes that man on the night of his twenty-first birthday when he declares triumphantly to his cousin McCaslin ("Cass") Edmonds, who has been a surrogate father to him, raising him in place of the superannuated Uncle Buck, "Yes. Sam Fathers set me free" (286). Faulkner underscores the fact that this is at once a choice of patrimony and identity, for he continues, "And Isaac McCaslin," a flat declaration of the name with which he begins the entire novel, as if "Uncle Ike" were the *genius loci* of Yoknapatawpha County and the novel's very own Presence (3). After Ike's declaration in the commissary, there follows a discussion of Ike's legacies, especially the Beauchamp, concluding in Ike's move to Jefferson and parting with Cass:

> and gone, and he looking at the bright rustless unstained tin and thinking and not for the first time how much it takes to compound a man (Isaac McCaslin for instance) and of the devious intricate choosing yet unerring path that man's (Isaac McCaslin's for instance) spirit takes among all that mass to make him at last what he is to be, not only to the astonishment of them (the ones who sired the McCaslin who sired his father and Uncle Buddy and their sister, and the ones who sired the Beauchamp who sired his Uncle Hubert and his Uncle Hubert's sister) who believed they had shaped him, but to Isaac McCaslin too. (294–95)

So Ike now really *is* who he is. Whatever house he may thereafter inhabit, we learn in "Delta Autumn" that he finds "the conviction, the sense and feeling of home," only in the woods in November, first in Major de Spain's hunting cabin and then in the tents that follow the dwindling wilderness (335). Ike even becomes identified with the divine wilderness itself: "coevals [. . .] the two spans running out together, not toward oblivion, nothingness, but into a dimension free of both time and space" (337).

"And that was all," we might have expected Faulkner to write. But he did not, as we know. The many ironies of Ike's decision have been often highlighted in criticism. I should not like to conclude, however, with a typical discussion of Ike as failure or copout, of the rightness of wrongness of his choice. I believe there is another way to look at it, through what we should learn from Ike's other father, Cass, and his very important legacy. Not the gun itself, which Ike would "own and shoot [. . .] for almost seventy years, through two new pairs of barrels and locks and one new stock, until all that remained of the original gun was the silver-inlaid trigger-guard with his and McCaslin's engraved names and the date in 1878" (196), but the relationship expressed by that juxtaposition of their names. For throughout the novel Cass is called Ike's surrogate father, "rather his brother than cousin and rather his father than either" (4). At the moment of their parting after Ike's relinquishment Faulkner describes their relationship in poignant terms: Ike is "looking peacefully at McCaslin, his kinsman, his father almost yet no kin now as, at the last, even fathers and sons are no kin" (294). That is, Ike repeats the patriarchal pattern of rebellion of son against father, an Oedipal declaration of independence.

We remember that in the *Saturday Evening Post* version of "The Bear" the figure that talks to Ike about his not being able to shoot Ben *is* his father.[3] And that scene marks the real legacy that Cass bequeaths Ike: the best advice he can give his son even though like all sons Ike is doomed to reject it. For Cass is not a total skeptic or cynic. He understands and sympathizes with Ike. We learn at the end of "The Old People" that Cass too has been vouchsafed a vision of the phantom buck; he too shares Ike's pantheism. But I think he recognizes it for what it is. Cass first reads Keats's "Ode on a Grecian Urn" to Ike when Ike is fourteen and has been unable to shoot Old Ben. And many critics have quoted Cass's lines about the poem: "*He was talking about truth. Truth is one. It doesn't change. It covers all things which touch the heart—honor and pride and pity and justice and courage and love. [. . .] They all touch the heart, and what the heart holds to becomes truth, as far as we know truth*" (283–84). It is extremely important to note the context of this exchange and to try to interpret the "*truth*" Cass sees embodied in Keats's "Ode."

Cass focuses not on the final lines of the poem about Beauty and Truth but on the second stanza. He quotes only the last two lines, but it is worthwhile to recall the whole:

> Heard melodies are sweet, but those unheard
>> Are sweeter; therefore, ye soft pipes, play on;
> Not to the sensual ear, but, more endear'd,
>> Pipe to the spirit ditties of no tone:
> Fair youth, beneath the trees, thou canst not leave
>> Thy song, nor ever can those trees be bare;

> Bold lover, never, never canst thou kiss,
>   Though winning near the goal—yet, do not grieve;
>   She cannot fade, though thou hast not thy bliss,
>   For ever wilt thou love, and she be fair!

The transcendent truth Cass means is that major theme of these lines and of Keats's poetry in general: the desire for transcendence itself. The unheard melodies are sweeter because they can be imagined as whatever we want. We can fill the blanks with our desire. And we can pretend there is no time, no change, no death. Ike is like the "Fair youth, beneath the trees" who wants the moment to last forever, but as Faulkner says later about Ike's moment of "glory" with his wife, such a moment "inherently of itself cannot last and hence why glory" (311). Cass understands that the Grecian Urn is an expression of desire and is thus itself a vessel full of significance but essentially empty, a symbol of the eternal absence of Presence.[4]

Now let us reinterpret Ike's existential decision. First, the context into which Faulkner introduces the allusion to Keats is that point in the discussion between Cass and Ike where Ike has just asserted that the blacks "are better than we are" (281), not only because of their virtues but "'what they got not only not from white people but not even despite white people because they had it already from the old free fathers a longer time free than us because we have never been free—' and it was in McCaslin's eyes too" (282), that is, the remembrance of Cass's citing Keats seven years ago. Why introduce the story now? Why not tell it immediately after the episode of the fyce, as Faulkner did in the other version of "The Bear"? Because it serves here not only to explain why Ike does not want Ben to die but also to imply that he is engaging in the same kind of mystification about the "old free fathers." Whether uttered by the Indians in Faulkner's stories about them or by Lucas in "The Fire and the Hearth" or Sam or Ike or the narrator himself, such words are only the signs of desire, a willful nostalgia, a longing for transcendence at least in the past, like all myths of a Golden Age, of Eden, of pure Origin (Glissant would add Genesis). For when we see some of the "old free fathers," like Ikkemotubbe and Moketubbe in such stories as "Red Leaves," "A Justice," and "A Courtship," they are as fanatical in their pursuits, as rapacious and cruel and stupid as men have always been. Faulkner demystifies his own nostalgia when he has Ike say in "Delta Autumn," "There are good men everywhere, at all times. Most men are. Some are just unlucky, because most men are a little better than their circumstances give them a chance to be. And I've known some that even the circumstances couldn't stop" (329). Not that Ike's substitute myth of circumstance is any better. It just reveals the fictive quality of both myths, exposes both as the rhetoric of desire.

What then of Sam Fathers? In Faulkner's "A Justice," Sam's two fathers are a black slave owned by Ikkemotubbe and Crawfish-ford or Crawford, not a Chickasaw chief but just a man of the tribe, and his mother is a black female slave (*Portable Faulkner* 27–45). Faulkner changes Sam's parentage evidently just for *Go Down, Moses,*[5] where we learn in "The Old People" that Sam's father is Ikkemotubbe himself. Now Ikkemotubbe was not always chief, or the Man, as the Indians called him. Old Issetibbeha had been succeeded by Ikkemotubbe's "fat cousin" Moketubbe (160). Instead, Ikkemotubbe had "run away to New Orleans in his youth and returned seven years later with a French companion" and with "the quadroon slave woman who was to be Sam's mother" (159–60). These details are reminiscent of Sutpen and Bon in Faulkner's *Absalom Absalom.* But more important, they are reminiscent of Carothers McCaslin. Ikkemotubbe murders Moketubbe's son with a poison that he demonstrates on puppies and causes his cousin to abdicate. No sooner is he the Man (du Homme) than he marries the pregnant woman to one of the slaves he had just inherited "and two years later sold the man and woman and the child who was his own son to his white neighbor, Carothers McCaslin."[6] Surely these details, altered as they are from "A Justice," are not without significance. Sam's father is a double for Carothers: he owns slaves and uses them and discards them without even acknowledging his "own." As Faulkner says in "Red Leaves," the Indians acted just "as the white people did" (*Portable Faulkner* 80). Moreover, in "A Courtship" Faulkner depicts the Indians' fanatical concern with genealogy and aristocracy, especially through Herman Basket's aunt, who "was the second cousin by marriage to the grand-niece of the wife of old David Colbert, the chief Man of all the Chickasaws in our section, and she looked upon Issetibbeha's whole family and line as mushrooms" (*Collected Stories* 364–65). They also have the same fanatical codes of honor, as in Moketubbe's wearing of the red slippers in "Red Leaves" or Ikkemotubbe's insane contest with David Hogganbeck in "A Courtship." And the Man must have a "House," so Ikkemotubbe, not considering his current domicile a worthy analogue to his white neighbors' grand houses, has his whole village and his slaves insanely drag through impenetrable wilderness an abandoned steamboat, which is equally a symbol of emptiness ("A Justice"). Finally, as Cass explains to Ike in "The Old People," Sam's two legacies make him "his own battleground, the scene of his own vanquishment and the mausoleum of his defeat" (162). Sam is defeated precisely because he himself cannot escape man's mad abstraction of purity of blood. As Glissant argues, Sam is *inextricably* both black and white, and neither Sam's nor Ike's—nor perhaps even Faulkner's—world is ready to accept the "Creolity" that goes beyond *métissage* (Anzaldúa's *mestizaje*—crossbreeding) to imply a "Relation" with the world at large that gets us beyond Being to Becoming.[7]

No wonder Ike must mystify Sam and claim he had no parents but the wilderness itself. Just as he must mystify not only his own parentage but his failed sexual relations too after his wife has terminated them forever as a result of his refusal to repossess his patrimony: "but still the woods would be his mistress and his wife" (311). Thus his mystification is a form of daydream wish-fulfillment. But then Ike has been dreaming and mystifying all along. As a child, before he even went to the Big Bottom, the Bear "ran in his knowledge before he ever saw it. It loomed and towered in his dreams" (185). It was

> not even a mortal beast but an anachronism indomitable and invincible out of an old dead time, a phantom, epitome and apotheosis of the old wild life which the little puny humans swarmed and hacked at in a fury of abhorrence and fear like pygmies about the ankles of a drowsing elephant;—the old bear, solitary, indomitable, and alone; widowered childless and absolved of mortality—old Priam reft of his old wife and outlived all his sons. (185–86)

But the Bear *is* domitable, as Ike learns in his very first year in the woods. That this narration is myth is emphasized by the allusion to Priam; that it is a false myth is emphasized by the fact that Priam did not outlive his wife. Moreover, the wilderness is "doomed" (passim), coeval with Ike himself— or is that just another of his myths? At least the lumber companies and logging trains are inescapably real.

Faulkner shows the process of mystification at work in "The Old People," when Ike listens to Sam's words fill the gaps in his lack:

> And as he talked about those old times and those dead and vanished men of another race from either that the boy knew, gradually to the boy those old times would cease to be old times and would become a part of the boy's present, not only as if they had happened yesterday but as if they were still happening, the men who walked through them actually walking in breath and air

and casting an actual shadow on the earth they had not quitted.
And more: as if some of them had not happened yet but would
occur tomorrow, until at last it would seem to the boy that he
himself had not come into existence yet [. . .] (165)

The operative words, as they are throughout the novel, occurring often
enough to reveal the process, are "as if" and "seem." Something of the
same process accounts for the phantom buck. Cass explicates its significance. Even though he too has seen it, it has no "substance," no "shadow"
(180). It is in effect the sign of the absence of the life that has died before,
which Cass self-indulgently and somewhat ludicrously speculates "must
be somewhere," since the impersonal heavens and the shallow earth "dont
want it" (179). The phantom is just that, the substanceless product of Ike's
and Cass's and Sam's wish. That is the meaning of Ike's frantic protesta-
tions, "'But I saw it!' the boy cried. 'I saw him!'" (180).

Faulkner reveals the same process at work in his narrative of Ike's
reveries in "Delta Autumn" about himself and the wilderness:

[. . .] the two spans running out together, not toward oblivion,
nothingness, but into a dimension free of both time and space
where once more the untreed land warped and wrung to math-
ematical squares of rank cotton for the frantic old-world people
to turn into shells to shoot at one another, would find ample
room for both—the names, the faces of the old men he had known
and loved and for a little while outlived, moving again among
the shades of tall unaxed trees and sightless brakes where the
wild strong immortal game ran forever before the tireless bell-
ing immortal hounds, falling and rising phoenix-like to the sound-
less guns. (337–38)

This is Keatsian rhapsody, escapism from war and time and death. In a
marvelous addition to Ike's reveries, written for the interstitial passage about
Old Man River that introduces "Race at Morning" in *Big Woods* (a story
that itself has a phantom buck, a "hant" seen by only a few, shot at and
never hit [181]), Faulkner has Ike fantasize again about his own participation in this immortality:

[. . .] the Big Woods, shoved, pushed further and further down
into the notch where the hills and the Big River met, where they
would make their last stand. It would be a good one too, im-

pregnable; by that time, they would be too dense, too strong with life and memory, of all which had ever run in them, ever to die—the strong irritable loud-reeking bear, the gallant high-headed stags looking longer than comets and pale as smoke, the music-ed and untiring dogs and the splattered horses and the men who rode them: himself too. Oh yes, he would think; me too. I've been too busy all my life trying not to waste any living, to have time left to die. (171, italics romanized)

As Cass says, all that must be somewhere where "memory" can keep it alive. At least isn't it pretty to think so. Faulkner would not like the allusion to Hemingway, and he may be fully complicit in these rhapsodies of transcendence (as are we all). But will-he, nill-he, Faulkner has exposed their source as the ultimate transcendental signified (as Derrida would put it, if not Lacan): the desire for the transcendent.

Ike's myth-making is painfully obvious in his continual temporizings in the commissary. He has concocted from various pre-texts a myth of Origins and Final Justice, a myth of Sacred History and Providential causality. We know it is a myth, not only because of the obvious fictions, say of God's conversation with John Brown, or just the ubiquitous *maybe*'s, but also because Ike has to keep altering it to meet Cass's objections. At one key point he stifles an interruption: "Let me talk now. I'm trying to explain to the head of my family something which I have got to do which I dont quite understand myself, not in justification of it but to explain it if I can. I could say I dont know why I must do it but that I know I have got to because I have got myself to have to live with for the rest of my life and all I want is peace to do it in" (275). This is existential choice, whose fatalism is fictional, a rationalization for what one wants to, chooses to do. Ike chooses to be a maverick on the border between the races. He even tries to cross over.

Typical of all these temporizings is Ike's bizarre application of the Abraham and Isaac myth to himself. If God chose Carothers and his immediate descendants for His plan to set the blacks free, "He must have seen" the need for Ike too: "an Isaac born into a later life than Abraham's and repudiating immolation: fatherless and therefore safe declining the altar because maybe this time the exasperated Hand might not supply the kid" (270–71). What kind of faith is this? If there is a Divine Presence or Providence operating through history, then how could Ike frustrate Its will? Is it not impious of him either to refuse the act of obedience that was the lesson of the original text or to doubt that the "Hand" would supply the kid? This is creative wish-fulfillment, and Cass recognizes it with one word: "Escape." Ike even temporarily admits, "All right. Escape" (271). We remember that a few stanzas later in Keats's "Ode" is the description of the procession toward the sacrifice that will never take place.

Furthermore, Ike is absent from his place in the central sacrifice of the novel; he is displaced from the center of his own myth. All along he has been primed for the task of killing Old Ben. When Sam says someday somebody's going to shoot him, even though Ike has not been able to during the episode of the fyce, he responds, "I know it. [. . .] That's why it must be one of us. So it wont be until the last day. When even he dont want it to last any longer" (204). Surely the phrase "one of us" refers only to Sam and Ike, the priests. So Ike does not hate and fear Lion but is "proud that he had been found worthy to be a part" of the last act—"or even just to see it too" (217). But mere observation is not the part assigned to him. For General Compson, over the objections of Cass, assigns him to ride Katie, the one-eyed mule that will not balk at the Bear. Nevertheless, Ike refuses to complete his pattern of romance, his feat, the sacrifice of the sacred totem. Instead it is Boon, laboriously portrayed as being unworthy, who kills Ben only out of a perverse love for Lion, and who is totally incapable of appreciating the significance of his actions, as is so pathetically symbolized by his madness under the gum tree. Instead of being a pure, serene, classical "piece of statuary," the figure of Ben with Lion at his throat as he falls is Gothic and grotesque, a gargoyle perched upon it.

Finally, Faulkner makes it clear that Ike's dream of freedom is also just desire. The blacks are not free; not the blacks on the McCaslin plantation in 1883, where sharecropping still enslaves them—and will for the foreseeable future; not Fonsiba and her husband in 1886, whose blindness to their plight is imaged in his lensless spectacles; and not Tennie's Jim's granddaughter in 1940, scorned and denied by yet another Carothers. And Ike is himself not free, however "peaceful" (passim). His wife's greed and prostitution teach him that "*[w]e were all born lost*" (300), and when Lucas comes to claim his legacy in 1895, Ike is "husband but no father, unwidowered but without a wife"—shades of Sam and Ben—yet he has "found long since" that lesson from Dostoyevsky's Grand Inquisitor section of *The Brothers Karamozov* that "no man is ever free and probably could not bear it if he were" (269). In "The Fire and the Hearth" Faulkner has given Ike a soliloquy at this moment of Lucas's advent: "*He knows.* [. . .] *That I reneged, cried calf-rope, sold my birthright, betrayed my blood, for what he too calls not peace but obliteration, and a little food*" (105). In other words, Ike wants to be "obliterated" from his own text, erased from the ledgers of his lineage. As before when listening to Sam, Ike wills that "faded and archaic script" of his indelible past (not just the ledgers, but the McCaslin deed in the courthouse in Jefferson) out of existence (165). He wants to absent himself, to negate himself, as he thinks in "Delta Autumn," "in repudiation and denial at least of the land and the wrong and shame" (334). This subvocal soliloquy in the presence of Lucas may undercut Ike's myth completely, but of course it only replaces it with other myths and codes and texts: the code of poker players who are not supposed to renege on bets; the code of boys who are not supposed to give up and cry "calf-rope"; the biblical text of Esau and Jacob and perhaps Judas; the myth of "blood" itself. Ike is supposed to have found his identity, but who is he? Isaac, son of Abraham? Esau, son of Isaac? Judas? The Nazarene he though "not in mere static and hopeful emulation" nevertheless imitates (295)? The Moses of the title of the novel, sent "to set at least some of His lowly people free" (248)? Is he still the little boy, a kind of wilderness Peter Pan, never to grow up? Or is he the primitive, the noble savage? Or the Dutch Uncle "to half a county and father to no one" (3)? His crossing is incomplete.

Ike is caught between two cultures, two apparent value systems, as he tries to free himself from the contamination of his white heritage yet finds no fully uncontaminated alternative. He is caught in the cracks between the different codes and texts he inherits, and he confuses them throughout. Though he claims to repudiate the McCaslin legacy, he still considers his pro-black feelings "heresy" (281). In "Delta Autumn" he is still enough of a racist to send Roth's mistress away to marry a man of her "own race" (346) and to view as "retribution" the fact that in America "*Chinese and African and Aryan and Jew, all breed and spawn together until no man has time to say which one is which nor cares*" (347). So he passes on to this woman and Roth Edmonds's child, to this great-great-great-grandson of Carothers McCaslin and his own distant cousin, the last of his legacies: the silver-mounted, buckskin-covered hunting horn General Compson had bequeathed to him. This symbol of the hunt, of a dead wilderness, a dead religion, he gives to a mulatto heading north perhaps to Chicago, where we know from the last story in the novel what the future holds for blacks, what Promise. So it too is an empty legacy, and Ike is still McCaslin enough and white enough to provide this kinswoman with a sign as empty as his coffeepot, but not to share with her and her baby his home.

In his attempt to obliterate his name from one lineage and write it into another, Ike attempts a permanent crossing. He tries to become an Indian, not as Indians are in Faulkner's other stories, but as they are in primitivism. This attempt goes the way of all adoption of pastoral and primitive modes. There is something ludicrous, something anachronistic in Ike's vision of

Ben in the Happy Hunting Ground, where "they would give him his paw back even" (313). Faulkner emphasizes Ike's inability to write his own text thus when he has Ike salute the snake in the ancient tongue as a spirit of the wilderness—but also and incompatibly as the Edenic serpent, "the old one, the ancient and accursed about the earth" (314). Ike cannot even attain a purity of myth. Nor a purity of identity. Not even Uncle Ike is a pure Presence in the novel. The name "Isaac McCaslin" is finally an overdetermined— and therefore literally indeterminate—sign.

Witness Ike's last attempt to mythologize in his vision of the dead:

> [. . .] not vanished but merely translated into the myriad life which printed the dark mold of these secret and sunless places with delicate fairy tracks, which, breathing and biding and immobile, watched him from beyond every twig and leaf until he moved, moving again, walking on; he had not stopped, he had only paused, quitting the knoll which was no abode of the dead because there was no death, not Lion and not Sam: not held fast in earth but free in earth and not in earth but of earth, myriad yet undiffused of every myriad part, leaf and twig and particle, air and sun and rain and dew and night, acorn oak and leaf and acorn again, dark and dawn and dark and dawn again in their immutable progression and, being myriad, one[.] (313)

The presence of the fairies tells us that this is mystification. It is Cass's pantheism again. It is a myth of the return to oneness, to harmony, to a lost perfect Origin. But as Cass knows, and as Keats's "Ode" insists, man is forever "dispossessed of Eden" (247). History is a series of endless dispossessions, and the fact that the plea embodied in the title of this novel is never fulfilled is significant. There is no Moses to take us to a Promised Land: his advent is always deferred. There is no unity, only difference and death. Ike's rapturous language (or is it Faulkner's?) at Sam's grave is simply the rhetoric of desire. He has been a maverick to no avail.

Perhaps, in Faulkner's vision here, to be man, *du homme,* is to be, as in Ikkemotubbe's mispronunciation of this French appellation, doomed. Glissant argues in his fine meditative essay that Faulkner eventually finds a way to extend his "intervention" into the process of tragedy beyond "the impossibility of a return to equilibrium [. . .] into multiplicity, [. . .] the suspension of identity, [. . .] the inextricable, which is its boundless home" (98). But we know that the aging Uncle Ike is incapable of accepting the crossbreeding such a surrendering of identity, such an acceptance of inextricable mixedness implies. That is the "boundless home" of at least Glissant's vision, if not of the later Faulkner. But it is not yet the achieved vision of *Go Down, Moses.* Ike's repudiation, while understandable, is finally no more efficacious than Bartleby's. The novel concludes not in tragic redemption through sacrifice, not in restoration of what Glissant calls "lost unity," but in a satire on the borders of the South as still gaping wounds. Ike's failed crossing is darkly mirrored in the failed crossing of another black McCaslin-Beauchamp, whose flight to South Chicago has been to no avail, whose body is returned to a funeral where there is no place even for the well-meaning Gavin Stevens. The absurdist implications of the novel are further figured in Gavin's escapist project of attempting to translate the *Old* Testament back into its original Greek! Neither Gavin nor Ike can restore such a lost unitary origin because it never existed: both the alpha and the omega of existence, then—some ontological *terminus a quo* and *terminus ad quem* of Being—remain mythic desiderata endlessly deferred.

2

Tragic Glory

A Bright Tragic Thing

> If I am still of this earth, it is the earth as history
> and the earth as dust.
>
> L.D. Clark, *A Bright Tragic Thing*

L.D. Clark's novel, *A Bright Tragic Thing: A Tale of Civil War Texas,* is a fictionalized account of the Great Hanging in Gainesville, Texas, in 1862, when Unionists were executed under the barest pretext of law in the early Confederacy. A great-grandson of one of the hanged, Nathaniel Miles Clark, L.D. Clark feels this history deeply; moreover, his grandfather wrote memoirs about the hanging of his father, which Clark has edited and published as *Civil War Recollections of James Lemuel Clark.*[1] The protagonist of *A Bright Tragic Thing,* Todd Blair, is a fictionalized version of Clark's grandfather. The novel is a *Bildungsroman:* it focuses on Todd's precipitate coming of age through the crisis of the imminent hanging of his father, Nathaniel Blair, who, like his fellow Unionists, is a maverick in north Texas, refusing to accept Texas's vote to secede, refusing to accept slavery itself. The Cross Timbers section of Texas borders on the Red River, beyond which lies a no-man's-land of Indian Territory between South and North. Like the "Border States" during the Civil War, it is a site of contending ways of life and ideologies—of cultures, if you will. The mantle of maverick on this border descends from father to son onto Todd, whose every instinct is toward violent rebellion against the tyranny of the Confederate faction in Milcourt (Gainesville). Yet Todd realizes that the enemy is his own people, and ironically he falls in love with the niece of the leader of that tyranny. Todd eventually is forced into a literal crossing of the no-man's-land between Texas and the Union, but his most significant crossing is his ability to negotiate, without necessarily making fully conscious his own Oedipal guilt, the inevitable death of the father that enables the succession of the son.

The title of Clark's *Bright Tragic Thing* comes from an Emily Dickinson poem, part of which serves as Clark's epigraph:

> Glory is that bright tragic thing
> > That for an instant
> > Means Dominion.

The key to the meaning of Clark's novel lies in the juxtaposition of *glory* with *the tragic,* a juxtaposition that yields a profound existentialist vision. That vision transcends Christianity, particularly of the evangelical kind, and focuses on the power of the individual to create his own meaning through words, stories, recollected history—a meaning not that wrests glory from the jaws of tragedy but that accepts the tragedy inherent in glory, the loss that fuels the brightness.

Throughout his introduction to his grandfather's *Recollections,* Clark uses the word "tragedy" to refer to the Great Hanging, as the aging Todd Blair does in the fictional account (12). That he uses the term with meaning beyond that of common parlance is suggested by both extrinsic and intrinsic evidence. A veteran of World War II, Clark attended Columbia University on the GI Bill and earned both undergraduate and graduate degrees. In the mid-twentieth century *tragedy* was a hot topic, from neo-Aristotelians especially at the University of Chicago to European existentialists. As he has informed me in private conversation, Clark took a year-long course in Greek literature and engaged in extensive conversations about the nature of tragedy.

In *A Bright Tragic Thing* the *tragic* manifests itself in a number of ways. First, the inescapability of the "curse" of slavery (76) as Nathaniel Blair crosses the Red River only to discover plantations in north Texas: "a danger you could not escape, wherever you went" (24). Six or so years later, eighteen-year-old Todd Blair wishes "we'd never come to the Cross Timbers in the first place, especially when I recalled how Pap had looked on this part of the world: his notion of settling in a frontier place out of the way of secession and slavery troubles—and how I'd suspected from the start [. . .] that those troubles could track you down in the Cross Timbers as well as the next place" (41–42). As he rides home after his father's arrest as a Unionist, Todd narrates: "Comanche's hooves beneath me, and Old Prince's behind me, clopped along steady and sharp on the road, through this country I'd ridden over so many times within the peace of that sound, only to have it contending now with the rhythm of despair. And still I wished,

and still I wondered, why Pap and the rest of us had ever delivered ourselves years ago to this disaster" (42). Another aspect of the tragic in the
novel is closely related to this inescapability: inevitability. Todd remembers an abolitionist's "declaring that no matter how rich and fine a plantation might appear, any social structure with slavery at the bottom of it lay
under a curse, and like the house built on the sand that structure would fall,
and great would be the fall of it" (76). Todd sees this inevitable conflict in
terms of us and them—plantation owners and farmers, slavers and
nonslavers, some, at least, as the previous quotation hints, with abolitionist
sympathies. As he visits Colonel Oldham, the figurehead the slavers use to
legitimate their cause and set up their mock jury and trial, to enlist his aid,
Todd comes to a startling insight, one we would today call "postcolonial."
Watching the young women on Oldham's plantation, Todd comments:

> Here we sat, a young man and an old man, enthralled by three
> young ladies on what passed for a fashionable stroll. [. . .]
> [W]hat we were truly contending about lay framed in the pic-
> ture before us, in the setting and the manner of the girls in walk-
> ing through it—a world sustained by the fine tall house behind
> us, with its fluted columns and its cluster of slave cabins in the
> rear, and spreading out from it around us and the girls the out-
> buildings and the tended fields. [. . .] [E]verything lying before
> our eyes in the scene completed by the girls walking through it
> was at stake in what was going on this moment in Milcourt, and
> beyond that in what was ripping the nation to pieces. (75–76)

What is at stake is an elitist, aristocratic way of life for a few built on the
backs of masses of human cattle. Son of a dirt farmer looked down upon
even by the aristocracy's slaves, Todd reflects further that the setting was
made for the girls, and they for the setting: they exist to reproduce it, to
reproduce the ruling class and its leisure as the basis of its culture. It cannot
last.

Yet at an earlier moment Todd, waiting for other Unionists to gather
into a force to liberate the prisoners, has another insight that militates against
an us-and-them dichotomy:

> I saw peopling the darkness other faces collected around [Peg
> Madill's]. None of them resembled Peg's except in this small
> feature or that tint of complexion, or in nothing at all—beyond
> what was everything: the kinship of ancestry, of race; the pro-

files of men in my own isolated community gathered from the
far-flowing human stream of those who had left the villages of
Britain and landed on wilderness shores to migrate west, west,
west. It was the face of my people, but suddenly the face worn
by friend and foe alike—and that was the terror. [. . .] I was out to
kill men of my own blood, and they were out to kill me. (52–53)

The great tragedy of the Civil War is that it pitted like against like, brother
against brother. For the Unionists, the other was not radically other. And
ironically, the curse of slavery is not extraneous to the Blairs themselves.
Even though they refused slaves as wedding presents (22), Nathaniel carries with him a wife who is herself the daughter of a plantation owner.
Seeing Colonel Oldham's "honest-to-God plantation mansion out here on
the wild rim of Indian country" (66), Todd reflects, "[T]his house recalled
one in Kentucky I'd never seen, only heard Ma describe, the house where
she was born and spent her girlhood" (66). Why does this realization make
him "uneasy"? Perhaps because of what Freud called the *unheimlich,* that
strange or foreign frightening thing that turns out to be *heimlich,* at home in
us, the dark truth we have suppressed. Was the other in the Civil War just a
mirror image of the self? As history repeats itself in "Delta Autumn,"
Faulkner's aging Uncle Ike discovers that you cannot really repudiate the
past.

Todd never consciously pursues this uneasiness. Instead, he focuses
on the inevitability not in some psychological inscape but looming on the
larger horizon: "It terrified me, this certainty that I was losing Pap to an
immensity of time never to be crossed" (37). Falling into a Romeo and
Juliet love affair with the niece of the real leader of the Confederate oppressors, Colonel Ticknor, Todd laments, "Yet crying out and kicking against
the barriers before us could not make them fall. As I knew. As I knew. [. . .]
The many obstacles that divided us—the what and the who—made defeat
seem inevitable" (217–18). The "what" is secession and the struggle over
an economic system based on fundamental immorality; the "who" is the
class difference that separates the Blairs from the Ticknors—and ultimately
Todd from the niece of his father's murderer.

Like Northrop Frye, Todd associates this inevitability also with the
seasons, with the tragic season of autumn:

For here was this familiar yet mysterious delay of autumn, forcing itself on me as a premonition of death. With an uncontrol-
lable quaking in my soul I knew that from now till Sunday [the

day his father was supposed to be released by the jury] I'd be in terror that the first blight of winter would arrive before my father could be freed: decreeing the end of his life as well as the dying of the year—cold to wilt the leaves, to strip the limbs, and by fate dire and unfathomed to pluck my father out of this life. (220)

The physical, seasonal life force deterministically *decrees* tragedy, the death of the father. Todd's analysis becomes positively metaphysical, moving beyond "fate dire and unfathomed" to entertain "the suspicion that all things including this [Romeo and Juliet] passion were ruled by a universal injustice all the more horrifying for being inevitable: a diabolic, indifferent urge for the perpetuation of generations, a passion that required the death of my father in the operation of its natural and merciless law" (220). He sees the life-force as not benign but "indifferent" to the "injustice" inherent in its determinism, a tragic necessity that "require[s]" the death of the father. Like most humans faced with such cosmic indifference, Todd here cannot face such absurdity and hence demonizes the life force into the "diabolic."

Tragic inevitability reaches its climax when Colonel Oldham, traveling with Todd to Milcourt to ensure that the jury's word will be kept and Nathaniel will be released, fatally encounters bushwhackers coming from Milcourt (hence it could not have been an ambush by Unionists, an interpretation that prevails both in fiction and history [*Recollections* 36–37]) and is assassinated. As a result, the jury's clemency is rescinded, and the remaining Unionists are given quasi-trials. Most, among them Nathaniel, are executed the Sunday they were to be released. Clark is at his absolute best in making us feel the agony of this tragedy: in Todd's last fracturing interview with his father, in his mother's finally standing up out of stupefaction to watch her husband hang.

Yet even here, at the moment of the killing of the two benevolent patriarchs, the Unionist Nathaniel and the Confederate Colonel Oldham, the tragedy is not reduced to melodramatic Manichaeanism. Nor does Clark leave the etiology of tragedy totally deterministic. For Todd's apocalyptic dream reveals not a Christian vision of final justice but an existentialist, psychoanalytic nightmare:

I saw Colonel Oldham slumping in the saddle, smeared, flowing yet crusted with blood, while I tried frantically to hold him up, while he went on sinking, sinking, slipping through my arms.—But no! he was not acting this out as true dying, rather as a ghastly pretense, a game: mocking also, playing the corpse and laughing in scorn at my stricken seriousness. And then! hearing the shots I'd fired, seeing a figure lurch and tumble from a horse—and that was also Colonel Oldham over there lurching and tumbling.—Besides, the Spencer was coming to pieces in my hands, and I couldn't make it fit back together. [. . .] Why, I too was at last infected with the mockery of the people passing, passing—all in play, all in play. And in horror every hope faded: any hope [. . .] in this game of apocalypse. (250)

The fragmenting of the Spencer repeating rifle marks Todd's castrating realization of his own Oedipal implication in the absurdist endgame of the killing of the father: Colonel Oldham dies twice in his dream, once from the shot of the bushwhackers, once from shots from Todd's own rifle. We remember Todd's inference that he resembles the son Colonel Oldham wished he had (74). Yet like Dostoyevsky's Raskolnikov, in his waking state Todd never becomes fully conscious of the *unheimlich* horror of his implication. He never seeks absolution—from his father or from us readers—for his guilt in the death of Colonel Oldham: if Todd had not sought him out one more time just to hedge his bets on his father's release, Colonel Oldham would not have accompanied Todd toward Milcourt and toward his murder. The encounter with the bushwhackers may be fate or may be the random chance of absurdity; Colonel Oldham's presence with Todd is not. Through what Aristotle would call his *hamartia,* his mistaken judgment, Todd is tragically responsible for the death of both his fathers, surrogate and real.

This tragic vision is neither Todd's nor Clark's final version of things. Intermixed in the novel is a glory that will not be eclipsed. Glory in the pulse of the land itself that the aging Todd refuses to leave: "a cadence, a rhythm, the rise and fall of life in this place, this land itself" (13). Glory in solitary oneness with the land: "All my life, off and on, I have found myself in some strange place where I sense, if only for a little while, that the land itself understands my solitary presence, and that a silence out of the earth responds to a silence in me" (65). Glory in his horse Comanche's precision pursuit of a buffalo: "[H]ow glorious that shone in my heart" (143). Glory through the notch in the hills behind his home Todd plans to use for his and his family's escape, an escape he can finally take only alone: "Ever since I'd first seen it that notch had told me of some great and wonderful place lying beyond it, a spot never to be reached except by passing through that notch—a passage waiting to be taken some day in assurance of a glowing future—" (210). And above all, the glory of Jenny Ticknor. In an image that tempers the association of autumn with tragedy, Todd compares the color of Jenny's hair to the "bronze light that streams unexpected some morning in the glory of autumn" (137). Their love-making catapults Todd into another realm: "When the culminating instant of panting release came, it was like a transformation into fire, like being wrapped in one flame with Jenny, a flame that burned us out of present existence and left us helpless and still and silent for a little space but in sure knowledge that soon we would rise up newborn, never to be the same again" (216). This positive image of regeneration at least tempers Todd's later depiction of it as "a diabolic, indifferent urge for the perpetuation of generations" (220). And leavening the tragedy is the *Bildungsroman* aspect typical of Clark's novels. Despite his nightmarish subconscious guilt and his macabre fear that all is a game, despite his theory of inevitability, Todd matures to become capable of significant agency. Early on he calls out the mob leader, Harley Dexter. When Harley contemptuously·dismisses him as a "boy" and suggests he's out of his league in dealing with matters of "*treason,*" Todd retorts, "I'll make you think 'treason.' And I'll make you think 'boy,' you bug-eyed sonofabitch, if any harm comes to Pap" (33). But this is just youthful bravado. Much more significant is his attempt to appeal to Colonel Oldham, an appeal that might have succeeded if not for either fate or chance. Todd saves Jenny Ticknor from bushwhackers and saves his mother and siblings from further persecution at the hands of the Confederates. Most significant is his standing up to Colonel Ticknor and Harley Dexter, the two leaders of his enemies.

Though Todd contemplates assassinating Ticknor, he stands up to him more impressively by articulating in his teeth his father's and the Unionists' position: "It ain't a crime, I reckon, to want to bring back the Union when they didn't vote to leave it in the first place" (195). Ticknor's Calhoun-like response— "The Union is over and done with. Texas is now the biggest and strongest state in the Confederate States of America—and it always will be. Texans decided this question in a free and fair election. The ones that voted the other way will have to abide by that decision"—is not unarguable. But Ticknor's fanaticism finally manifests itself in his rejection of Todd's ultimate appeal that, after all, he had saved Ticknor's niece from rape and murder: "YOU DID YOUR DUTY AS A MAN. I MUST DO MY DUTY FOR MY COUNTRY. SEE THAT YOU DO THE SAME" (260). Whatever Ticknor knows in his heart of hearts, he has allowed himself to become a "madman [. . .] gone insane for his cause:" He is an essentializer to the point of being a fascist.

Instead of enlisting in the Confederate army, as Ticknor had threateningly urged, however, Todd prepares to strike out for Union lines. He has no immediate revenge in mind. But when Harley Dexter gets the drop on him, his Spencer apparently unloaded, Todd rises to the occasion, tricks Harley into a gunfight, and kills him with the remaining chambered round. Todd and Comanche escape north, join a Union cavalry detachment, and return years later victorious. Out of tragedy Todd has forged a meaningful existence, a self capable of mature, defining action.

Out of the mixture of tragedy and glory, then—Todd calls the Great Hanging episode in his life "that enthralled existence in the ordeal of slaughter and glory" (296)—comes possibility. Even at the moment of Pap's hanging, Todd is moved by the juxtaposition of the father he can't watch and the vision of his stolid mother behind to push to the verge of that possibility: "That sight [of Ma] and the quivering of the giant limb with it tore my heart loose and swept it away through the terrible world holding us prisoner to where maybe that world came to the frontier of—what? If not of hope at least of a pause, an arrest, on the emptiness of the future" (267). Such emptiness has no absolute meaning. It is a boundary situation.

Toward the end of the novel Todd lays over his experience narrative emplotments designed to fill the void, to make sense of his experience. Over the cave he hides in till his family is safe and the time is propitious for his escape north Todd lays this interpretation:

> Because this entering and leaving the cave seemed to mean that I was in a tomb myself: just as Pap was—as the Lord had once been—I too biding time till the resurrection, and as though my own at least was at hand. This last, this ancient act beginning in despair and ending in victory, brought a glimmer of solace in contradiction to the fright of my dead father's presence: as if having Pa and the Lord with me could bring me one day out of this cave to stay, and into a new life—. (271)

Clark teases us with this Christian rhetoric, as if we are headed for a reaffirmation of its metaphysic. After having killed Harley, Todd throws his body in that cave from which he himself has emerged, and then rolls "a big rock over the mouth of the cave" (281). To the metaphor of resurrection Clark adds the Christian rhetoric of "remorse" (296), employing the traditional conceit of tomb/womb: "remorse entangled with the regret that I'd buried him so near my father's grave, and also with a new and strange sense of fellowship created between us by the sharing of that cave: a tomb for him, for me a place of symbolic death and resurrection" (296). After the war, Todd further overlays history with the rhetoric of sacrifice and expiation:

> Being near that spot once more, with war gone from the world, in course of time I had another change of heart, coming to wonder why I'd ever regretted killing [Harley]. Instead, I now felt entitled to the consolation of that sacrifice performed by my own hand: and that the worst of the lynchers, in paying for my father's blood with his own, had in a sense died for his cohorts as well, and even expiated the crime the whole town was guilty of for allowing the massacre to take place. Let that, I concluded at last, be sufficient to keep me at peace with the bones of my father. (299–300)

Lurking within this apparently Christian rhetoric of consolation, however, is the troubling return of the repressed: that Harley Dexter, trammeled up with the corpse of Todd's father, is himself, like Colonel Oldham, a double for the father, a negative version of the authoritative superego. In killing him, especially after his making fun of Todd for seeming to "jack off on his play-purties" (274), Todd commits a displaced version of Oedipal rebellion—in this instance, killing the dark side of the father.

Yet, uncrippled by the return of the repressed, Todd effects a crossing, a negotiation of conflict. His final vision eschews Christian for an existentialist metaphysics that combines both the psychoanalytic and the sociological, as well as both tragedy and glory. Employing, to borrow a phrase Clark uses anent Todd's and Jenny's vows, "those best of all words" to tell his story, his history (218), Todd comes to the realization that, "gleaming as visions of immortality," the glorious moments of his life are finally inseparable from the dark ones, "the torment inseparable from the rapture" (301):

> I realize that I cannot long to recreate the marvel of that life without simultaneous consent to seeing my father subjected to a hideous death. [. . .] My blood courses to a deeper conviction that I need not after all shut my eyes to the immolation of my father in order to value the brightest splendor of existence: that indeed life of this intensity cannot exist without acceptance of the immolation; and on the verge of delirium I discover in myself the ability to reconcile the contradiction of such acceptance. It may be that this endeavor comes to no more than pitting my

will against the inexorable laws of circumstance, never to be
actualized in time, yet in these rare moments I glimpse a silence
outside time where I have the power to offer up myself in my
father's place. It comes to me as a great consolation, this ever-
potential surrender of my own life, this willingness to submit to
vicarious sacrifice. This and this alone, in brevity but in mighti
ness, inspires in me consent to a boundless universe where the
father and the son must each be willing to yield up life in per-
petual sacrifice to redeem the other. (301)

"It may be" that such an "endeavor" is meaningless, Todd admits, but he
chooses a vision of a "boundless universe" where the acceptance of tragic
"immolation" and the willingness to undergo it in a reciprocal Oedipal
sacrifice has the "potential" to redeem existence from meaninglessness
precisely because humans—not some transcendent or even immanent god—
choose to endow such words with meaning, with glory. Such "Dominion,"
to return to the Dickinsonian epigraph, is tenuous indeed. But Todd's "consent" to it is a Nietzschean gay/tragic affirmation: if he had to journey
through it all over again, says the aging Todd, "Oh yes, I would go" (302).
Todd's affirmation is the logical culmination of Clark's fiction about the
Cross Timbers, a story that is *his story,* too, if not strictly history. If it is also
about "the earth as dust" (300), then Clark has created an existential quin-
tessence for us to wonder at.

Todd Blair, as opposed to Ike McCaslin, finds a rhetoric of adequa-
tion that enables crossings. Having literally crossed over no-man's-land,
that border between South and North and for Todd between tyranny and
freedom, to join the Union cavalry, Todd returns to Milcourt triumphant
but still vengeful. Nevertheless, his coming to accept Harley's death as
redemptive sacrifice (perhaps even for his own suppressed guilt) allows
him to bridge self and other in civil war, to bridge generations, to bridge
over loss. At the heart of his rhetoric is the trope of sacrifice, a willing
surrender of both father and self to an immolation that is endemic to existence, that enables endurance, that accepts the transience of glory as sufficient transcendence. How can the son substitute himself for the father at
whose death he becomes the new father, head of the household? Clark, a
product of his own time, offers refuge in another trope, one celebrated by
the New Critics of his graduate school years, *paradox.* Paradoxically, Todd's
gesture of substitution resolves the Oedipal crisis inherent in his dream of
Colonel Oldham. Paradoxically, the sacrifices of the Civil War made the
country stronger, eventually strong enough to resist Axis aggression, to

survive the cold war, to realize the ideals of the Civil Rights movement. Clark's novel looks backward but reflects back on his own time. As in Faulkner's fiction, Clark's perspective as a southerner, through the final trope of Todd's forgiveness, offers a way to negotiate a crossing that perhaps can only be made by an insider.

If so, Clark is an unsentimental insider who recognizes, at least subconsciously, that all rebellions are Oedipal; and that thus we are all interimplicated in them; that they, like the glorious passion of love, like the tragic season of autumn, require the death of the father "in the operation of" a "natural and merciless law." Moreover, the aging Todd Blair's accommodation with Milcourt, with its Confederate veterans—at a distance—and his finding the words to tell his story represent a crossing achieved at great cost. The tragic death of Jenny means that they will not embody reconciliation in a marriage and long life together: a reconciliation between slave owners and dirt farmers that would have symbolically resolved issues of race and class that festered for another hundred years and linger yet in the deep South. And the tragic death of Todd and Jenny's son means that the issue of Oedipal rebellion—of son against father, of sons against *patria*— is not resolved either. Like Uncle Ike, Todd merely escapes the cyclic return of the Oedipal crisis because he remains a maverick to the normal pattern, "grandfather to everybody and nobody, childless, my wife dead for years" (10). Yet Todd's story (the childless Clark's novel) is perhaps the offspring that offers a vision of reconciliation through pendant and provisional tragic glory.

3

THE BORDER OF BECOMING

THEODICY IN *BLOOD MERIDIAN*

> If God meant to interfere in the degeneracy of
> mankind would he not have done so by now?
> Wolves cull themselves, man. What other creature
> could? And is the race of man not more predacious
> yet? The way of the world is to bloom and to
> flower and die but in the affairs of men there is no
> waning and the noon of his expression signals the
> onset of night. His spirit is exhausted at the peak of
> its achievement. His meridian is at once his
> darkening and the evening of his day.
>
> Cormac McCarthy, *Blood Meridian*

Cormac McCarthy's *Blood Meridian; or, The Evening Redness in the West*
is a dark parody of the Western. His central protagonist, the unnamed, un-
capitalized "kid," is a parodic, unheroic avatar of Kit Carson, a maverick
who leaves his home in Kentucky to go west through St. Louis and make
his fortune. The novel is a grotesque *Bildungsroman* in which we are denied access to the protagonist's consciousness almost entirely. Yet the kid
seems to grow somehow, especially in conflict with an adversary. From
almost the beginning the kid is shadowed by his—and the novel's—major
antagonist, another maverick, the judge: "Our animosities were formed and
waiting before ever we two met," proclaims the judge ominously (307).
The "meridian" of the title is bloody indeed: it is on one level a border
between civilization and violence, on another between past and future. As
the kid crosses west underneath it "in him broods already a taste for mindless violence. All history present in that visage, the child the father of the
man" (3)—not in some Romantic or Platonic, Wordsworthian sense, but in
a sense far darker. Nature on this planet is red in tooth and claw, and man is

a part of nature, as McCarthy's epigraphs attest, as the hermit the kid meets early in his wanderings attests: "[Man] can know his heart, but he dont want to. Rightly so. Best not to look in there" (19). The child sires his own adulthood in the sense that ontogeny recapitulates phylogeny: history is a bloody record of man's inhumanity to man, and the kid enters into a black baptism of blood. The key question of his crossing, however, is whether it is "entire" (passim): whether the kid does not withhold something that redeems him from his gang's Faustian bargain with evil.

This chapter's epigraph represents the judge's theory of history: that civilizations rise slowly and fall precipitately. He is a modified Gibbonesque historian; he concentrates on fall without decline. Here the judge is attempting to explain magnificent ruins, like those of Chaco Canyon, whose Anasazi inhabitants were excellent masons, a skill apparently lost by their descendants. His long story has important aspects to which I shall return later. But the theory of history embodied in the image means that, according to the judge, the moment civilizations reach their apogee, they are so spent after rapacious and predacious striving, in which there is no room for meekness, that their high noon does not yield to the waxing shadow of gradual decline but rather to immediate eclipse. Thus the mysterious vanishing of the Anasazi.

The subtitle of the novel—*The Evening Redness in the West*—may also refer to the bloody rising and setting of civilizations in an impersonal universe that watches them violently come and go with indifference. Thus all the imagery of void and vortex in the novel and of bloody sunscapes: "They rode on and the sun in the east flushed pale streaks of light and then a deeper run of color like blood seeping up in sudden reaches flaring planewise and where the earth drained up into the sky at the edge of creation the top of the sun rose out of nothing like the head of a great red phallus until it cleared the unseen rim and sat squat and pulsing and malevolent behind them" (44–45; see also 185, 187). The image of the phallus is not gratuitous, for the founding of civilizations is accompanied by War and its attendant Rape. The Comanches wantonly sodomize the corpses of Captain White's ill-fated filibuster. Captain Glanton's men sodomize the bodies of the fallen peaceful Tiguas. The judge sodomizes and then mutilates the bodies of little boys and girls all along the path of Glanton's army. And these rapes themselves are not gratuitous, for they are the sign of (male) dominance over every culture that stands in the way of an advancing one. The very bashing of skulls, eviscerating of abdomens, castrating of genitalia is erotic. War is rape. Rape is war. That's why they're both so attractive to males on the rise.

One wants to demur: "Well, at least that's how McCarthy portrays the world." But McCarthy won't let us take refuge behind the lace curtains of refinement. As one McCarthy scholar puts it, we readers take a "frighteningly complicitous joy" in the "baroque opulence" of McCarthy's lyricism of violence (Shaviro 111). Behind those lace curtains lurks the visage of a sado-masochist. McCarthy insists that "culture is just [. . .] ideological facade" (Pughe 378). It is the function of ideology to obfuscate the fact that not only nature but civilization itself is red in tooth and claw: witness the relatively recent rise of the civilizations of England, France, Germany, Russia, the United States, and now China, to pick only the most major—and most egregious. The ascent has been up hecatombs of human corpses. The Holocaust is not a unique event. *Pace* Pughe, *Blood Meridian* represents no "regress" into barbarism.[1] The barbarism has always been there as a driving force of so-called progress. There really is no meridian, no border between barbarism and civilization; they are one and the same.

Yet something else resides in the judge's opening gambit: "If God meant to interfere in the degeneracy of mankind would he not have done so by now?" This is the kind of statement one makes in a theodicean argument, an argument over the Problem of Evil: How could a good God permit evil to exist in the world, physical as well as moral? that is, natural disasters as well as man-made? The judge begs the question from the beginning here by assuming as proved one of the terms of his argument: "the degeneracy of mankind." The traditional Judeo-Christian answer to the Problem of Evil is to locate its origin in the Fall of Man, after which he merely continues to degenerate. Yet the judge is a sophist, a consummate liar, who laughs at those who believe his rhetoric as "fools" (116). He is therefore not trustworthy here as philosopher. But the judge is not the only one to raise theodicean topics. The hermit rebukes the kid:

> The way of the transgressor is hard. God made this world, but he didn't make it to suit everybody, did he?
> I dont believe he much had me in mind.
> Aye, said the old man. But where does a man come by his notions. What world's he seen that he liked better?
> I can think of better places and better ways.
> Can ye make it be?
> No.
> No. It's a mystery. A man's at odds to know his mind cause his mind is aught he has to know it with. (19)

The last refuge of those who justify the ways of god to men is to portray man's intelligence as limited, too limited to plumb the depths of God's power and wisdom. The hermit here speaks similarly to the voice from the whirlwind in Job: Can you make a world? No? Then shut up. You have no grounds on which to stand to complain of evil and injustice.

That McCarthy recalls Job is evident in the narrator's, not the judge's, reflection on dust devils ("dustspouts") in the void of the desert: "Out of that whirlwind no voice spoke and the pilgrim lying in his broken bones may cry out and in his anguish he may rage, but rage at what? And if the dried and blackened shell of him is found among the sands by travelers to come yet who can discover the engine of his ruin?" (111). The rhetoric here captures Jobish complaint but complicates it by removing the Cause of evil. It is like Job demanding an answer from a whirlwind that has vanished.

To address the Problem of Evil is to assume causality in the cosmos, in human history. However, it is as if Blind Chance alone rules the world in *Blood Meridian:* witness all the imagery of random and chaotic physical violence and human interaction. McCarthy offers as a central image for such randomness the anecdote of the wayward wagon train, that happened to cross paths with Anglo renegade marauders posing as Indians to cover their tracks, metaphorically, and to excuse their savagery. Yet one cannot forbear seeking causality, and even an ex-priest conjectures that a "cynical" god must direct these seemingly random intersections (153).

Contradicting a theory of randomness is the apparent pattern of Manichaeanism: a good God of Light is opposed by the fell Prince of Darkness. Indeed, critics have read the judge as the "devil" he is called by the reverend whom he accuses of his very own sins (7). Sepich interprets the novel as a Faust legend: like Milton's Satan, the judge can make gunpowder; he and Glanton have a "terrible covenant" between them (126); the kid joins Glanton's gang, surrendering the judgment of his performance to the gang—a performance the judge finds lacking, so he comes at the end for the kid's soul and rends him asunder. Similarly, Daugherty reads *Blood Meridian* as a "gnostic tragedy" in which the world is dominated by the judge as dark "archon" who wills to be suzerain over all and who triumphs over the resistant kid; the only hope lies in the flickering light of the epilogue, a sign of the good God, who is alien from us.

The judge himself indulges in some Manichaean theodicy: he points to any man at random and presumes to instruct the kid, who is now a man, that the Problem of Evil originates in man's dissatisfaction, "that men will not do as he wishes them to. Have never done, never will do" (330). But the judge then teases the kid with a Manichaean etiology: "Can he say, such a man, that there is no malign thing set against him? That there is no power and no force and no cause? What manner of heretic could doubt agency and claimant alike?" Who is this "claimant"? The God of Job, Who claims ultimate agency, who *can* make a world? The judge insists through rhetorical questions that man's rage for order, meaning, etiology obviates belief that all is sound and fury signifying nothing: "Can he believe that the wreckage of his existence is unentailed? No liens, no creditors? That gods of vengeance and of compassion alike lie sleeping in their crypt and whether our cries are for an accounting or for the destruction of the ledgers altogether they must evoke only the same silence and that it is this silence which will prevail?" To believe in such Epicurean meaninglessness is beyond human capacity; it is to stare into the abyss and go mad.[2] Man demands to know, and like Job, he cannot tolerate the silence. He peoples his universe with "gods of vengeance" and competing gods "of compassion."

Beyond Manichaean good and evil, the judge offers a strange theory of causality. Attempting to negotiate with a Mexican sergeant Glanton's gang's purchase of revolvers, the judge explains, "It is not necessary, he said, that the principals here be in possession of the facts concerning their case, for their acts will ultimately accommodate history with or without their understanding" (85). Here is a theory of historical destiny in which humans may be witting or unwitting agents, but it makes no real difference. The judge rearticulates this theory later in the metaphor of life as a dance:

> The participants will be apprised of their roles at the proper time. For now it is enough that they have arrived. As the dance is the thing with which we are concerned and contains complete within itself its own arrangement and history and finale there is no necessity that the dancers contain these things within themselves as well. In any event the history of all is not the history of each nor indeed the sum of those histories and none here can finally comprehend the reason for his presence for he has no way of knowing even in what the event consists. In fact, were he to know he might well absent himself and you can see that that cannot be any part of the plan if plan there be. (329)

So agents are just actors in some cosmic plan, which they themselves do not, cannot understand, for, as the hermit opined, their minds are part of the field of study, both knower and known. Moreover, if humans were to understand the horror of the plan, they might "absent" themselves, like Bartleby, by preferring not to play. Whatever they do, they cannot understand the plan, "if plan there be," because they cannot know "in what the event consists"—the *happening* of the universe, its essence.

Then how can the judge himself understand history, the dance, the cosmos? Unless he is a cosmic agent himself, the "beast" (331) come round at last to dominate the world's stage in its transition from its age of warriors to the new, bourgeois era of tradesmen, the counterfeiters of the kid's delirious dream (see Daugherty)? As Bell points out, the judge "has no serious philosophical adversary in the text" (122). His confrontation with the kid seems strangely reminiscent of Milton's *Paradise Regained,* the preternaturally intelligent Tempter confronting a Messiah who is taciturn, who eschews worldly knowledge. Yet the kid has not Messiah's intelligence to respond to his Adversary. Or at least McCarthy seems to deny him the consciousness we desire him to have. Thus it is we readers, we critics who must be the judge's interlocutors.

The judge definitely seeks dominance, as is especially evidenced in his urge to taxonomize everything. The whole earth is his "claim," and he resents anything that remains outside the grasp of his mind and free (198–99). Those who interpret the judge as some kind of malevolent deity or demiurge may be right. But as Bell suggests (124), he also represents Enlightenment Man, that Eurocentric impulse to conquer the world and dominate it by not only military but cultural and scientific imperialism. Manifest Destiny is such imperialism's ideology.

Yet the judge's belief in his own agency seems not restricted to a super being. No longer speaking strictly for himself and his own megalomania, the judge generalizes: "The man who believes that the secrets of the world are forever hidden lives in mystery and fear. Superstition will drag him down. The rain will erode the deeds of his life. But that man who sets himself the task of singling out the thread of order from the tapestry will by the decision alone have taken charge of the world and it is only by such taking charge that he will effect a way to dictate the terms of his own fate" (199). The judge's own sophistry trips him: Has he not just defined a philosopher, any philosopher? Thus any man, Everyman, who attempts to know has already begun to master. Yet the judge contradicts himself through the oxymoron of the philosopher's dictating "the terms of his own fate." If it's "fate," not even Zeus can dictate his own terms: witness the fall of Troy.

Perhaps the judge means *extraordinary* men like himself can somehow be the agents of, can master Fate—if not super beings then perhaps the Nietzschean supermen he believes ought to dominate history. When one Irving protests that right should make might, the judge explodes in impatience: "Moral law is an invention of mankind for the disenfranchisement of the powerful in favor of the weak. Historical law subverts it at every turn. [. . .] Decisions of life and death, of what shall be and what shall not, beggar all question of right" (250). The way that history manifests its "law" is through the triumph of the strong over the weak. So the judge is not only Nietzschean but social Darwinist, and he *does* have an ethic, the ethic of the warrior class. Black Jackson reminds the judge of the scriptural warning that he who lives by the sword, dies by the sword: "What right man would have it any other way? [. . .] War endures. [. . .] War was always here. Before man was, war waited for him" (248)—in the war of all living creatures with each other to survive. War merely awaited "its ultimate practitioner" and war "endures because young men love it and old men love it in them" (249), as each generation sends another group of heroes to seek glory in slaughter. War is "the ultimate trade" (248), the ultimate "game" (249) for this *homo ludens:* "Men are born for games. Nothing else. Every child knows that play is nobler than work. He knows too that the worth or merit of a game is not inherent in the game itself but rather in the value of that which is put at hazard. [. . .] But trial of chance or trial of worth all games aspire to the condition of war for here that which is wagered swallows up game, player, all. [. . .] What more certain validation of a man's worth could there be?" What greater stake than his very existence?

Surprisingly, in the midst of this rhapsody, the judge's theory of fated historical agency becomes thoroughly intertwined in a theory of free human agency: "This enhancement of the game to its ultimate state admits no argument concerning the notion of fate. The selection of one man over another is a preference absolute and irrevocable and it is a dull man indeed who could reckon so profound a decision without agency or significance either one. [. . .] War is the ultimate game because war is at last a forcing of the unity of existence. War is god" (249). Obviously, some men choose to play the game and some, the weak, do not. Without human will, there would be no war. Some deity may perform the ultimate act of "preference" in war, but it is man's will-to-power that provides the fighting—and the "significance." In an existential sense, man is god, creator of his own destiny, of his own meaning.

The narrator himself seems swept up in the judge's rhetoric of agental destiny. He describes Glanton's horrific scalp hunters as riding "like men invested with a purpose whose origins were antecedent to them, like blood legatees of an order both imperative and remote" (152): "Deployed upon that plain they moved in a constant elision, ordained agents of the actual dividing out the world which they encountered and leaving what had been and what would never be alike extinguished on the ground behind them" (172). "Ordained agents" seems to be a pregnant oxymoron of the narrator, and in his opening celebration of the age of the warrior he is about to describe, he seems to be a bit of a Nietzschean himself: "[N]ot again in all the world's turning will there be terrains so wild and barbarous to try whether the stuff of creation may be shaped to man's will or whether his own heart is not another kind of clay" (4–5).

The question, if this novel is a theodicy, is whether there is any other agency that counts, that does not serve the warrior ethic and a brutal imperialist Manifest Destiny. There would seem to be a couple of possibilities. In answer to a question whether there be life on other planets, the judge propounds a theory of infinite possibilities, concluding,

> The universe is no narrow thing and the order within it is not constrained by any latitude in its conception to repeat what exists in one part in any other part. Even in this world more things exist without our knowledge than with it and the order in creation which you see is that which you have put there, like a string in a maze, so that you shall not lose your way. For existence has its own order and that no man's mind can compass, that mind itself being but a fact among others. (245)

Yet the man who singles out the thread of order from the tapestry of this world has already begun to master it, to find the clue to its labyrinth. So even if the mind of the philosopher is doomed to be the examining agent in a field that contains itself as one of the objects of study—and even though we know from science that, indeed, the future of this planet is "unspeakable and calamitous beyond reckoning" (245)—questioning would seem to be better than despair. First, one must resist, as the kid does in the San Diego jail, the counsels of despair, especially as they are proffered by the malevolent intelligence of the satanic judge, who seeks above all to control, to dominate.

There is in the novel a healthy skepticism toward knowledge for the sake of dominion, as exercised by the judge. Tobin, the ex-priest, in Pauline fashion suggests the wisdom of this world may just be foolishness with the Lord: "Whatever could it mean to one who knows all. [The Lord has] an uncommon love for the common man and godly wisdom resides in the least of things so that it may well be that the voice of the Almighty speaks most profoundly in such beings as lives in silence themselves" (123–24).

Could the lowly kid, silent during so much of the novel, be the recipient of God's love?

McCarthy himself is wise enough to know that if one is going to wrest a Christian existentialism from our contaminated world it will be hard won. There is no room for sentimentalism. The major question for such an interpretation is whether the kid's actions, his exercise of his own free agency, are redemptive—or just foolish. The kid is a maverick within Glanton's gang. When no one else will help and when failure will mean death at his hands, the kid removes the arrow out of Brown's thigh. For the first time, having been thrown, in an almost Heideggerian sense, into a field of violence, he crosses over some kind of border between violence and if not civilization then compassion. The ex-priest remonstrates, "Fool, [. . .] God will not love ye forever. [. . .] Dont you know he'd of took you with him? He'd of took you, boy. Like a bride to the altar" (162–63). Such a warning seems ominously foreboding of the ending, when the naked judge takes the kid into his arms in the jakes and kills him, ravaging his body.

The judge is certainly angry with the kid for failing to commit entirely to the ethic of the warrior. The kid has conferred with Toadvine about the senseless slaughter of the Tiguas, killing the people they had contracted to protect. He does not shoot the wounded Shelby but hides him, leaves him to work out his destiny with General Elias's Mexican army scouts. The kid refuses the ex-priest's advice to kill either the judge or the judge's fool, both of whom are tracking them. Trying to trick him, the judge pretends admiration for the kid's refusal to shoot him. Then he berates the kid for being neither "assassin" nor "partisan" (that is, a loyal member of Glanton's irregulars, as if they were engaged in a legitimate war): "There's a flawed place in the fabric of your heart. Do you think I could not know? You alone were mutinous. You alone reserved in your soul some corner of clemency for the heathen" (299). The judge tempts the kid, weak from his desert fast, to self-accusation, self-abnegation:

> You came forward, he said, to take part in a work. But you were a witness against yourself. You sat in judgement on your own deeds. You put your own allowances before the judgements of history and you broke with the body of which you were pledged a part and poisoned it in all its enterprise. [. . .] If war is not holy man is nothing but antic clay. [. . .] Only each was called upon to empty out his heart into the common and one did not. (307)

The kid steadfastly insists that the judge is the one who is radically different, other—in being totally devoid of humanity. How are we to decide who's right, the kid or the judge? Is there not significance in the fact that, after he has escaped not only from the wrath of the Yumas but from Glanton's gang itself, from its most ferocious member, the judge himself, the kid is saved in the hell of the Mojave Desert by the Digueños, a peaceful, *un*warlike tribe? Has he not been vouchsafed a form of salvation? The judge tracks him down as the last of Glanton's gang, as the final participant in that "terrible covenant." Is there another salvation waiting?

What is most interesting to me in the judge's rhetoric is that he has prefaced his remonstration of the kid with the guilt trip, "Dont you know that I'd have loved you like a son?" (306). Like the Kentuckian kid Elrod, so like himself, whom the kid killed not long ago, the kid might have retorted to the judge, "I'm not your son." Yet the judge here represents the father the kid never really had, the one he ran away from in Kentucky. He is the cultural superego, at least the superego of their subculture of the warrior. And in order to understand their relationship and their last embrace, we need to examine another of the judge's anecdotes.

In order to explain the failure of the Pueblo descendants of the Anasazi to match their achievements, the judge tells a convoluted story of two sons. One's father senselessly kills a traveler, apologizes later to his son on his deathbed. The son scatters the stones marking the grave and the bones therein, runs away and becomes "a killer of men" (145). The other is the son of the murdered traveler, who is an "idol of perfection" among the family lares. The judge propounds a theory of Oedipal rivalry: "The father dead has euchered the son out of his patrimony. For it is the death of the father to which the son is entitled and to which he is heir, more so than his goods. He will not hear of the small mean ways that tempered the man in life. He will not see him struggling in follies of his own devising. No. The world which he inherits bears him false witness. He is broken before a frozen god and he will never find his way" (145). These sons are deprived of fathers "to grapple with" (146). Only by wrestling with the father can the son define himself, his own, free being. Elrod is an orphan, turned like others of his generation—and like the kid—into killers of men. Moreover, he appears to be very like if not identical with the grandson of the slain traveler ("His grandaddy was killed by a lunatic and buried in the woods like a dog" [323]). He wants to define himself against the kid, now a man, obviously a warrior of long standing. So he comes back to his camp to kill him and loses the shootout. At least he had his *agon*.

So the kid and the judge are doomed to grapple. As he leaves Kentucky, one of the few things he notes on the horizon is a hanged parricide. He has not killed his own father. Now, though he has put it off as long as he can, he must wrestle him. His father was an erstwhile schoolteacher before he became just a drunk, but he could read and write and quote "from poets whose names are now lost" (3). The kid "can neither read nor write and in him broods already a taste for mindless violence" (3). Is this violence similar to that of the Pueblo descendants: "All progressions from a higher to a lower order are marked by ruins and mystery and a residue of nameless rage" (146)? Is the illiterate kid doomed, then, to attack the literate judge, his surrogate father?

Or is the kid a figure for a silent Job—or perhaps a Jacob— and is the grappling with the judge similar, perhaps, to the wrestling with an angel? Can the judge be both devil and angel? When the kid tells the judge, who claims to be the one who will always be present in the dance, "You aint nothin," the judge responds, "You speak truer than you know" (331). In Augustinian Christianity (and in Goethe's *Faust*), evil is a negation.[3] On a more mythic level, must this Messiah-*manqué* wrestle with the Father Who has subjected him to this trial, Who will not let the cup of his agony pass? I am chary of such a reading, for the kid himself seeks reassurances from the ex-priest that the history they are living is no "parable" (297). But McCarthy has teased us into mythic thought, will-we, nill-we: his signs are overdetermined, pregnant with multiple levels of meaning.

There are perhaps some signs for a Christian existentialist reading of the end of the novel. The kid carries a Bible with him in his latter days, though he cannot read it. He seeks to help the desiccated old Penitente, whose garments may be suggestive of the Virgin. He kills only when he cannot avoid it, and he tries to avoid confrontation with the judge. But if the kid is redeemed in the end, it is because Christian existentialism, à la Dostoyevsky, finds grace in the abject—in the mire and the filth and the blood and the disemboweled viscera of human existence.[4] The kid's association with these murderers begins and ends in a jakes. As Swift once suggested in one of his scatological poems, speaking literally of the shit in the commode, we must foul our hands in search of hope. The judge has insisted to his benighted followers, "Your heart's desire is to be told some mystery. The mystery is that there is no mystery." At this the ex-priest, pipe in teeth, comments sagely, "[A]nd no mystery. As if he were no mystery himself" (252). One remembers the hermit: "It's a mystery": Has God "set" a "way" for the heart's desire (19), despite the judge's sophistry?

I may be fouling my mind in such a search for hope (and since I am an atheist, I have no vested interest), but one's final response to the novel depends on one's reading of the epilogue. The mystery of the novel may be that the posthole digger seems part judge and part kid, both at once. Just as the judge signals the death of the Old West—buffalo gone, the last of the true warriors about to die, the judge's mapping of the terrain nearly complete—the posthole digger represents the fencing in of the wild Western range, the bringing of order, the coming of civilization. We have already contemplated the evils of civilization, but it is also the envy of men. The city builders develop the "tools, the art, the building—these things stand in judgement on the latter races" (146). The human race seems represented by the wanderers on the plain, *"the gatherers of bones and those who do not gather."* Yet the posthole digger not only brings order, he releases divine sparks: *"with his steel hole by hole striking the fire out of the rock which God has put there."* Are the kid's acts of compassion such sparks? Is there another ceremony other than war that uses "the sanctity of blood" (331) to cement human bonds? Can the kid's death be read as a bloody sacrifice? Isn't he the imperfect scapegoat for the judge's ultimate failure to control everything? Isn't he the free bird who escapes the judge's zoo? He does not escape Death, but who does? Where is Death's sting at the end? The judge may have come to claim the kid's soul—"This night thy soul may be required of thee" (327)—and the scene of his death may be horrible, but what the soul leaves behind cannot *matter.*

Daugherty thinks the fire of the epilogue is the sign of the alien gnostic god, and he also speculates that the posts represent McCarthy's own art, novel by novel. I think McCarthy holds out the possibility that at its best, civilization might produce the philosophers and city builders and artists as well as artisans that can bring some *"light"* beyond just the gray dawn to us mortals on the darkling plain. For the order thus wrought seems *"less the pursuit of some continuance than the verification of a principle, a validation of sequence and causality"*—a principle of causality that might go some distance to explain the Problem of Evil—or that at least might, through our questions, point us in the direction of mystery. The people on the plain, perhaps like the kid, the readers of this novel, *"cross in their progress one by one that track of holes that runs to the rim of the visible ground."* The judge has mockingly demanded of the kid, "[E]ven if you should have stood your ground, [. . .] yet what ground was it?" (307). It is *this* ground that we cross, this strange borderland, noticing *"each round and perfect hole."* From this crossing provided by art, we might infer meaning in the mystery of the darkly absurd as we attempt to cross the meridian of becoming, where our only, awesome destiny is to be the meaning-makers.

PART II

NORTH OF THE BORDER

In this part I focus on mavericks north of the Gadsden Purchase border and after the Civil War. Roughly the first half of these works deal with conflicts between "cowboys and Indians," so to speak; the second half with conflicts between "outlaws and lawmen," so to speak.

The United States was free to concentrate now on subduing Indian threats to its western movement, often using as an excuse for military intervention Indian raids on its new Hispanic citizens—and even on Mexicans south of the border. Since the Treaty of Guadalupe-Hidalgo in 1848 and the Gadsden Purchase in 1853–1854, however, Indians, who were not granted the same citizenship as their old enemies the new Mexican Americans, complained against the injustice (and inherent racism) of the policy of not just protecting their enemies but of prohibiting their lifeways, especially those of the Navajos and Apaches.

Broken Arrow's Tom Jeffords in the early 1870s tries to escape the role of Indian fighter and its senseless killing by crossing into the Chiricahua culture of the great chief Cochise and effecting peace. Tragically, neither his crossing nor the peace can last. In the early 1880s *Buffalo Soldiers'* 1st Sgt. Washington Wyatt confronts not only Victorio, one of the last great Apache chiefs, but also a crisis of identity that has pursued him, as an African American, from South to West. In the feature film *Geronimo: An American Legend* we confront the figure of the uncompromising eponymous warrior with radical ambivalence, embodied in the figure of Lt. Charles B. Gatewood, who brings Geronimo in at last in 1886 only to have betrayed him and his people into a form of genocide.

Meanwhile in the early 1880s, as the Anglo settlers move into the Southwest, creating boomtowns with a vengeance, the boom was subject to the predation of outlaws, and their threat brought equally predatory lawmen. *Tombstone*'s Doc Holliday lives on the edge—of the law, of life itself—until he confronts his alter ego, Johnny Ringo, whom he understands only too well, as a substitute for his friend Wyatt Earp, to whom he bequeaths not his death but his life wish. Doc Holliday's woman, in the novel of that title, crosses several boundaries in her self-creation, refusing to be objectified as just Doc's woman but emerging as her own person, Kate Elder.

Around the same time as Wyatt Earp and Doc Holliday are playing avenging angels, Gore Vidal's Billy the Kid, in the film of that title, identifies himself with the Territory of New Mexico and nostalgically defies the system of law and order employed to protect the rich and confine the anarchic individual. At the end of the century emerges one of the West's famous "bandit queens," Pearl Hart. The eponymous novel about her records the story of her robbing a stagecoach in desperation and winning the ignominious distinction of being the first woman sent to the dread Yuma Territorial Prison. Out of abjection she not only asserts her own identity but paradoxically dissolves it in her solidarity with the other oppressed of the Southwest—and the world.

4

BROKEN ARROW

CROSSING AS GESTURE

> I didn't think I would sleep but I must have.
> Because I awakened out of a sick nightmare.
> And I wanted to run. . . . It wasn't being brave
> that made me stay. It was something else. . . .
> Something deeper maybe. . . . 'Most every man
> I've ever known came to a time in his life when
> he decided to do something no matter what it cost.
> I figured this was it for me.
>
> Michael Blankfort, "Arrow"

Written to be a voice-over during Tom Jeffords's night camp as he approaches his daring meeting with Cochise, great chief of the Chiricahua Apaches, the probing lines of the epigraph were omitted from the film *Broken Arrow*. Yet the director, Delmer Daves, captures their essence in his wide-angle shot of Jeffords the next morning riding through the vast, apparently deserted, hostile expanse of alien Apache country as he approaches Cochise's Stronghold in the Dragoon Mountains. The film retains these final lines of the screenplay's existential moment: "I never felt so lonely—and so dog-scared in my life."[1] Though he has declared earlier, "I tell you, Mill—I'm sick and tired of being in the middle—with people asking me which side I'm on. I've been willing to take a chance in Cochise's territory to find gold. All right, now I'll take a chance on something else," this maverick Jeffords has taken "a chance" precisely by thrusting himself into the "middle." Jeffords has entered a nightmare boundary situation, a no-man's-land, as a lonely stranger filled with awe and dread at his momentous choice—to try to bridge two enemy cultures on the border. Bridge them he does, at terrible cost—a loss that seals the peace yet signs his ultimate failure.[2]

The film opens with incipient bridging: having saved an Apache boy wounded by white men,[3] Jeffords is released by a scouting party looking for the boy: "They wanted to kill me all right, but they let me go . . . I learned things that day: Apache mothers cried about their sons; Apache men had a sense of fair play." Before he can leave, however, he is forced to watch the Indians attack and slaughter, sometimes slowly, another group of miners. One of the leaders of the Apache band, Goyahkla, known to us as Geronimo, comments on what Jeffords has witnessed: "Learn it—learn it well! This is Apache land! You have no right here. Where Cochise lives, no white man can live."

Seemingly absolute separation: Cochise, we know from history, has tried peace with the invading Anglos. Invading, because as far as Cochise is concerned, Anglos and Mexicans traded for the land without consulting its dominant, indigenous inhabitants.[4] Yet in the late 1850s and early 1860s Cochise kept a peace for a half-dozen years with the Anglos, until betrayed under a flag of truce in the infamous Bascom affair—a betrayal from which he narrowly escaped and as a result of which his own brother was humiliatingly hanged. So now his claim to the land is absolute, his war against the Anglos total. And the murder of Mangas Coloradas under another flag of truce and the Camp Grant massacre have merely hardened him in his resolve.[5]

Yet Jeffords is already embarked on a crossing in his consciousness. When Jeffords returns to Tucson, he rejects Colonel Bernall's offer to scout for the army, and he mocks the colonel's West Point plans for defeating Cochise in six months. Jeffords evinces his great respect for Cochise and his Chiricahuas as adversaries:

> Cochise can't even read a map, but he and his men know every gully, every foot of mountain, every water hole in Arizona. His horses can go twice as far as yours in a day — and his *men* can run on foot as far as a horse can run. He can't write his name but his intelligence service knows when *you* got to Fort Grant and how many men you've got. He's stopped the Butterfield stage from running, he's stopped the U.S. Mails from going through. And for the first time in Indian history he has all the Apaches from all the tribes fighting under one command. Ah, you're not going to string him up in six months, Colonel, not in six years.

Confronted by Tucsonans, some of whom have lost loved ones recently and resent Jeffords for his incipient sympathies, Jeffords sets the record straight: first, with regard to the attack on the miners, which he witnessed; second, with regard to who started the war: "Ah now hold, let's get the facts straight here. Cochise didn't start this war. A snooty little lieutenant [Bascom] fresh out of the east started it — he flew a flag of truce which Cochise honored — and then he hanged Cochise's brother and five others." Already alienated from Slade, whose wife was just killed by Apaches and who suspects Jeffords is an Indian-lover, Jeffords's final exchange with the Tucsonans is the most significant:

> *Jeffords* (to Slade): You want to know why I didn't kill that Apache boy? Well, for the same reason I wouldn't kill your boy or scout for the army. I'm sick and tired of all this killing . . . Besides, who asked us out here, in the first place?
> *Lowrie:* I don't know, Tom. I don't claim the white man's always done right. But we're bringin' civilization here, ain't we?

Lowrie's version of Manifest Destiny gets ludicrously truncated, however, as he continues: "Clothes and carpets—hats an' boots an' medicine. Why I got a wagonload of first-class whiskey waitin' for me in the east. I could sell it at a dollar a bottle if it wasn't for Cochise." Civilization reduced to its basest accoutrements and commodified. To the Tucsonans, the West is merely market. But behind Jeffords's remark is a growing awareness, fully developed in the novel, that the United States is simply an imperial power, conquering those in the way of its destiny—although in the novel Jeffords says, in effect, that it is Yankee know-how that is "being tested": that all we need are "trained colonizers" (Arnold 427–28). Screenwriter Blankfort and director Daves instill in Jeffords an even more revisionist consciousness. Jeffords says to the astonished Cochise, "My people have done yours great wrong." This admission, like Ike McCaslin's about what the white men have done to the black, is heresy to the prevailing ideology.

In the novel Jeffords daydreams that perhaps he and Cochise together can find a way to stop the war, to find lasting peace. In the film, although he has come ostensibly just to petition Cochise to let the mail go through unmolested, Jeffords spontaneously extends his mission, endeavoring to get Cochise to think about the inevitable "tomorrow" when the dwindling Apaches will be no match for the ever-increasing Anglos. Cochise ruthlessly terminates the topic: "I will not talk of that with you!" Jeffords persists: "Is it not possible that your people and mine can someday live together like brothers?" Such is the promise of Jeffords's daring venture.

Daves sets the audience up, then, to be sympathetic with Jeffords as he starts his crossing. The problem is that the crossing becomes attraction-repulsion: repulsion from the crass white world and attraction to the primitivized, romanticized Indian world. Jeffords is in danger of crossing over and not just walking a mile in Cochise's moccasins and returning to the other bank but going native. Welcomed by Machogee, the boy he has saved, admired by Cochise, he falls in love at first sight with Sonseeahray, the beautiful young Indian woman he encounters during her puberty ritual as White Painted Lady. Jeffords has asked the tame Apache Juan to teach him Apache language and customs so that he can learn them "in here"—in his heart. His respect for the Apaches grows in proportion to his contempt for his own kind. Indeed, the film portrays Apache village life as almost idyllic, their rituals and religion as richly meaningful, their political and social interaction as bound by respect and honor, a code of word-as-bond.

Meanwhile, the Tucsonans grow increasingly distrustful of Jeffords as his deal with Cochise holds and the mail goes through but at the same time Cochise continues his war and successfully raids a wagon train guarded by Colonel Bernall, who along with most his men is killed in the action. They finally accuse Jeffords of being in collusion with Cochise. Jeffords slugs Slade to the floor and demands, "Anybody else want to call me a renegade?" *Renegade* used to be a much more powerful word than it is today. For centuries it was employed as a term of utter opprobrium against Christians who went over to Islam and thus *denied* (Spanish *renegar;* Latin *renegare*) not only their European heritage but their Christian faith. Thus Jeffords reveals his own anxiety about having crossed over. The Tucsonans sense the gap between them and try to string Jeffords up, yelling, among other comments almost lost in the crowd, "He's a copperhead! He sold us out!"

The near-hanging of Jeffords is not in the novel. It was fabricated for the film in order graphically to express not only irrational hatred among the Tucsonans but the depth of Jeffords's alienation. General Howard's intervention saves him, but the alienation continues and deepens yet, around the metaphor of *selling out*. For this Gen. Oliver Otis Howard, one-armed Civil War hero, has been sent by President Ulysses Grant to negotiate lasting peace with the Apaches. He seeks Jeffords's help. Jeffords insists he will not "sell Cochise down the river." What constitutes a "fair peace"? Jeffords declares, "Equality! The Apaches are a free people. They have the right to stay free — on their own lands. [. . .] [A] clear territory that is Apache — ruled by Apaches . [. . .] No soldiers on it." Jeffords's crowning achievement is to broker this peace, so that Cochise breaks the arrow of war.

Jeffords's demands for equality, freedom, and self-rule are an expression of his belief in the democratic ideals on which his country is supposed to be based. The major symbol of the treaty presented dramatically in the film is the map Cochise asks Jeffords, not Howard (because he does not speak Apache, but symbolically Jeffords is elevated to chief negotiator), to explain to his people. Jeffords first explains the signing of the map to Cochise: "This is a way of showing to all people for all time any agreement that you make." He then explains to the assembled chiefs. "I have in my hand here a map. This is a sort of picture writing. It shows the Apache territory — fifty thousand square miles — that you have agreed upon. This piece of paper will go back to Washington where the Chief of all white man lives. If you make a treaty of peace, this will be part of that treaty."[6]

Some Apaches were not happy with the treaty, such as Goyahkla, who now declares his independence under his Spanish name, Geronimo, for it took away from the Chiricahuas their livelihood by raiding, forced them to farm and raise cattle, and made them dependent on the U.S. government for rations of food and blankets. Moreover, in time it would be interpreted as forbidding forays into Mexico. But the southern Arizonans were even more unhappy, for, as portrayed in the novel, they felt Jeffords and Howard had given away far too much land. The screenplay includes a scene, cut from the finished film, of Howard and Jeffords's being scorned upon their expected triumphal entry into Tucson. Of course, Cochise's response would be (and is in the novel) that the white man did not *give* the land to the Chiricahuas but simply acknowledged their right to it as traditionally theirs.

Jeffords's opinion would square with Cochise's, especially since they had become like brothers. The film structures the story so that the peace negotiations are interspersed with scenes of the deepening love and eventual marriage between Jeffords and Sonseeahray. Cochise brokers the marriage—and even kills the jealous lover Nahilzay, his chief warrior, for attacking Jeffords and thus breaking Cochise's protective word. So Jeffords's motivation for the treaty is mixed, contaminated in a sense: "I prayed that a decent peace would come from the meeting of these two men. I wanted it for my country. I wanted it for Cochise and his people . . . and I wanted it . . . because I loved a girl." When Sonseeahray, after their wedding night, worries, "Sometime . . . will you grow tired of me and go back to your people?" Jeffords proclaims, "That is a bad thought, Sonseeahray. Never think it again. *You* are my people." Jeffords has crossed over so far that after Sonseeahray is killed in Slade's ambush, he demands that one of the survivors be brought to him so he might torture and finish him with a knife—as if he were an Apache avenging himself for another Anglo atrocity.

There is a richer meaning to Jeffords's telling Sonseeahray, *"You* are my people," however. And it speaks to the reason so much of the film is devoted to their love story. In the novel, Sonseeahray is killed in a cavalry raid well before General Howard's advent. Blankfort constructs the screenplay so that the love story is integral to the last moment. He invents the story of Slade's ambush, thus causing the film to come full circle back to Slade's anguish and unrelenting hatred of the Apaches. Perhaps he made the love story so prominent for reasons of Hollywood: to increase appeal and thus profit. But as cultural critics we can read out the implications that flowed, perhaps unwittingly, through Blankfort's pen and Daves's camera.

Proclaiming Sonseeahray his people places Jeffords in the space between cultures, not fully one nor fully the other. She is a figure for his ultimate desideratum, a cure for his existential loneliness. The very morning after he has seen her for the first time as White Painted Lady, he declares to her, "All my life, I have been mostly alone. I wanted it that way. But when I saw you in the wickiup, and you touched me, you prayed for me, I felt bad being alone, and I knew that I needed to see you again before I left so that I could find out if it was the same as last night. [. . .] Now when I go away, I will be lonely for someone for the first time in my life." More than the typical Western loner, Jeffords has just been through a dark night of the soul on the way across the gap between his and Cochise's people. It is as if this wonderful person comes to meet him in the arroyo of his decision and comforts him. On a mythic level, it is as if the matriarchal goddess of life, the "Earth Woman" as she is identified by the screenplay during the marriage ceremony (129), has entered the space between to welcome the patriarchal sky god represented by Tagliato, the Redbeard (novel).

Broken Arrow is not the first story of a European colonizer falling in love with a native "girl." One thinks of the godlike bearded Cortés and La Malinche/La Chingada; Capt. John Smith and Pocahontas. In some sense the figure is the same as in the story of Carothers McCaslin and Eunice. It is a figure for cultural dominance, cultural imperialism. The colonizer is male, the colonized female. The male appropriates and plows the female (La Chingada) even as he appropriates and plows the land. He inseminates her with his culture. Sonseeahray begs to know Jeffords's language. And it is no accident that Howard has been "nicknamed the Christian General" and that Jeffords likes the way he reads the Bible he carries with him everywhere. From the beginning of the novel Cochise says the white man has something special, in the light of which the Apaches must make peace with him, must learn from him. That specialness is cultural superiority conferred by the Right Religion. In their postcoital matinal reverie Jeffords hoots aloud then explains, "I think it was a word that was made by Adam when he opened his eyes and saw Eve." Sonseeahray: "Who are they?" Jeffords, a bit surprised: "Don't you know?" Sonseeahray, ingenuous in her ignorance, ready to be instructed: "Oh, the world is so big and I know so little." The film is fully complicit with this cultural imperialism, for as sympathetically as it portrays the Chiricahuas, it suppresses several positive portrayals of their religion and culture and negative portrayals of Anglo religion and culture.[7] In the novel Cochise is a social Darwinist, believing finally that the strong win, the weak lose in the course of history. The film glosses this truth with the ideological justification of Manifest Christian Destiny. The coupling of Jeffords and Sonseeahray signifies the coupling of the United States with the Chiricahua Nation—supposedly in *equality* but really with the latter in the feminine or recessive position.

The death of Sonseeahray, however, far from being the seal of the peace is the sign that there can be no coupling. First, because Jeffords and Sonseeahray cannot really bridge the gap between cultures. Theirs is a union in the gap, in no-man's-land. Neither side will accept their miscegenation, as Cochise warns:

> *(to Jeffords compassionately)* [I]t will not be easy for you.
> . . . You are an American. Where will you live? Here? — There will always be Apaches who have suffered from white men who will hate *you* for it. Tucson, maybe? — Will there not always be whites there who will hate your *wife* because of the color of her skin? You will go far away maybe — in new places — but your eyes will never see anything — always they will be turned backward — toward home.
> *(he turns to Sonseeahray, his voice is even gentler)* And you Sonseeahray — they will look at you as at a strange animal — and make jokes.

A contemporary Arizona audience knows that the state antimiscegenation ordinance stayed on the books until the U.S. Supreme Court overturned it in 1977! Within the context of the film, the miscegenation will not overcome Jeffords's loneliness but simply compound it. He will not have completed a successful crossing over and back. He will not have completed even a full crossing over, a full going native. The children Sonseeahray envisions will ride no white horses. They will remain mavericks.

Machogee is a kind of sign of the possibility of future crossed generations. Befriended and healed by Jeffords, giver of his amulet to Jeffords, greeter of Jeffords in Cochise's camp when he comes upon his first peace mission for the mails, Machogee dies attacking the supply train. The camera pans his dead body on the plain. Even though historically Cochise had sons, at least one of whom eventually joined Geronimo upon his father's death while another submissively moved the Chiricahuas he could onto the San Carlos Reservation, the film portrays him as virtually childless, his hopes for progeny symbolically dashed in the death of Machogee and (in the novel) in the death of Sonseeahray and Jeffords's uterine offspring upon her death.

At this deeper, more symbolic level, there can be no successful union between Jeffords and Sonseeahray, for there can be no lasting brotherhood between Anglo and Chiricahua Apache. However much the film highlights Cochise's resolve to keep the peace, to keep his sacred word no matter Jeffords's and his loss—he insists that there are rogues on both sides, Geronimo and Slade, but that the peoples themselves have not broken the peace—we know that it failed miserably. That even before Cochise died the U.S. government was trying to renege on its promise to let the Chiricahuas stay on their own land. That the Tucsonans and other southern Arizonans would never give up that much potentially exploitable land. That the genocide the novel finally discloses was virtually completed. That the Chiricahuas as a nation were obliterated, scattered as far away as Florida. That Cochise kept his word but we did not. Sonseeahray's death becomes a broken seal, Jeffords's great painful choice resulting only in irremediable loss.

Yet Jeffords is a figure not for the nineteenth-century Indian agent, who went on to work for the government in its dealings with the Apaches, but for the twentieth-century revisionist, from historian to critic to audience. He offers us absolution for the sins of the fathers, a position from which to condemn the treatment of the Apaches even as we still benefit from it, whether we participate in the West's current economy—as I do, teaching at the University of Arizona in Tucson—or just visit its national parks and monuments and forests, like the Chiricahua Mountains or Cochise's Stronghold. In an important sense, Jeffords's existential dilemma represents our own ambivalence.[8]

5

LATERAL FREEDOM

BUFFALO SOLDIERS

. . . fighting men we have more in common with
than we dare admit.

John Horse, army scout, in *Buffalo Soldiers*

Charles Haid's 1997 Turner Network Television production, *Buffalo Soldiers,* features three mavericks: Victorio, great Apache chief, who in the
early 1880s has refused to live where the United States dictates away from
his native homeland, Warm Springs, New Mexico, and has gone on the
warpath; John Horse, Black Seminole scout for the U.S. Army, with great
experience patrolling the Southwest border—and a great love of his own
freedom; and especially Washington Wyatt, freed slave from Mississippi,
now first sergeant in the United States Army, Tenth Regiment, H-Troop:
part of the Buffalo Soldiers, on patrol in Texas and New Mexico during the
last years of the Apache Wars, as two of the remaining chiefs after Cochise,
Victorio and Nana, try to bring their Mescaleros and Mimbreños together
to fight a last-ditch total war against the Americans. Wyatt is no maverick
initially, however, for he has chosen the army as a career and does everything he can to carry out orders. His commanding officer, Col. Benjamin
Grierson, opines that he is the best soldier he has ever served with. But as
the film progresses, Wyatt is forced to make a crucial choice of identity: to
remain in the pyramidal, hierarchical structure of the army—and thus of
the dominant white, patriarchal society—or to move laterally toward fellow oppressed people of color.[1]

Wyatt is trying to make a career in the army by carrying out orders and
going by the book. His fort commander, General Pike, and Maj. Eugene
Carr, the leader of C-Troop, on loan from the Sixth Cavalry in Arizona, do
not want him to succeed, for they are racists. Wyatt explains to his regi-

mental commander, Colonel Grierson, his chosen path: "Being an ex-slave in Mississippi's as bad as it gets. You're colored, new-freed. I did what all good Mississippians couldn't, to prove something Carr and the general would never believe anyway"—that is, to prove by being a good soldier that he is a man, free and equal. Grierson himself owns he never did really want the army, and he pointedly asks Wyatt, "Is this what you and your fellows bargained for with your new-found freedom?" But Wyatt responds, "I chose the army, Sir." When Grierson lies wounded, he implores Wyatt to take command of the Buffalo Soldiers and carry out their mission: "The mission matters. This regiment, H-Troop. They matter. If we fail in this men like Pike will use it to force men like you out of the army. We—You can't let that happen. We've come so—so far." Wyatt responds to this white man who sacrificed a more brilliant career to lead the Tenth, "Always knew what you tried to do for us, Colonel."

Indeed, Pike, who offers Grierson a way out of his ignominious command, sees the Buffalo Soldiers as inferior. When Sergeant Christie returns having been outflanked by the powerful and elusive Victorio, Pike expostulates with condescension about the black noncoms, "Their kind relays orders; they don't give them." "Kind" superficially means noncoms, but implicitly means blacks. Not as explicitly as Carr, who refuses to lead "niggers," Pike is nonetheless a racist. By his order the Buffalo Soldiers are evicted from their barracks for Carr's newly arrived white C-Troop. It is Carr who wants the barracks wiped down with lye, the bunks "kerosened"; it is Pike who has the blacks not on patrol stripped to their waists and wielding picks to dig a new latrine looking like field darkies. Of course, the racism is fully institutionalized: "Keep your troops back, Captain Calhoun [who has been assigned temporary command of H-Troop and is leading them out to find Victorio]. Parade regulations: colored companies fifteen yards behind white." As Wyatt and his men dismount to ride through the adjacent town, Wyatt explains further to Calhoun: "Colored soldiers not supposed to ride through town with fanfare. Regulations, Captain."

Pike's racism of course extends to the Apaches. The reason Christie and not Wyatt has pursued Victorio is that Wyatt has caught Texas Rangers chasing the marauding Victorio onto Mescalero Reservation land under army protection—and hanging Apache children to extract Victorio's whereabouts from their captured mothers. Wyatt dispatches Christie and brings the Rangers back to the fort under arrest. Pike seethes, "I pray you didn't let Victorio slip through your fingers, sergeant, just for the sake of two Apache brats." Pike frees the Rangers. The Buffalo Soldiers speculate why: "'Cause they aren't Apaches. 'Cause they kill Apaches. 'Cause they're white." When the captured great chief and prophet Nana sings into the night disturbing Pike's sleep, he grabs one of Nana's band and shoots him in the head.

So Wyatt attempts to forge an identity for himself and his Buffalo Soldiers that is accepted and respected by the white army in particular, the white society by extension. He wants to be accepted as a soldier and as a man. So as not to give men like Pike and Carr an excuse to "fail" him, so to speak, he is scrupulous in obeying orders. He is deferential to a fault to his superiors. Sometimes he uses such deferential behavior to his advantage, as when he chooses to return to the fort with Nana instead of reinforcing Carr down on the Gila River: he tells Pike in a way that mocks the general's previous stance, "Lacking proper leadership skills, I relied on my limited field experience." Carr threatens him: "One of these days, Mr. Wyatt, you're not going to be able to hide behind army regulations."

If Wyatt has learned how to accommodate prejudice with mild resistance, he nevertheless faces an insidious threat. From the beginning he has shown himself vulnerable to compassion for the Indians. He arrives in time to save a third Apache boy, and he sarcastically asks the captain of the Rangers which of the two hanging boys is Victorio. As he splits the troop and heads back with the captive Rangers, he instructs one of his corporals to return the boy to his mother. When Grierson asks him what he thinks of Nana, Wyatt replies from the depths of a capacity in his own soul: "I think he's the most alone man on this earth." Grierson: "Alone? Nana? With the U.S. Army at his throat, the Apache Nation at his feet?" Wyatt: "Half himself buried and the other half left to wander, looking for what's dead and gone. And it's him." It would seem that Wyatt's ability to appreciate this aloneness stems from his own profound loneliness as he tries to carry out his choice. Grierson prods Wyatt to feel proud that he captured "the one man who had the power to turn a murdering renegade like Victorio into a holy crusader," but all Wyatt can feel is the loss of seven men, including the gallant but inexperienced Calhoun.

At this moment of vulnerability, there is grumbling in the ranks of the Buffalo Soldiers. They are appalled at Carr's filthy trick of bringing in the dead bodies of homesteaders and using them to vindicate his failed campaign by making it appear Wyatt was at fault for not reinforcing him. Surprisingly, John Horse, Pike's personal scout and, apparently, spy, sticks up for Wyatt. But when he comes to the Buffalo Soldiers' campfire looking for some gratitude from Wyatt, he is surprised at the cold shoulder: "Damn, are you such a stupid nigger?" Horse himself is half black, half Seminole Indian. "What kind of nigger you think I am, breed?" seethes Wyatt. Horse's response is Wyatt's first challenge to his self-definition, self-representation: "I don't understand you. I don't understand who you are." Wyatt: "I'm a First Sergeant in the United States Army." Horse: "In the army? Army bears you no love. None of you. They endure you. They endure you till they wipe all the tribes from the slate with our blood. You have no pride, First Sergeant. You have no pride." Stung to the core, Wyatt retaliates: "One thing's for sure, Scout, I didn't leave it in a bone on the floor next to Pike's boots."

Horse's own self-identification here, however, problematizes Wyatt's entire project: "till they wipe all the tribes from the slate with *our* blood" (emphasis mine). Horse is a walking embodiment of a relationship between black and Indian that perhaps he only begins to feel ironically when he uses the hair of Nana's captive daughter to wipe off her contemptuous spit: a commingling of blood. He confronts Wyatt even more directly, when he picks up on his men's mutinous mutterings. The Buffalo Soldiers have been grumbling even more loudly at the white officers' complete ignoring of the death of the blacks during Calhoun's ill-fated skirmish. The brother of a dead Buffalo Soldier complains, "We're not soldiers, we're sponges, goin' around soakin' up the blood and the guts. And for what? Till I joined this here th'army, I ain't ever known me no Indians, never even cared to meet one. Now I've killed a dozen. And I have to wonder why." Another responds cynically, "'Cause some white boy with gold braid on his arm tells us to, that's why, and we let him. Every one of us gave him the right to tell us what to do, when to do it. Now we might as well be back on the block, the mess we made of this thing." What thing? The campaign? The war? Their service in the army? Freedom itself?

At the critical moment of Grierson's wounding, Horse wonders whether they ought not all be heading back to the fort with him. The men wonder too, aloud, and Horse picks up their complaint in midsentence and makes it radical: "[. . .] fighting men we have more in common with than we dare admit." Wyatt again resists, cynically glancing at Nana's daughter and interpreting Horse's sentiment as coming from a new-found conscience: "No tellin' where you find one these days." Horse represents himself in terms of freedom: "I am a free man, Wyatt. I come and go at *my* pleasure, for *my* reasons. Can you say the same?" Pulling his service revolver, Wyatt resists by affirming the self he has worked so hard to construct. Those "without the balls" to continue after Victorio may accompany the scout and Grierson back to the fort. Anyone else who remains will obey him, and he will meet mutiny with summary execution and dismemberment. Horse stays, acknowledging Wyatt as "the Man," and Wyatt immediately puts him to the test by threatening to blow the Apache woman's head off if Nana does not reveal Victorio's rendezvous. The secret extracted, the men complain at the forced march, and Wyatt insists, "We have our orders." One protests plaintively, "I thought you was in charge now, Sergeant." Wyatt screams, "I AM!"

When Horse saves Wyatt from the Apache sniper they are pursuing, Wyatt stares at him but refuses to shake his hand. He cannot. For to do so would threaten his commitment to the army and its hierarchy. Moreover, Horse challenges hierarchy with lateral identification,[2] sympathy with an enemy they have more in common with than Wyatt, at least, dare admit. Even as the Indians are humanized before his very eyes—the most child-like of the soldiers marvels as they play in the water, "Nev' think they might do that, play splash n' such"—Wyatt maintains his hardline position anent the surrounded Victorio. The parleying Victorio continues Horse's assault on Wyatt's consciousness. In a poignant touch, Victorio's probing questions and retorts are conveyed through the translating scout:

> *Victorio/Horse:* Are you a slave?
> *Wyatt:* No, I am not a slave.
> *Victorio/Horse:* You were a slave.
> *Wyatt:* Yes, I was.
> *Victorio/Horse:* Why do you fight for those who were your mas-
>   ters, Washington Wyatt?

Wyatt does not answer but instead reminds Victorio that the Buffalo Soldiers have his remaining band of Mescaleros surrounded. Victorio defiantly affirms, "We will fight you and fight for our dead. We will not be slaves like you." Wyatt still refuses the direct challenge to his identity: Victorio has said that the ex-slave is *still* a slave, to the army: "Why do you murder my people for those who made you less than cattle?" Their exchange had begun with a compliment on the name "buffalo" soldiers; now Victorio diminishes the buffaloes to a domestic herd.

Wyatt is like the colonel in *Bridge on the River Kwai.* He stubbornly fails to see what he is about to do. He does not realize how his obedience to a hierarchical order perpetuates the master narrative of European culture. He is a collaborator with the enemy: an enemy who enslaved millions of Africans and now commits genocide against the Indians. The master has freed the slave but not into full participation in American society. Blacks have no jobs to speak of, but may enlist in the army, where they virtually cannot be officers, must be segregated.[3] Here they are being exploited to exterminate another Third World people. Wyatt experiences an existential *crise de conscience.* And he now resists with all his might, threatening to annihilate every man, woman, and child and to put all the blame on Victorio's head.

As the Buffalo Soldiers reluctantly shoulder their arms to obliterate the Mescaleros, and as Victorio and his men and older boys shoulder their arms in return—women and children huddled together in the middle wailing—some of the soldiers plead with Wyatt: "We can't do this. Wyatt, *we* can't do this." "How can you do this, Wyatt? How can you live with this? It be on your soul, Wyatt." Shutting his ears to these sirens of mutiny, Wyatt orders his men to fire on his shot. Some begin to cry. One prays the Lord to have mercy on their souls. But they will not finally mutiny. He has taught them well.

What causes Wyatt to depress the hammer of his revolver and not shoot, what finally breaks through and forces the existential crisis to the forefront of his consciousness is an Apache boy: the boy he had saved from hanging, sent back to his mother at the beginning of the film. The boy walks out of the huddle, looking Wyatt in the eyes, first quizzically then reprovingly, as if to say along with his men, "How can you do this? How can you now kill me whom you saved? I don't understand you."

Wyatt rips pages from the book. He releases the Apaches, urging them to go to Mexico. He plans to falsify his report. He countermands the order for the troop to dismount as they ride through the town outside the fort. He brazenly leads his troop onto the parade ground as Pike and Carr are playing soldier. It is the Fourth of July. The healed Grierson returns his salute. It would appear that Wyatt has won respect for the Buffalo Soldiers. They are now full-fledged Americans. It is their Independence Day too.

But the ending is subversive. Wyatt has forever altered his relationship to the book, to the army—and to the Indians. The closing hymn, the "Battle Cry of Freedom," celebrates a "welcome" not only to "our Brothers" the Buffalo Soldiers as they ride into the fort but also to "our Brothers" the Indians, for both black and Indian are embraced in the lines, as the camera switches from Buffalo Soldiers on parade ground to retreating Apaches on the landscape:

> Although he be poor
> He shall never die a slave,
> Shouting the Battle Cry of Freedom.

The white boy who salutes the Buffalo Soldiers as they ride through the town is the same boy Horse saved from the homestead destroyed by Victorio at the opening of the film. The ending seems to say that the future lies in a nonhierarchized, lateral brotherhood that embraces that boy, the Apache boy, and the Buffalo Soldiers—a brotherhood from which the hierarchy is excluded, for Pike sits his horse dumfounded, pointedly failing to return Wyatt's salute.

Yet once more history tempers our response: Victorio and his band were slaughtered by Mexican soldiers, as the director, Charles Haid, suggests by erasing them from the landscape in the final wide-angle shot. Blacks had to wait till after World War II to gain equality in the armed services and a modicum of civil rights. But at least Victorio did not die a slave. And when Wyatt insists, "You do not use the word 'sir' for the First Sergeant. You only salute—," *officers,* he would have said, his self-interruption, and his return of his men's salutes—even Horse's—point in the direction of respect based on merit, not rank, not race, not class. The respect Wyatt merits at the end of the film is earned by his refusal finally to be complicit with the master script of Manifest Destiny, especially as it entails not only a myth of cultural but racial superiority. He has had to jettison the belief he had built his postslavery identity upon. The decision was excruciating. But through it he arrives at identification with fellow resisters. As much as he is in uniform in front of his troop at the end, he is an ironic figure for resistance to imperialism.

But only ironic. For his figure cannot erase the historical complicity of African American soldiers in the subjugation of another oppressed people. Late-twentieth-century multicultural consciousness wants to erase that complicity and to substitute solidarity. It can do so only through the wish-fulfillment of fiction—or denial.

6

Geronimo Framed

> For many years the One God made me a warrior. No gun, no bullets could ever kill me. That was my Power. Now my time is over. Now, maybe, the time of our people is over.
>
> Geronimo in *Geronimo: An American Legend*

Walter Hill's 1993 feature film *Geronimo* frames the story of this *American Legend* as he calls him in the subtitle. The story is framed first by a voice-over narrative derived from the memoirs of Lt. Britton Davis. Davis serves as a controlling point of view for the audience. Geronimo's legend is of course always already framed, even for Apaches: framed by Geronimo's own words as told to S.M. Barrett; framed by the memoirs of other Americans on the scene, notably Lt. Charles B. Gatewood and Gen. George Crook; framed by other witnesses and intervening histories, oral and written. As opposed to the coeval Turner Network Television made-for-TV film *Geronimo,* which follows Geronimo's own narrative—as if it were not filtered through amanuensis, translator, screenwriter, director, and actors—Hill's film accepts framing as inevitable for those of us who would try to view, understand, interpret this legend a century removed.[1] But the reflective moviegoer realizes that he or she is invited to identify not with Lieutenant Davis but with Lieutenant Gatewood, whose consciousness is forced to engage most deeply with the significance of this moment of Southwestern history—and with the consciousness of the enigmatic Goyakhla, known to us by his Anglicized Spanish name, Geronimo. They are both mavericks in relation to their cultures: Geronimo because he cannot bring himself to follow the old chief, Nana, and become a tame Apache; Gatewood because he respects the enemy he fights and loathes the general he serves yet operates anyway as an agent of cultural domination. Gatewood crosses over to Geronimo only to absorb his power and finally obliterate it.

Davis's framing voice-over provides the late-twentieth-century audience a guiltless retrospective. Like him, we never killed any Apaches: "I'm

quite content to go to my grave knowing that I've never killed an Apache."
Like him, we are sympathetic to the two major protagonists of the film,
Geronimo and Gatewood. Like him, we admire Gen. George Crook and
hate Gen. Nelson Miles. Like him (though unlike Crook), we are led to
understand Geronimo's and to abhor our own government's broken word.
Davis's resignation of his commission because of his fractured idealism—
"I thought the U.S. Army kept its word. [. . .] I'm ashamed. And you have
my resignation"—costs him the career he and his family desired, but it lets
him, and us, off the hook of responsibility, complicity.

History tells us that Davis resigned much earlier, finding an offer to
manage a ranching and mining enterprise too attractive to resist. And that
he resented Geronimo for the breakout at Turkey Creek, branded him "a
malcontent" there and "faithless" later when Geronimo broke his word to
Crook at Cañon de los Embudos.[2] Hill chose to fictionalize him, however,
to make him a better stand-in for us, a better guiltless witness. Freed from
guilt, we can better lament our country's treatment of the Apaches. We can
be the idealists Miles despises ("There's always something messy about
them" because they're "more worried about keeping [their] word to a savage" than "fulfilling [their] duties to the citizens of this country"). Therefore we can, in our revisionist history and art and rhetoric, acknowledge
both collective guilt and sympathy in the changing process of legend. It
may be messy, but it's necessary.

In his eulogy for the late Arizonan Barry Goldwater, Secretary of the Interior Bruce Babbitt, himself scion of a frontier Arizona family, compared
Goldwater to Geronimo: his love of this land, his fierce defense of liberty.
Those are astonishing words from an Anglo Arizonan, words for which he
would have been branded a Tom Jeffords-style Indian lover a century ago.
In the case of Geronimo, the most hated of all the Chiricahuas, he might
have been strung up. That Babbitt could get away with such revisionist
rhetoric within a hundred years of Geronimo's death measures how much
the legend has been transformed. Hill's film presents Geronimo about as
admirably as he can be portrayed. He is brutal. He kills men, women, and
children indiscriminately. But when accosted by Crook for such heinous
behavior, Geronimo responds, "Not murder. War. Many bad things happen
in war." Crook: "You killed women and children." Geronimo: "So did you."[3]
Unpleasant as it is to acknowledge, the warfare of the Apache wars is
Clausewitzian *total war:* the war of people against people, where the objective is to annihilate the opposing people entirely. Major Carr in *Buffalo
Soldiers* and General Crook in *Geronimo* can protest shock and outrage at

the *depredations* of Victorio or Geronimo, but in the context of total war, they make perfect sense. As Gatewood says about Apache scouts, there's a kind of morality to it once you understand it. The same kind of morality that must have justified in the minds of Truman *and* his nemesis MacArthur the dropping of atomic bombs on Asians.

The film endows Geronimo with bravery and a fierce defense of land and liberty—and culture. After bolting the reservation at Turkey Creek[4] Geronimo exhibits both brutal efficiency and a warrior code of honor when he attacks the mining camp yet spares the one brave miner (whose own polemic is that of colonizers since Cabeza de Vaca: the Indians have done nothing with the land, never will). Even while sparing him, however, Geronimo insists that the land belongs to the Apaches and that he will kill the miner if he ever sees him on it again. Geronimo opens his negotiation with Crook at Cañon de los Embudos with an appeal to the One God over all, a setting up of a religious, culturalist defense of his breakout, but Crook interrupts him, rejects his rationale out of hand, and pronounces the traditional condemnation of Geronimo: "The Apache were doing fine farming corn—the problem was Geronimo—I knew Cochise. He was a king. He was a wise ruler of his people. I knew Victorio. He was a proud leader. And I know Geronimo. He doesn't want to lead or rule or be wise. He just wants to fight."[5] Geronimo polemically protests, "I didn't start this trouble. The Army killed the Dreamer." "He was calling for war," Crook retorts, but the film portrays the Dreamer as an Apache religious revivalist of sorts, prophesying the rising of the dead chiefs and insisting that the Apaches are the true keepers of the land. It is the army, from Gatewood to Carr (who leads the enforcing troop to Cibecue Creek), that interprets the shaman as a military threat to be, as Davis's voice-over puts it, dealt with immediately. Geronimo, who has traveled from Turkey to Cibecue Creek to hear what the shaman has to say, insists to Carr, "He's not done nothing. We're not bothering no one." But the tragedy is that, aside from rare individuals like Jeffords and Gatewood, Anglos made no attempt to understand the Apache ways. Even the unsentimental scout Al Sieber thinks Carr was wrong to shoot the shaman.

Crook refuses to listen to Geronimo's justification, so Geronimo shifts the argument. Ironically (for those who would portray him as renegade), he sounds like Cochise and Victorio: "With all this land, why is there no room for the Apache? Why does the White-Eye want all land?" This is perhaps the key moment in the entire film. Larry Gross's revised screenplay at this moment gives the stage direction, "Crook makes no reply — stares hard at Geronimo" (70). Gene Hackman as Crook, however, perhaps with Hill's direction, plays Crook here as exasperated but also speechless: he takes off his hat and rubs his hair. He does not stare at Geronimo but looks around. When Geronimo realizes he will get no answer to this all-important question, he asks, "How long in Florida?" The import seems to be that Crook, the army, the government have no answer that can be articulated. Crook comes close in a candid moment with Sieber after his resignation. "Settlers, prospectors, land speculators—they won't admit it, but the truth is they'd all like to see the Indian dead. They see the army as their weapon."

Even though Nana capitulates, Geronimo resists, uttering an ethos of endurance and defiance: "When I was young, the White-Eye came and wanted the land of my people. When their soldiers burnt our villages, we moved to the mountains. When they took our food, we ate thorns. When they killed our children, we had more. We killed all White-Eye that we could. We starved and we killed. But in our hearts we never surrendered." Biographers tell us Geronimo was warned by a whiskey trader that he would be hanged if he surrendered now.[6] But in order to portray his maverick decision more heroically, the film invents a scene between the Apache chiefs. Mangas is sympathetic with Nana and others who are too old and tired to fight any longer. But Geronimo warns that Crook will make them all prisoners. Nevertheless, Nana says, fatally, they have to trust Crook, and Geronimo concludes, "Go if you must. I have made my decision. I will not surrender to the White-Eye." He refuses to be a farmer on the reservation. ("Some Apache are good farmers," he tells Gatewood on his visit to Turkey Creek. "Others miss the old ways. I am not good farmer, Gate-wood.") Like the Victorio of *Buffalo Soldiers,* then, he refuses to relinquish his land to the white man, to give up his freedom to become a virtual slave. And even veteran Indian fighter Sieber says if he had been born an Apache, he'd be fighting alongside Geronimo.

Thus Geronimo has been reconstructed to fit a late-twentieth-century American ideology. He is a freedom fighter for whom extremism in the defense of liberty is no vice. He is truly, then, an *American* legend, not really different from Daniel Marion the Swamp Fox. He is a resister of tyranny, of colonization, of imperialism. He allows draft resisters to deplore the infamous actions of their government in its immoral wars, to refuse to participate (like Britton Davis), to sympathize with Ho Chi Minh, with Fidel, with Che. Goldwater's ghost will not like the drift of this analogy. But history makes strange bedfellows. Or is it theory? Or just rhetoric? C.L. Sonnichsen, eminent student of the Southwest, deplored the apotheosis of the modern Geronimo, resulting from a consciousness as well as conscience awash with guilt. He wants us to recall Geronimo's ignominious, ludicrous character in later life. But the heroicization of Geronimo and other Apaches is less about them than it is about us inheritors of their conquest. Hill's film (and Gross's revisions to the screenplay) will not let us rest complacently in a heroicized Geronimo. It forces us, through Gatewood, to confront our own radical ambivalence.

When Geronimo finally does surrender, he says simply, "Once I moved about like the wind. Now I surrender. And that is all."[7] Only we don't get to witness this moment, except through the narrative of Davis. How could this fierce defender of land and liberty come to this pass? The moment is anticlimactic. The real drama takes place on the top of Montaña Aviripa. And in order to understand it, we need to understand the relationship between Geronimo and Gatewood. For while the passive audience may identify with Davis, the thinking critic identifies with Gatewood, another figure, like Tom Jeffords, who attempts a crossing—and a bringing back.

Gatewood and Geronimo admire and respect each other from the beginning. As they elude the vindictive Tombstone posse, they bond through humor, warrior skill, and gifts. Geronimo wants Gatewood's field glasses, asks if he may have them, provided he scare the posse off. When he shoots the jug out of the Tombstone City Marshal's hand, Gatewood compliments him on a great shot. Geronimo: "Not so great. I aim for his head." As the posse hightails it, Geronimo admires not only the binoculars but Gatewood's men's respect, implied in their gift of them to him. So Geronimo gives Gatewood a large piece of turquoise, endowing it with meaning by saying, "Blue stone is valuable to Apache." Gatewood realizes the worth of the gift and can only mutter a dignified thank you.

Because of the economy of film time, their relationship can be only cryptically incremented during the film: Geronimo requests Gatewood as custodian at Turkey Creek, which position he is not allowed to fill, so Geronimo asks him to visit. The screenwriters substitute Gatewood's for the historical Davis's visit to Geronimo's farm (Debo 233). After Geronimo's comment about not being a good farmer, Gatewood is seen eating with Davis and articulating his sympathies. He is familiar with the type who fights lost causes, for his brothers and father fought for the Confederacy. Though his father made him serve the new flag after the war and sent him to West Point, he still knows "what it's like to hate the blue coat." Sieber infers Gatewood's ambivalence. The latter protests that the fight at Cibecue Creek would not have happened if he'd been there. The former accuses him of a lack of honesty: "I just—uh—figure you're a real sad case. You don't love who you're fightin' for and you don't hate who you're fightin' against."

Davis comments on Gatewood's sympathy for the Apaches (and says Sieber is just as taken by them in his own way).[8] But Gatewood is no Davis. He does serve his new flag. He is an officer. And he follows the orders to bring Geronimo in for the last time. Meanwhile, the film must convince us that Gatewood is not only a thinking man but a warrior worthy of this special relationship with Geronimo. So in an interpolated scene, we watch Gatewood win a single contest with an Apache who sets out to test Gatewood's bravery, to win credit with his own people. Executing the deft maneuver of dropping his horse, Gatewood coolly shoots the Apache down, but shows respect for his corpse. Later in another interpolated scene Gatewood shows both courage and morality as he pursues the butchers of the Yaquis and kills them when they try to capture Chato, Gatewood's Chiricahua scout.[9]

Meanwhile, in another interpolated scene, the film is also at pains to show a more humane side of Geronimo. One of his warriors lies wounded, in obvious consternation at slowing down the Apaches' legendary swiftness of movement among the mountains. Geronimo gently reassures him that there is no great haste to move, that he needs to rest, get better. At this moment, Geronimo, who has been portrayed as influenced by religion and visions throughout, now receives his final vision, the Iron Horse, which he interprets as a sign of his Power, a good omen for the Apache.

Thus cinematically prepared as worthy and as worthy of each other, the two protagonists meet for the last time. Gatewood has been chosen by Miles for a secret mission to find Geronimo and bring him in—since Miles's enormous army is incapable. Gatewood protests, "Begging the general's pardon, sir, but why not leave him to the Mexicans? He can't continue to keep raiding across the border. He can't afford to lose any more warriors, can't replace them." But Miles appeals to political necessity (read, Tucsonan hatred, Washingtonian embarrassment, Anglo greed). Gatewood speaks his conscience: "I don't think you or the government intend to keep this promise." Miles has no patience with this idealist either, insists peremptorily that Gatewood has his orders. Gatewood's conscience applies Scripture: "What does it profit a man to gain the whole world and lose his soul?"

Yet Gatewood follows his orders. As Gatewood leaves the disappointed Davis behind to guard the supplies, he praises the young lieutenant as a fine officer and enjoins him to "stay noble." He then offers a justification for his actions that sounds like a lame version of Manifest Destiny: "We're trying to make a country here. It's hard."[10] Obviously, Gatewood has made a decision to follow orders, and he is trying to justify it to himself. His ambivalence is inescapable. He *doesn't* love what he's fighting for, hate what he's fighting against. He *is* enormously sympathetic with the Apaches.

He *has* bonded with Geronimo. Yet he has an ethos of honor, nobility. And an interpretation of Geronimo's last breakaway that surprises.

When Gatewood and Chato achieve the arduous ascent of Aviripa, they are met by an angry Mangas, who demands of Gatewood, "Why did you bring him [Chato]? He is an enemy to his people."[11] Gatewood's reply surprises us: "He thinks you are." Mangas smashes Gatewood across the face, and Geronimo hastens forward to demand, "Have they taught you to lie, Gatewood?" What can Gatewood possibly mean? Chato has articulated no such opinion. The answer may lie in the figure of Nana, Apache patriarch and holy man, who earlier is upset with Geronimo for jumping Turkey Creek. When, aware that Nana is "angry" with him for renewing war, Geronimo approaches Nana for his blessing, Nana testily replies, "You ask my blessing after this thing is done." He feels Geronimo has brought down upon them the wrath of both the Americans and the Mexicans. Geronimo protests that they have been fighting the Mexicans for years and that the Americans will never catch them. But Nana instead sends for Crook, saying with all the authority of his position, "We will talk with him. I ask that you do this." When Geronimo spooks and does not accompany Nana and the others to San Carlos, even his Apache brothers seem to consider him a maverick, a renegade. And even his sympathetic biographer titles her chapter about this last resistance, "Geronimo Brings Disaster to His People": he incurred a wrath in Washington that resulted in the cashiering of Crook, the assignment of Miles, and the deportation of the Chiricahuas to the East. And in a scene wherein Gatewood and Davis confront dead prominent Americans in a bushwhacked stagecoach, the film presents both Davis and even Gatewood as disgusted, disappointed in Geronimo and his renegades. Davis: "They didn't have to kill them just to get their horses." Gatewood, with a sigh of world-weariness, "No—they didn't."

Geronimo rejects Gatewood's reasoning, defiantly demanding, "If I kill White-Eyes forever, I am still Geronimo, an Apache. Who are you, Gatewood?" Geronimo's crucial decision is to remain the self he has fashioned as warrior. Gatewood is caught between competing identities: Apache sympathizer and army officer. He can only weakly respond, "Just a man like you, and I want to go home. I want to see my family." He knows this sentiment can have an appeal to the Apaches, whose families are mostly on the reservation. But he also knows that they are in the process of being shipped to Florida. His position as a negotiator for his government is compromised, untenable. So he shifts to personal appeal, between men, between worthy warriors. Understanding Geronimo's religious side, Gatewood now appeals between gods.

Taking his cross from his neck, Gatewood offers it to Geronimo, explaining that it has "Power" for him, that it represents his god, who is "a God of peace. A God of life, not death. What does your god say?" Geronimo: "Usen is not here with us on the mountain. Tell me, what is in your heart?" Gatewood: "The war is over. [placing the cross in Geronimo's hand[12] [. . .] Our fight must end here." Because Usen, the Apache god, is not present, we feel a shift of power toward the Christian god, like the shift from the Old Testament god of wrath and vengeance to the New Testament god of peace and love. Geronimo's next speech is all about revenge and its failures for him: "No matter how many I killed, I could not bring back my family." He capitulates: "Usen, the Apache god, is a god of peace. I gave you the blue stone. You give me this. It will be peace."

In other words, the peace is between these two men—"*Our* fight must end here"—on the seeming basis of an alliance between their two gods of peace. Yet as Geronimo leads his people to the rendezvous with Miles, not Apache but Christian sacred music provides the background, the hymn "Deal Gently with Thy Servants, Lord"—an ironic title if there ever was one: the Lord didn't heed that prayer! As promise after promise is now broken; the Chiricahua scouts, including the loyal Chato, stripped of their rank and arrested; the remaining Chiricahuas shipped to Florida and Alabama; Gatewood exiled to Wyoming lest he prove a continuing embarrassment to the army's failure;[13] Geronimo a prisoner of war till death, never allowed to return to his native land, the film leaves us with a sense of gross injustice. Yet as attractive as Davis's final, self-righteous position is, the critical observer is not allowed refuge within it.

Geronimo would seem to offer the final rationale for the triumph of the white man. He begins by saying the reason is inexplicable: "No one knows why the One God let the White-Eye take our land. Why did there have to be so many of them? Why did they have so many guns, so many horses?" But he proceeds to a theory of personal and tribal history: "For many years the One God made me a warrior. No gun, no bullets could ever kill me. That was my Power. Now my time is over. Now, maybe, the time of our people is over." As the train recedes into the distance, the background music is Apache, followed by the Whisper of Geronimo's Power as it has manifested itself in his visions. The import of these last sounds is indeed that the time of the Apache, of the Indian, is on the point of vanishing; that the Iron Horse was not the sign of Geronimo's Power but that of the Anglo.

The religious music, then, Geronimo's own capitulation to not only the Power of the Anglo god but the Anglo theory of history, these signs reveal that Gatewood has not reconciled his clash of cultures with a theory of mutuality but with a theory of dominance. If we identify with Gatewood, despite these powerful forces of the ending, we cannot erase the hanged scout's words: "Don't trust the White-Eye. With them there is no right way. [. . .] The One God will welcome me." Or Chato's last words to Geronimo: "You were right to fight the White-Eye. Everything they said to me was a lie." We cannot reconcile these two conflicting positions. We do not only suspect, with Gatewood, that Miles's promises would not be kept, we know the subsequent history of this band, a gesture toward which occurs when Geronimo predicts that one of the women on board the train will probably die with her child from the coughing sickness. Unlike Davis, we cannot easily slide into the position of Lone Ranger, American Adam inheriting the West with a clean conscience. Like Gatewood, we remain in exile, lost in the gap between two worlds. The framing of *Geronimo* relieves us of no responsibility.

7

TOMBSTONE

VIOLENCE AND THE SECULAR

You're a daisy if you do.

Doc Holliday in *Tombstone*

Thus Doc Holliday teases Frank McLaury, who believes he's got him dead to rights at the OK Corral.[1] But just like Johnny Ringo at the end, Frank turns out to be "no daisy," as the wickedly puckish Doc kills them both. Through his cavalier wit and insouciance, Val Kilmer's Doc Holliday steals the show in George Cosmatos's 1993 *Tombstone*. Not that Kurt Russell does not do a fine job as Wyatt Earp. Author of the recent *Wyatt Earp: The Life behind the Legend,* Casey Tefertiller says of the film,

> The original script by Kevin Jarre gave an authentic portrait of the West and told much of the Earp story as it had actually occurred. After a change of directors [Cosmatos replaced Jarre himself], the finished movie emerged as a jumble of authenticity and overdone violence; an interesting combination of facts and flaws. President Bill Clinton took a copy of the film with him to Russia to show as a symbol of American culture. (343)

The film definitely contains a mixture of authenticity and violence; and it is definitely a symbol of American culture. But whether the mixture is a jumble, whether the violence is overdone depends on our interpretation of what screenwriter, director, and actors have finally produced. As I read it, the film turns mavericks Wyatt Earp and Doc Holliday both into existential heroes, caught in an apparently apocalyptic whirlwind of vengeance yet planting daisies in the graveyard, turning the *danse macabre* of violence into a *danse de vie* of life-affirming, secular friendship and illicit love.

Tefertiller's thesis is that in times of lawlessness American culture sanctions extremism in the service of not so much liberty as order:

> In the 1990s of drive-by shootings and gang warfare, the streets of some major cities became more dangerous than Tombstone ever was in the 1880s. Americans brought up the same old questions, trying to find solutions without compromising precious legal standards. With this backdrop [*Tombstone*] arrived on the market, retelling the tale of the marshal who made his own justice. It is inevitable that America rediscovers Wyatt Earp whenever lawlessness reigns. (343)

Perhaps. Certainly the film makes Wyatt a reluctant champion of vigilante justice. Historically, Wyatt was nearly always a lawman—city, county, or federal—up through his residence in Tombstone. In the film Wyatt turns down requests by U.S. Marshal Crawley Dake and Tombstone mayor John Clum to become a lawman again. He has gathered his brothers Virgil and Morgan to make their fortune in Tombstone: "Now all we gotta do is keep our eyes on that brass ring, fellas." He is a maverick, wandering from his own apparent destiny, refusing the identity conferred on him by the past and by popular culture. Only on the morning of the famous gunfight near the OK Corral does Wyatt join his brothers and get sworn in as deputy town marshal. Virgil, on the other hand, after Clum's second request for help from the Earps, has had both a crisis of conscience and a crisis of identity. Walking out of the pool hall and onto the street, he saves a child from being run down by reckless "Cowboys," the name of the locally dominant terrorizing rustlers, and he stares into the eyes of a woman, apparently the child's mother ushering her brood along the boardwalk. The eyes evince fear; the face bears a long scar, perhaps the result of some form of Cowboy discipline. Accepting Clum's offer to succeed slain town marshal Fred White, Virgil rejects Wyatt's philosophy of non-involvement: "You got us involved when you brought us here. I walk around this town and look these people in the eye and it's just like someone slappin' me in the face. These people're afraid to walk down the street. And I'm trying to make money off them like some God damn vulture. If we're gonna have a future in this town, it's got to have some law and order." From the moment they arrive in Tombstone, the Earps have ignored the plight of the townsfolk in the grip of the Cowboys. Indeed, the film opens on a scene of Cowboy power, as they avenge the death of two of their numbers by Mexican police, who were obviously trying to protect Mexico from Cowboy rustling raids.[2] They kill several of the police at a wedding, finally shooting their captain in the arms of his bride. Marshal White informs the newly arrived Earps that there's no real law in Tombstone, "only real law around here's the Cowboys." And their law, of course, is anarchy with impunity.

After Cowboy leader Curly Bill Brocius, on an opium high, kills Marshal White, new Marshal Virgil Earp tries to bring order to the chaos by imposing a gun ordinance: no carrying guns in town. But the Clantons and McLaurys, scions of two big ranchers in Cochise County who fence horses for the rustlers, don't like the ordinance and don't like the Earps. Ike Clanton has already confronted Wyatt, calling him "law-dog" and telling him "law don't go round here." Wyatt has assured him he's "retired," but it is Wyatt who arrests Curly Bill for the shooting of White and retains his prisoner against Ike and his boys who are trying to take Curly Bill out of town. After Wyatt's pointing a gun at Ike's head and threatening to turn it into a "canoe," Ike backs down but affirms twice, "I'll see you soon."

Ike's threats continue after he thinks Doc has cheated him. Billy Clanton threatens Doc. Tom McLaury threatens Wyatt. The morning of the shootout, Clum tells the Earps that the Cowboys have been telling everyone in town that they're going to clean the Earps out. Only on this morning does Wyatt take a badge and only reluctantly. Nor does he want to arrest Ike and his band, prefers to let the liquor wear off, thinks risking lives to enforce a misdemeanor is foolish. But as Morgan has done earlier—following what he thinks is Wyatt's ethic—Wyatt now backs his brother's play, still hoping that Doc's carrying the shotgun—that "street howitzer"—will back the Clantons and McLaurys down, still wondering, "How the hell did we get ourselves into this?" When Doc's wink provokes Billy's draw, Wyatt laments, "Oh, my God." Standing unscathed amid the holocaust, Wyatt says sarcastically to Clum, "Now I guess we did our good deed for today, Mayor." As the Cowboys bury Frank and Tom McLaury and Billy Clanton, Morgan and Wyatt Earp almost wish it had been they that were killed. In all his previous days as a lawman, Wyatt had only ever killed one man, and he had earlier warned Morgan how terrible it feels. Morgan acknowledges, "You're right. It's nothin' like I thought." Jarre's directions to the actor read, "A look of unutterable sadness in [Wyatt's] eyes. This is the one thing he didn't want for his little brother" (59).

Wyatt becomes an avenging angel only after the Cowboys have bushwhacked both his brothers, killing Morgan.[3] Even after the shotgunning of Virgil, the shotgunning of the Earps' and Clum's houses with the women inside, Wyatt counsels Morgan, "We gotta get out of here." But Morgan is incensed: "Who ever heard of that? They're bugs, Wyatt. All that smart talk about live and let live? There ain't no live and let live with bugs." As he himself is dying, Morgan warns, "You were right, Wyatt. They got me good. Don't let 'em get you, brother, you're the one." Wyatt screams a complaint as much against the gods as against the Cowboys: "Why? Why him?" Agonizingly alone in this vortex, both brothers gone, both of the women in his life walking away from him, Wyatt relinquishes, donning the role destined him from the beginning. The priest in the Mexican village, quoting Revelation, has prophesied an avenging pale rider on a pale horse, hell coming with him. The four men in black coats as they approach the OK Corral march in front of a flaming building, a hellish backdrop. When Wyatt kills Frank Stillwell, who has stalked the Earps to Tucson under Curly Bill's orders to "finish it," Wyatt screams at Ike, whose cowardice has saved him again as it did at the shootout, "All right, Clanton. You called down the thunder—well, now you got it! The Cowboys are finished, you understand me? I see a red sash, I kill the man wearin' it. So run, you cur! Run tell all the other curs! You tell 'em I'm comin' and Hell's comin' with me."

The next scenes detail hellish vengeance, with Cowboys executed sometimes without even the illusion of a fair fight, as when Wyatt substitutes his Buntline Special for an opium pipe and shoots the startled Cowboy in the mouth. When it looks as if Wyatt and his faithful few are trapped by Curly Bill and a passel of Cowboys, Wyatt, protesting an eternal negative to the universe, miraculously avoids being shot and kills Curly Bill, one or two others, and rescues his band. McMasters asks where he is. Doc archly responds, "Down by the creek, walking on water." After the death of Ringo, Wyatt says, "All right, let's finish it," and Doc responds, again archly, "Indeed, sir, the last charge of Wyatt Earp and his Immortals."

Wyatt Earp is portrayed, then, as an agent of divine justice. The last four of Wyatt's riders—Wyatt, Doc, Turkey Creek Johnson, and Texas Jack Vermillion—are explicitly called in the screenplay "THE FOUR HORSE-MEN," that is, of the Apocalypse, of Revelation, and Jarre describes them on their last charge as "airborne, grim-faced avenging angels on winged horses, now even more majestic in the twilight, like a myth made flesh, awesome, superb, and unutterably beautiful. They ride by in a flash, cresting another rise and passing into legend" (93). At least the director spares us this last cresting. Robert Mitchum's voice-over signals the successful ending of the holy vendetta: "The power of the Cowboys was broken forever."

Why endow Wyatt with such mythology? Is the film really religious? Have we returned to the opening church, with the Christ the priest supposedly stands for in the final pulpit, all judgments eschatological? After all, Doc Holliday is receiving the last rites of the Roman Catholic Church, and when he pretends hypocrisy, Wyatt brushes aside his pretense. But before we can believe Wyatt and Doc to be apotheosized, we have to reconcile the theme of divine justice with the theme of Faust.

The traveling troupe, which includes Josephine Sarah Marcus and one "Fabian," puts on at the legendary Birdcage Theatre a brief morality play entitled *Faust; or, The Devil's Bargain.* Doc whispers to his "sweet soft Hungarian devil" Kate Elder, "Is your soul for sale, dear?" and Curly Bill asks Johnny Ringo what he would do if the devil approached him for such a sale. Johnny responds ominously, "I already did it." Upon learning that the beautiful actress he had seen on the street has played the devil, Wyatt exclaims, "I'll be damned," and Doc puckishly responds, "You may indeed. If you get lucky." When he encounters her on horseback, despite his earlier resistance to her, Wyatt exclaims, "Oh hell!"

The implication would seem to be that the major players here have all sold their souls to the devil. Wyatt engages in an adulterous affair even as he takes the law into his own hands. And his horse is not white but devilishly black. Johnny Ringo claims to have sold his soul, and since his first violent action is to shoot a priest in defiance of his apocalyptic prophecy, his signal action in the middle of the film is to call for the bodies and souls of his adversaries, and his final shootout with Doc is the fulfillment of their blood sport, it would seem he has done so indeed and the devil has come to claim it at the end. Curly Bill would seem to have met a providential, condign punishment in being cut in half by the same kind of weapon used to make the Mexican captain kneel; moreover, Wyatt now wears a marshal's badge, as if the death he deals were recompense for the murdering of Fred White. Finally Doc, a dark, defiant figure from the start, wonders if Kate, who erotically seduces him away from any reformist path, be not the "Antichrist."

Are Wyatt and Doc angels, however dark? or are they devils, like Curly Bill and especially Ringo? Or is such mythologizing merely a function of the rhetoric with which we mystify history that seems larger than life? Perhaps it is another version of the rhetoric of desire. Heroic romance seems to persist as a genre in order to combat the ennui of banality, the ultimate insult of which is the increasing insignificance of the individual in a world drowning in humans. We seem to fear that no *one* individual, no One Just Man, can make a difference. So in our art we pretend that he (and occasionally she, as in the current Xena cult) can. Romantic, Byronic heroes (Jarre explicitly calls Ringo "Byronic" [2]) exalt the individual if only in defiance.

Wyatt and Doc transcend defiance—but not in the realm of the Transcendent. Jarre has raised the issue of the Transcendent explicitly. Right after the Faust play, Morgan wonders aloud that in the vastness of the universe God would take the trouble to create such an insignificant being as himself. He asks boyishly if Wyatt believes in God. After Wyatt's noncommittal response, Morgan waxes rhapsodic about the spiritualist notion that when people die, they see a light in a tunnel: "[They] say it's the light leadin' you to Heaven." Wyatt scoffs. At the moment of Morgan's death, he returns to the topic: "'Member what I said about seein' a light when you're dyin'? It ain't true. I can't see a damn thing." The horizon of this world—so spectacularly filmed so often in *Tombstone*—is portrayed in the film as the human limit.

The violence of *Tombstone* strikes me, then, as not being allied with the sacred, ultimately, but with the secular. The apocalyptic and Faustian tropes are the rhetoric of desire for the Transcendent. They are the tropes of man the myth-maker, attempting with Promethean energy to endow existence with significance. And yet these tropes yield to others at the end. Unlike McCarthy's kid, though Wyatt's time as a warrior is over, he does not have to pass away in cataclysmic Faustian fashion. He is instead redeemed by Doc's secular sacrifice, a sacrifice that enables Wyatt to effect a crucial existential crossing.

Doc hates Ringo because they are kindred spirits:

> *Doc:* You must be Ringo. Look, darling, Johnny Ringo. That's the deadliest pistoleer since Wild Bill, they say. What do you think, darling? Should I hate him?
> *Kate:* You don't even know him.
> *Doc:* No, that's true, but I don't know, there's just something about him. Something around the eyes, I don't know, reminds me of—me. No, I'm sure of it, I hate him.

Both displaced patricians, both educated speakers of Latin, both hollow men:

> *Wyatt:* What makes a man like Ringo, Doc? What makes him do the things he does?
> *Doc:* A man like Ringo got a great empty hole right through the middle of him. He can't never kill enough or steal enough or inflict enough pain to ever fill it.
> *Wyatt:* What does he need?
> *Doc:* Revenge.
> *Wyatt:* For what?
> *Doc:* Being born.

Faulkner's Addie Bundren informs us in her only soliloquy in *As I Lay Dying* that her father told her the only reason for being born is to get ready to stay dead a long time. Like Faulkner's intellectuals, Ringo—and Doc, too, who understands this alter-ego reminder of himself—is cursed with consciousness, the consciousness of the meaninglessness of human existence. Like Ahab and Job's wife, he would curse god and die, curse the cosmos for bringing him into consciousness. Like other dark Romantic heroes, he inflicts on others the pain of his own existence. But he can never fill the void at the center of his being, a void which mirrors the void of the universe.

Doc's own void is linked to his Keatsian knowledge of imminent death from consumption. That makes him an absolutely fearless fighter. When Wyatt tries to keep him out of the shootout as not his fight, Doc responds, "That is a hell of a thing for you to say to me." As Billy and Frank reach for their guns in the opening gambit of the famous gunfight, Virgil proclaims desperately, "That's not what I want." But Doc winks at Billy Clanton because he does want the fight. It is as if only that adrenaline rush convinces him he's alive. In our first glimpse of him, he provokes Ed Bailey into attacking by apparently disarming himself, only to stick Bailey with his hidden knife. Seeming to emerge from the reclining odalisque,[4] Doc's life is an erotic *danse macabre* as he dances from danger to danger with his Hungarian devil: "Doc can go on day and night and then some. That's my lovin' man." Ambiguously, Kate means Doc's staying power in both poker and sex. When Wyatt tries to talk him down from his thirty-six-hour binge, Doc responds, "Nonsense, I have not yet begun to defile myself."

Doc—and Ringo by extension—have a death wish, a wish that culminates in their *danse macabre* to the death at the end.[5] The camera wonderfully represents such a *danse* as it spins around the circling combatants. "I'm your huckleberry," Doc says to Ringo as they are about to engage in blood sport earlier. He repeats the same term of endearment as he approaches him to take Wyatt's place in their private shootout. Ringo blanches, and Doc jibes, "Why Johnny Ringo, you look like somebody just walked over your grave." Ringo's eyes finally widen, as he grinningly, madly says, "All right, lunger. Let's do it." Mortally wounded, Ringo tries to raise his phallic pistol for one last, orgasmic shot, and Doc urges, "Come on! Come on!" But Ringo turns out to be "no daisy at all." They do not die together in a love embrace.[6]

Yet Doc's teasing with Bailey—"Why Ed Bailey, we cross? Does this mean we're not friends any more? If I thought you weren't my friend, I don't think I could bear it"—points to the ironic difference between him and Ringo. Creek Johnson opines Doc ought to be in bed rather than out fighting with Wyatt:

> *Creek:* Why the hell you doin' this for, anyway?
> *Doc:* Wyatt Earp is my friend.
> *Creek:* Hell, I got lots of friends.
> *Doc:* I don't.

Doc's fidelity to Wyatt is absolute. As with another dark, Romantic hero, Sidney Carton, Doc gives secular meaning to Christ's dictum, "Greater love hath no man than that a man should lay down his life for his friends." So Doc takes Wyatt's place in a gunfight Wyatt can't win and Doc in his condition well might not.

The hole at Doc's core is not empty after all. The friendship therein—solitary, brutal, but faithful—bonds these two even as they face death together. The nod they exchange after the gunfight behind the OK Corral speaks volumes. Doc finally utters a deathbed confession: despite his cynicism, Wyatt is "the only human being in my entire life who ever gave me hope." No true existential nihilist has hope. Wyatt's friendship has given meaning to Doc's desperate existence. So Doc attempts to bequeath a legacy to Wyatt: "I was in love once, my first cousin. She was fifteen. We were both so—. She joined a convent over the affair. She was all I ever wanted."[7] Wyatt lauds this unconventional, illicit love, and Doc pushes his lesson:

> *Doc:* What did you want?
> *Wyatt:* Just to live a normal life.
> *Doc:* There is no normal life, Wyatt. There's just life. Now get
>   on with it.
> *Wyatt:* Don't know how.
> *Doc:* Sure you do. Say good bye to me. Go grab that spirited
>   actress and make her your own. Take that beauty and run
>   and don't look back. Live every second, live right up to the
>   hilt. Live, Wyatt. Live for me.

As Doc dies, then, he passes on to Wyatt his clouded joie de vivre. And the film ends with Wyatt taking Doc's advice. He has resisted Sadie Marcus. He has tried to remain faithful to Mattie, his common-law wife. But the film has portrayed Mattie as already an opium addict, and Wyatt's efforts with her are for naught. Meanwhile, he is attracted to Sadie as the liberated woman who lives on the edge, would die for fun, wants to live on "room service": "That's what I want. I want to move and go places and never look back and just have fun. Forever. That's my idea of heaven. Need someone to share it with, though. [. . .] Oh, I know, don't say it, I'm rotten. I've tried to be good but it's just so boring. Oh look, I don't have time to be proper, I want to live. I'm a woman, I like men. If that means I'm not ladylike, then I guess I'm not a lady. At least I'm honest." According to conventional morality, Sadie would indeed be considered unladylike, immodest, a homebreaker. Allie Sullivan Earp, Virgil's wife, whose recollections furnished a good deal of Frank Waters's *The Earp Brothers of Tombstone,* hated Sadie for breaking up Wyatt's relationship with Mattie. Sadie, going now by the name of Josie, tried her best to suppress the story, though her own memoirs have now been published as *I Married Wyatt Earp.*[8] There is even the suggestion that Sadie was a vamp, playing Sheriff Johnny Behan off against Wyatt Earp. Her vampishness is hinted in the film through her being photographed nude under a veil at Fly's studio right before the shootout (a famous photograph reproduced on the cover of her memoirs).[9]

But the film's portrayal of Wyatt's choice of Sadie is positive.[10] He is following Doc's advice to live up to the hilt. The *danse macabre* of Tombstone violence is replaced with Wyatt and Sadie's final dance, a life-affirming dance of love: free love. Robert Mitchum's voice-over bestows on Wyatt and Sadie the film's final blessing, as they dance in the snow outside the theater in Denver: "Wyatt and Josephine embarked on a series of adventures [. . .] . Up or down, thin or flush, in 47 years they never left each other's side." If Doc's love, the only thing he ever wanted in his life, died in a convent, Wyatt's love has planted a daisy on Doc's grave. He would probably say, as he does when he dies with his boots off, "I'll be damned. This is funny."

The way to the daisies, however, is not only through Doc's death but through the violence itself. It is a rite of passage, what Kristeva calls a ritual of defilement—in this case to cleanse the abjection associated with violence. Doc's purgation afterward is effected through his confession of his incestuous love, his tears as he begs Wyatt to let him die alone, his passing on to Wyatt the daisy of his flickering life-urge. Wyatt's purgation is effected through his expression of thanks to Doc and his declaration of undying love to Sadie. The snow that falls upon them as they dance at the end is the cleansing analogue to the rain that falls on the Jobish Wyatt as he begins his transformation into avenging angel.

Sadie has complained to Behan about the death of Fabian, shot gratuitously by a couple of Cowboys: "What do you care? It was your friends that did it. [. . .] They tried to take my watch. He cursed them for cowards and they shot him. I don't understand any of this, I only know it's ugly. [to the Cowboys] You're all ugly and he was beautiful, he tried to bring something fine into your ugly world and you shot him for it." The tragedy of human existence is that violence seems necessary to define beauty, to endow it with value. Violence seems necessary to provide the environment in which the daisy can grow. Although Wyatt has not yet the courage to seize that beauty when Sadie soon thereafter stops at Hooker's ranch, he has come to know its value, as he tells Doc, apparently too late: "I spent my whole life not knowing what I wanted out of life, just chasin' my tail. But now, for the first time I know exactly what I want. And who. And that's the damnable misery of it." Redeemed by Doc, in a very secular sense, Wyatt survives the violence—indeed, is mythified and ennobled by it—and is vouchsafed a rare long, happy life. No tragic hero after all, he becomes an epic hero, the Beowulf of the American Southwest. And the closing scene returns us to church—not the church of some Vision of the Last Judgment but the church of the opening, aborted wedding, now, in a sense, consummated in front of a temple of art. Wyatt is remade, reborn. Through Doc's agency, through his substitution for Wyatt in what should have been the final act of Wyatt's tragedy, Wyatt has crossed the Valley of Death, of violence to a kind of existential freedom—free from restriction, order, law (which he finally really has left behind): living on room service.

Tefertiller has it only half right, then. We may resurrect Wyatt Earp in times of violence so we can fantasize about an avenging angel. Kevin Jarre's and George Cosmatos's Wyatt is finally, however, like them (and me), an aging child of the sixties. But unlike us, their Wyatt is free, dancing free love in the city square, in the face of convention and authority—the ultimate existential hippie fantasy.

8

"I'D BECOME MY OWN MOTHER"

BIG NOSE KATE IN *DOC HOLLIDAY'S WOMAN*

> Who was hidden within that small frame, behind
> those voluptuous breasts? Who was it who re-
> sponded with delight to the caresses of men? Who
> mourned, murdered, fought unceasingly for life
> despite all odds? Would she show herself in the
> mirror? . . .
>
> She looked wanton, mischievous, despite her
> fragile bones. I liked her, this illusion, if that's
> what she was. Actually, she seemed more like a
> mother, dredged up out of my own body. Not the
> mother who had borne me, but the woman I would
> have chosen had I had a choice in the matter.
>
> *Doc Holliday's Woman*

If *Tombstone*'s Doc Holliday has filled the void within him through loyalty, friendship, and a joie de vivre that he passes on to Wyatt Earp, Jane Candia Coleman, in *Doc Holliday's Woman,* renders us a Kate who escapes loneliness, emptiness—and even worse, subordination—through the assertion of self and through a passionate love of life, a jouissance she shares in a tempestuous relationship with Doc. Coleman places Kate on a border between despair and hope, between entrapment and freedom. Coleman too employs the West, especially the Southwest, as a borderland in which choices of existential moment are made. Springing off from Kate's own memoirs, Coleman regales us with a fictionalized biography that explores a female maverick on the border who defies male tyranny and frees herself through her own agency.

Mary Katherine Harony is a Hungarian noblewoman, whose father follows the Hapsburg Maximillian to Mexico. Already the young Kate is a rebel, who boldly tells the emperor she does not want to go. She already interprets her mother's passive acquiescence as a sign of a male tyranny she vows to resist: "On the verge of womanhood, I thought how dreadful it was to relinquish happiness simply at the desire of one's husband. [. . .] I made a vow. Never, I thought, never would I go against the yearnings of my heart at the whim of a man—or a woman. Never would I compromise as if I were no one, nothing, a piece of furniture moved here and there, an orna-ment packed and unpacked, placed on a shelf" (4). What Kate resists, then, is objectification.

Before such defiance achieves full realization, however, Kate is the victim of further male tyranny. First, she and her family are the victims of male political power struggles as Maximillian is overthrown in Mexico and they must flee to the United States, settling in Iowa. Unfortunately, her parents both die. Then her foster father, Otto Schmidt, rapes her in his barn. She hits him on the head with an axe and, fearful of a male-dominated legal system, runs away, stows away on a riverboat, and becomes the mistress of its captain, who impregnates her. Though Kate says this Captain Fisher "banished" her "loneliness" by introducing her to the mysteries of sexual passion, for which kindness she is grateful, Blanche Tribolet, an octoroon madam and her first female friend, provides her a feminist reinterpretation: "Kind! Let me tell you, he was not kind. He made a baby, then left you. This is kindness? In this life, trust nobody except yourself, and sometimes not that" (48). Yet despite her admiration for Blanche's relative indepen-dence as a business woman, Kate realizes that even Blanche depends upon a man, her keeper, and bitterly concludes, "We're all kept, if you think about it" (57). When Blanche's keeper in a fit of temper slashes her throat with impunity, Kate unleashes her anger at objectifying men and avenges her friend by blasting his head open with Blanche's hidden derringer.

Not all the tyrants Kate seeks to escape are male. Two of the biggest in the novel represent the reality principle: Fate and Death. Both take her parents in Iowa. In the form of Plague both take her son and the husband she marries to legitimate him in St. Louis. Given sanctuary by her husband's gambling friend, Doc Holliday, Kate resists falling in love with him: "'I've had enough of dying.' I faced the mirror. 'It's like I'm cursed'" (84). Even as they fall into a furious affair, their passions are forged not only in their bones but in their dread and defiance of the reality principle: "his [passion], for life, a staving off of the inevitable; mine, the need to comprehend the enemy, death. Love was a fury raging against fate, and we were its victims" (85). Ironically, the consumption-ridden Doc leaves Kate because he fears she will consume him. Their last night together, she says, "There was something of my own savagery in the way he took me, as if he was trying to blot out reality, as if in the whole world there were only the two of us on a tangled bed in the light of a dying fire" (88). This fire consumes them both, and throughout their lives they cannot live with it and cannot live without it.

Kate has already begun to assert herself, to free herself from these tyrannies: from oppressive men, by striking back; from Fate and Death, by the will to live. After the death of her husband and her consequent impoverishment, Kate has an extraordinary scene naked before her mirror, worth quoting at some length for Coleman's craft in female self-birthing:

> Who was I now? What name best suited me? How different was I from before? [. . .] I slipped out of bed, pulled off my nightgown, and stood looking at myself in the mirror, something I had never done. Women were discouraged from becoming familiar with their bodies, from doing anything more than bathing them hurriedly, often beneath a sheet or gown. Bodies were a source of wickedness. I knew that only too well, yet I was curious.
>
> Who was hidden within that small frame, behind those voluptuous breasts? Who was it who responded with delight to the caresses of men? Who mourned, murdered, fought unceasingly for life despite all odds? Would she show herself in the mirror?
>
> Whoever she was, I pitied her at first. The shadows beneath long blue eyes, the down-turned lips, the sag of narrow shoulders spoke clearly of sorrow. But as I watched, she smiled, and light shivered across her face and caught in her eyes. Not dead yet, she seemed to be saying. Badly hurt, but not broken.
>
> I reached out my hands to clasp hers, and she did the same.
> "Help me," I pleaded, and she nodded.
> Always.
> She looked wanton, mischievous, despite her fragile bones. I liked her, this illusion, if that's what she was. Actually, she seemed more like a mother, dredged up out of my own body. Not the mother who had borne me, but the woman I would have chosen had I had a choice in the matter. (65–66)

This alter-ego in the mirror is the mother to Kate's new self. She represents the life urge within her, resisting the reality principle. She is "wanton" and "mischievous" because she defies the conventional definition of bourgeois womanhood. She delights in her "voluptuous breasts," in her entire body, in her passionate desire for the bodies of men. And she is a survivor.

It is this mirror self who, when Kate dresses up for Doc, helps her read her heart and decide who to be for and with him:

> What I saw was my mother, breathless before a ball. What I saw was that buried part of myself armed for battle.
> "You're beautiful," she said. "So is he."
> "Him!"
> Her laughter chimed like distant bells. "Oh, Kate," she said. "What a fool you are."
> "I've had enough of dying." I faced the mirror. "It's like I'm cursed."
> "Then fight. I hate quitters."
> She was gone. All I saw was myself dressed for battle, armed with a necklace the color of blood. (83–84)

The battle imagery is significant: Kate will fight for her life, fight for the object of her desire, fight not to be consumed. The necklace is especially significant: the red color of the garnets implies not only the violence of her passion but violence itself, the blood Kate can never escape. The blood on her own hands from the men she has killed (or nearly killed, in the case of Otto); the blood on Doc's handkerchief, which will eventually kill him; the blood all around them in Fort Griffin and Tombstone and elsewhere, which is the price of life, the very matrix of life, the bloody show of both birth and death.

Kate's new self is unconventional. She early opines anent reputation, "What was that, anyhow, but a method devised to keep young females from thinking for themselves?" (57). In other words, she sees that reputation is a form of discipline imposed by a patriarchal society and, unfortunately, so thoroughly internalized by women that they become its enforcers. When her male escort, Anson McGraw, is murdered for their money in Wichita, Kate can't get a job because of her reputation: "In my search for work, I'd been ushered out of the bank, the grocery stores, and the homes of women who called themselves 'decent'; it was a quick and bitter education" (105). Wyatt Earp, law officer, has no luck in finding McGraw's murderers or the money and, faced with a destitute and desperate Kate, suggests she seek employment in his brother Jim's wife's brothel. Kate asserts her will to live in the teeth of convention: "Given the choice between living and dying of starvation, I always chose living, and opinion be damned. Opinion didn't put meals on the table. Work, any kind of work, did" (108).

As she triumphs over her circumstances thanks to her relationship with the rediscovered Doc, Kate exults in her unconventional identity: "Doc and I were together and on our way to more adventure. And it suited me. The days of parlors and propriety were long gone and buried. I was a new person. I was Kate. Harony [her family name], Elder [her assumed name], Melvin [her married name]; Big Nose Kate [her nickname]; Mrs. Doc Holliday [her common-law name], and I liked who I'd become. I bowed to no one, said what I liked, urged on by Doc, who was as wild as I" (218). Even when Kate tries to go home again to her new-found siblings, she finds that she has crossed over a permanent border. When she curses in front of her younger sister Mina, the latter chastises her in the manner of a proper, "respectable" bourgeois wife. Kate again asserts her autogenesis: "To hell with her! I thought, but I didn't say it. I'd become my own mother. My rules were mine, and if they shocked some, they didn't shock the friends I'd left behind" (260). Not only does Kate birth her self, but she is her own superego. Unable to complete the recrossing, Kate returns to the West, where she continues to bring forth her own self, created by a series of choices.

An aspect of Kate's unconventionality is her defiance of traditional religion with its cosmic superego. At the death of her husband and son, she laments, "My prayers were, as ever, meaningless. No one heard" (60). She has the following exchange with Doc at the beginning of their relationship:

> "Sometimes I don't know who I am or why I do things," I confessed. "I'm not who I was raised to be at all. Everything I learned turned out to be fairy tales."
>
> "That's usually the case." There was bitter knowledge on his face.
>
> "Why?"
>
> "The world kicks us around. Wars happen. Look at Nancy [Blanche's Negro servant, anchorless after Blanche's murder]. She's lost. Look at you. You lived through two revolutions. The Civil War ruined my life. Killed my mother. We can change with the world or we can die. Dealer's choice."
>
> "It isn't fair."
>
> "Nobody said it would be. Kids believe. Then they find out it's bullshit."
>
> "Where will it end?" [. . .]
>
> "In the grave." (84–85)

Doc's metaphor of the card game provides them a hedge against an impersonal, inherently unfair Fate: the human agency one assumes in *dealer's choice.* Faced with a world devoid of traditional religious meaning ("it's bullshit"), they can at least choose the terms of their own existence. They cannot beat Death, but they can at least enter it having chosen how to live.

Kate tells Josie Earp, with whom she sympathizes as a fellow rebel ("She was honest. She didn't give a hoot in hell for gossip or disapproval. Those huge brown eyes held more than a hint of arrogance" [298]), that all they can do as they await the showdown in Tombstone is pray, but both have forgotten how, and, Kate says, "[W]hen the time came, as it did two days later, I was frozen in terror and my mind was blank" (299). Her descriptions of Doc and Wyatt have painted them as pagan gods, and the folk-demon La Llorona dominates Kate's mythology surrounding the shootout, from the ominous scream she hears in Tucson to the aftermath: "The scream I hear is my own, and La Llorona's, filled with anguish" (301).

When Kate tries to get Doc to convalesce at her brother Alexander's home in western Colorado, Doc asserts it's too late. On Kate's persistence, he remarks with admiration, "You'd take on God Himself, wouldn't you?" "God, the devil, or anybody else," Kate blasphemously replies (317). Of course, such rhetoric is mere bravado. Doc's death is inevitable. But neither of them takes refuge in some comforting metaphysics.

The West represents for Kate a kind of secularized promised land, whose possibilities, like its horizons, seem boundless. As she crosses Indian Territory with Doc, fleeing prosecution, she compares themselves to "Adam and Eve in the garden that was the Texas prairie" (191): "We were free, and we had only ourselves to rely on. There was a greater freedom in that, as if we were the only two people in the world" (191). From her first arrival in the West she has felt, "[I]t's so big, it makes me feel that way, too. Like I can do anything. Like there's no limit to what I could do" (98). With Wyatt in their brief affair she has exclaimed, "You don't know what it's like to be out here. Free" (124). With Doc, "I began to feel that there wasn't anything I couldn't do; that I could grow until I filled the space that surrounded me. I loved, and even my heart seemed to expand, taking everything inside—the prairie, the sky, Doc's happy presence at my side—with a hugeness I'd never known was possible" (192). As they enter Arizona, "I was enchanted by what I could see, and I could see a hundred miles, reaching out to gather in the space, lifting my face to the skittering wind" (251). She begs Doc to dance spontaneously in the desert, and he "waltzed me as if we'd both gone mad but didn't care" (251). (Shades of Wyatt and Sadie at the end of *Tombstone.*) Even in her straitened circumstances, Kate proclaims, "Besides, with the optimism of my youth, I figured I wouldn't always be homeless and on the edge, fighting for survival. [. . .] This job [as one of Bessie Earp's whores] would keep me alive until I could go out and find [Doc]. I never thought of suicide like so many of the girls. What kept me going was the hope of freedom, and Doc" (108–9).

Kate's expansiveness yields her a kind of will-to-power, an indomitable energy to join with and preserve the object of her desire. When she learns from the rancher Abel Cochran that Doc resides near his ranch in Fort Griffin, Kate exults internally, "Doc was waiting at the end of the trail. To get there, I'd have stripped naked and run the distance, and never mind the heat, the dust, the threat of Indians, or the drama I'd left behind me" (141). When Doc is in danger of being lynched for the killing of Ed Bailey in Griffin, Kate will move heaven and earth to free him: "I was fighting mad and thinking clearly. The way I saw it now, Selman, Larn, the whole crew of Bailey's supporters didn't have a chance against a woman with her mind made up" (180). She daringly sets a fire to distract the town, gets the drop on the crooked Sheriff Larn, and springs Doc to flight across Texas and Indian Territory. Even Doc never gets over the fierceness of her drive.

Yet Kate finds the "freedom" she seeks to be not limitless but circumscribed. Not only by the impersonal forces of Death and Fate but by personal forces. Personalities. Hers. Doc's. Wyatt's. The larger human agency that brought together in Cochise County two opposing forces bent on destroying each other. And by radical loneliness, emptiness. This last threatens to swallow Kate from virtually the beginning. As she lies contemplating her escape from the convent, longing to be comforted by her nun friend, she complains, "I wanted to call her back, to lay my head on her starched breast and confess. Let another hear my sins and bear them! I was not equal to the task. I was a child wanting, crying out for comfort. None came. I was alone, the loneliest person on the earth" (30). She comes to see all her friends, all humans, as ineluctably lonely: "There was so much sorrow in the world—Wyatt with his memories, Doc with his broken dreams and diseased lungs, me with my loneliness. Was everyone like us? I wondered. Did everyone wander the earth looking for solace?" (126). Such a vision is, to steal a phrase from Faulkner's Father Compson, the mausoleum of all hope and desire.

Wyatt's memories of his first wife, the albatross of his second, his insulting of Kate—all conspire to weigh him down. But he is lucky enough to find "solace" in Josephine Sarah Marcus, his third and life-long wife, with whom he achieves happiness. And he is lucky enough to find a male friend like Doc. Conversely, Doc's broken dreams and lungs find some solace in Wyatt's friendship. But their bonding presents a threat to Kate:

[Doc] saved Wyatt's life and formed that peculiar bond that exists between partners in battle. I understood indebtedness, but I couldn't approve. It was as if Wyatt and Doc (and I because I was there) became a family, only I was on the edge of that family, privy to nothing, shunted aside while they followed their male pursuits, left to nurse my annoyance into a fine rage. [. . .]

I felt I'd lost a friend, a lover, a fellow adventurer, and not to any person I could complain about. Being men, they wouldn't understand. They were simply doing what men do—attending to business, gambling, talking, planning their next move, the profitable future—secure in the fact that one would defend the other. How could I complain about that without seeming like a scold? (238–39)

In a world between men, Kate is shunted aside, silenced. Even when Doc apologizes to Kate for his outrageous behavior toward her and takes her to Tucson for the fiesta, they are interrupted by Morgan Earp with a message from his brother that Doc is needed in Tombstone immediately.

Kate has vowed early that she will never be "an ornament" moved about by men. She continues, "And with one exception, for which I never forgave myself or the man responsible, I have kept that vow" (5). Perhaps the exception is Johnny Behan, who manipulates Kate to bear false witness against Doc. But more insidiously, perhaps it is Doc himself. Kate's affair with him is love-and-hate. If he worries about her consuming him, the feeling is mutual. At their reunion in Griffin, Kate responds with aggression to Doc's wonted teasing. He wants her to understand, to excuse that teasing, but she reflects,

> Somewhere in my tangled past, I'd made a vow that if I ever got Doc back, I'd try to behave better. But I hadn't realized how hard it would be to do, or how vulnerable I always felt around him. He had the power. All I had was love. (152)

Even when they are most in love as they flee across Indian Territory, like Adam and Eve in a garden, Kate reflects problematically, "I stood by his side, feeling like we were two parts of a whole, as if I had, in truth, been created out of his body, out of a piece of rib, and that the mystical joining would remain forever" (189). If she is a rib, she is inherently subservient.

Manipulated by the Earps into Arizona and into a darker purpose than anyone was acknowledging (Coleman leaves implicit the suggestion that Wyatt was being brought to Tombstone by the bankers, merchants, mining interests to counterpoise the lawless but dominant Cowboys), Kate decides to try to "free us both" if she can (259); if not, at least free herself. Her attempt to return to her siblings fails, but she nonetheless wants "a home of my own, not like Mina's, but a place in which I belonged, in which children belonged. And I wanted Doc in it. [. . .] [T]he more I thought, the more sure I became that I was right, that we needed some stability, financial and otherwise. I'd seen too many derelicts, men and women, grown old and helpless before their time" (260–64). So she makes love to him furiously, "fighting for both our lives" (264). When Doc refuses to go, she moves to Globe, opens a restaurant and boardinghouse, and obtains independence through agency: "I was a success, and honestly, too. And though Doc wrote regularly urging me to return in his nastiest fashion, I paid no heed. I was proving my own worth using my mind, my hands, the labor of my back, and the feeling was glorious, especially for me, who had always needed someone else, used men—and women—to survive" (269).

This is Kate's final self, self-reliant, no longer objectified but an individual in her own town, her own chosen economy. She returns to Tombstone when she hears Doc is in trouble, falsely accused. Having heard from Mattie that Wyatt and she had an affair, Doc is insufferably cruel to her. In defiance, she slaps him and vows to get even. Perhaps drugged by Behan to get the incriminating affidavit, Kate nevertheless at some subconscious level does get even with Doc. Violently. In an action that might have resulted in his being hanged. Her blood necklace at this moment associates her with Kali, Medea.

To Doc's sarcastic insistence that she leave Tombstone forever, that all she came for was his inheritance, Kate responds in her most defiant defensive moment: "I don't want your money, Doc. I've never wanted that, no matter what you think. You can't give me what I want. It's not in you. You called me a whore. Well, I'll tell you something. It's you who's the whore. You took what I had and spit on it. You took my heart like it was trash, but it was all I had" (282). Doc cannot give her what she wants because it's not in his nature. He has said as much in his refusal to go to Globe: "What would I do in a hotel? Run the desk? Act the part of inn-keeper? I'm not right for it" (265). Allie Sullivan Earp, Virgil's feisty wife, tries to tell her as much after Kate's miscarriage of their child: "You'd have tied that kid around his neck [. . .] . You think you own that man, but you don't. [. . .] I'm telling you—squeeze too tight and you'll kill what you've got. You'll have a man you don't know anymore and don't care about—*if* he hangs around that long. Doc's a man. That's why you love him" (258). His manliness, his wildness is why she offered him her heart to begin with.

Kate accepts Doc's apology, his admission that she is "the only good thing" ever in his life and that he shat upon her (285). And she agrees to go to the fiesta: "We'd dance, eat, laugh, make love, and why not? What good had suffering done? Never again, I vowed, because never again would I lose myself in him" (287). Yet in Tombstone she begins to feel "pushed aside" again, "made to behave, to watch while he got shot at by a gang of thieves" (295–96). So after she has been forced merely to observe, to be a spectator while men determine the course of events, she tries to exact from Doc his promise to return home with her. But her domestic dream is never fulfilled, and she begins to understand and to accept why. Allie had been right: "You can't domesticate wild creatures. And Doc was a wild thing. Hemmed in, caged, he paced and burned and ate at himself from the inside out. I should have known that from the first, and maybe I did in some small corner of my mind, but that never stopped me from trying. My idea of home was something I hadn't had since I left Hungary, and it was romanticized, vague, composed of longings that had nothing to do with reality" (306). Longings that are not related to reality because the only reality is death and the antidote to it is not some bourgeois dream of perfection or perfectibility or afterlife but life itself. The sisterhood Kate shares with Blanche and Bessie and Allie and the "girls" and even briefly with Calamity Jane. But especially the dance she shares with Doc.

At her nadir in the brothel Kate is determined: "I had made a shambles of my life and I could not go back and redo, only go forward hoping. For what? For love and life and decency. For laughter. Above all for that" (116). Kate dances in the meadow before Wyatt, in the desert before Doc. In their first fight they have this exchange:

> "Go away," I said. "I wouldn't invite you to my funeral."
> "Will you come to mine?"
> "I'll dance on your grave." (82)

Doc in his morbid sense of humor never lets Kate forget this ironic promise. His own dance is desperate, and from it he gets the rush that keeps him alive: "But the way I see it, we all dig our own graves out of our lives, and Doc was no exception. Awaiting death, he lived as he chose, tempting fate every day, laughing at it, hating it, trampling it underfoot when he could" (262). In Tombstone "[h]e was ready to shoot, to strike, and loving every minute of it" (295).

When the dance is nearly over, Doc writes to Kate, *"You always said you'd dance on my grave [. . .] . The bugs are winning, so pack your dancing shoes and let's say a proper farewell"* (315). After Kate gets to Colorado, Doc predicts she will "dance and laugh" when he is gone (318).

Kate protests, wishes they had led a normal life together. But Doc understands and teaches her the final meaning if not of life then of their tempestuous lives together and apart: "'I thought you'd figured it out. If we'd been like other people, none of this would have happened. Think what we'd have missed! By now, we'd have been bored to tears with each other and with life. As it is'—he spread his hands—'we've got a hell of a lot of living to remember. And maybe we've made a difference somewhere, left our mark. Who knows?'" (318). Kate and Doc have defied boredom by laughing and dancing and fighting and making earth-trembling love. And they have certainly left their mark. Kate can't have her cake and eat it too. But she can have her female selfhood *and* her passionate dance with Doc. The twin reality principle of Fate and Death allows no more, but no less.

Yet the aging Kate laments in the epilogue,

> As I'd foreseen, the world without Doc was an empty place, bereft of laughter.
> All I had left was myself. (321)

Mattie dies "clutching the emptiness that was all she ever had" (323). Kate's emptiness strangely becomes filled, however, with a man who can handle horses, the one to whom she had sold the great paint Gibran after her and Doc's heroic, frolicking escape across Indian Territory, whose "housekeeper" she becomes (324): "Life isn't going to be so empty, after all, I thought, and leaning back in the seat, I took a deep breath of the clear desert air" (325). Doc was right. Kate dances on his grave in the only gesture that makes sense, that provides solace in this lonely world.[1]

9

L'ÉTAT C'EST MOI

GORE VIDAL'S BILLY THE KID

> I'll tell you what, Pat, I got more friends around here than you. You? You're just rollin' through town, you're just blowing through. Me? I'm permanent, like the cactus.
>
> Billy in *Gore Vidal's Billy the Kid*

If Val Kilmer stole the show in *Tombstone,* he *is* the show in William Graham's 1989 Turner Network Television version of *Gore Vidal's Billy the Kid,* much as is Paul Newman in Arthur Penn's 1958 version, *The Left-Handed Gun.* Leslie Stevens moralized Vidal's original 1955 script for the 1958 film, however, so that Billy's intemperate revenge against one of Tunstall's murderers at Pat Garrett's wedding leads an angry Pat to accept the heretofore rejected badge as sheriff of Lincoln County, vowing to get rid of the Kid as a menace to society. Pat's embrace of his wife after the shooting of Billy suggests the establishment of law and order.

The major intervening film, *Pat Garrett and Billy the Kid* (recently rereleased in a director's cut), represents the very idea of law and order as problematic: "I'm outlawed, for sure," Billy says to friends and a recently deputized former outlaw, "Wasn't long I was a law ridin' for Chisum and old Pat was an outlaw. The law's a funny thing, ain't it?" Sam Peckinpah gives us almost the perfect tragic absurd: the death of Billy becomes the death of Pat, who shoots himself in the mirror immediately after killing the Kid, whose own assassination is juxtaposed to Billy's shooting of chickens in the beginning of the film and invaded by the figure of Billy at the end. Both deaths are meaningless incidents as the "destiny" of New Mexico, as Governor Wallace hints, becomes intertwined with Manifest Destiny and the triumph of corporate will-to-power over the anachronistic rugged individualism of the West. James Coburn's Pat warns Kris Kristofferson's Billy early:

Pat: It feels like times have changed.
Billy: Times maybe, not me.

But Pat's own change to a lawman as a way of staying alive ("No matter what side you're on, you're always right") avails him nothing.[1]

Yet as this fine film waxes on in a slow, painful *danse macabre* that embodies existential ennui, Peckinpah robs it of its inevitability. Billy decides after his escape from execution that Mexico might be best after all and is headed away from his confrontation with Pat, when he chances upon his Hispanic friend Paco being butchered, Paco's daughter being raped by some of Chisum's men: "That ties it: I'm going back." The implicit motivation is that he stays in New Mexico to fight Chisum's power, the power of the Santa Fe Ring, the power Pat Garrett has come to represent. Bob Dylan's haunting refrain—"Billy, they don't like you to so be free"—gets reduced from metaphysical potentialities of being to a political meaning that "they" don't want Billy around to stop their consolidation of power. Billy's enigmatic smile at his old friend and surrogate "daddy" as he shoots him represents on one level the embracing of alter-egos in a dance of death. But like Ike McCaslin's failure to kill the bear, it also represents Billy's failure to confront power and triumph. It makes his action at Paco's death site a meaningless gesture and, I think, fatally flaws the film.

William Graham's version of Gore Vidal's play remains closer than Leslie Stephens's to the Vidal original[2] and obtains greater aesthetic integrity than Peckinpah's film. Kilmer brings to the role a depth only Newman before him was capable of, but Kilmer plays less a psychotic Billy (Newman's Billy is susceptible to manic bouts of wildness, illness, and depression) than simply an anarchic Billy. When Kristofferson's Billy refuses to change, the decision seems superficial, and it is certainly not related to his righteous motivation to return and fight Chisum. Kilmer's Billy not a little resembles Studi's Geronimo: when Governor Wallace asks Billy how he survived after his mother's death from consumption, Billy responds that he started gambling when he was about twelve, then went into ranching,

Billy: Then I went to war, like you did, for Mr. Tunstall.
Wallace: You see, mine was a war to preserve the union.
Billy: Mine was a war to preserve, uh—
Wallace: What?
Billy: Sir, if you kill my friend, then I have to kill you in order to
    preserve—everything.

Billy's war is to preserve the Code of the West, an Old Testament code of eye-for-eye justice, what Hegel calls a religious code that predates a society based on law, where one relinquishes revenge to the state. Billy remains a maverick on the border. He refuses to cross over into the new world order because he identifies himself with New Mexico, the land itself, the cactus. He is never going to leave; he is never going to die.

Billy asks Governor Wallace why he wants to civilize the territory:

> *Wallace:* You like it the way it is?
> *Billy:* I like it.
> *Wallace:* So then you liked it when they murdered your friend,
>   John Tunstall?
> *Billy:* No. But I liked it, when I killed Sheriff Brady, who killed
>   him. I like things squared.

When Billy first learned that Brady was coming with Dolan to enforce a writ of attainder on Tunstall's property, his advice is for Tunstall to leave immediately, hide out, then "swoop down" and retake what's his. When Billy is warned by Tunstall's drunken cousin that Brady is after him for witnessing his murder of Tunstall, Billy seizes the initiative and kills Brady and his deputy Morton. Billy has no faith in the law, for he has seen it be manipulated, has seen assassins wearing badges. He himself is manipulated by the prosecutor to look totally lawless, and his deal with Wallace for exoneration falls through. Wallace lamely apologizes for their deal's being botched but then out of guilt justifies himself by reminding Billy that he broke the law, that he's killed people (Tunstall's assassins):

> *Billy:* So've you, General.
> *Wallace:* That was war.
> *Billy:* What do you think this is, you fool? [. . .] I never kilt a
>   man but I was right.
> *Wallace:* The law, what about the law?
> *Billy:* Ol' Tunstall saw what law we got, and you know it.

Pat Garrett sees the future and throws for the main chance, asking Governor Wallace for the vacated sheriffship of Lincoln County and rationalizing his choice as "settl[ing] down," "fitting in," getting married and becoming a property holder. Ironically, Billy has suggested that after Governor Wallace's amnesty he and Tom O'Folliard and Charlie Bowdre and even "old Pat Garrett" might settle down to ranching together. But Pat is already making his move and advises Billy to "move with the times" himself. Even Valdez Gutierrez, father to both Pat's wife and Billy's lover (Celsa), tells Billy toward the end, "Billy, for your own sake, go, leave Fort Sumner, leave the Territory. [. . .] [B]ecause this is no place for you any more. [. . .] People [. . .] change. You don't. We want new things: order, safety. *¿Pero tu?* no, you don't. So please, William Bonney, leave us. *Todos tus amigos están muertos.* Hear me. All of your pistolero friends are dead. And now God waits to strike you down." The Hispanic belief system may interpret him as a rebel to be struck down, or as a martyred saint, or the *indios* among them may see him as a returned god, but the film portrays him as a man stubbornly clinging, in the threat of change, not just to a code but to a concept of identity.

Governor Wallace's plan to exonerate Billy may go awry, but he arranges for Billy to be placed only under house arrest, in handcuffs, and guarded by the obtuse Deputy Bob Ollinger; in other words, Wallace allows Billy to escape, is happy when he does, but wants Pat Garrett to make sure he leaves the territory. When Pat shows Billy his badge back in Fort Sumner, tells him he's been appointed and intends to run for the office next election as well, Billy asks what he should run for, and Pat tells him, "Old Mexico."

Billy's ultimate response to Pat reveals what we have had a few glimpses of: that not only does he identify Fort Sumner as his home and the home of his sweetheart, which and whom he refuses to leave, but he identifies his very self with the entire Territory of New Mexico. When at his wedding celebration Pat seems to be lecturing Billy about his wild ways, Billy retorts, "Don't you lecture me, Old Casino. [. . .] Do you know, you and me are just alike: gambling men, shoot pretty good, we know the country. Hell, we *are* the country." And Billy likes the country as it is, uncivilized. As they ride into Lincoln together, still friends, for Billy's rendezvous with Governor Wallace, Billy asks Pat plaintively, "Hoo, look at all those people. Pat, don't you ever just want to get out and ride and ride like we used to?" When the photographer asks him for his name and address, Billy responds, "My name is William H. Bonney. My address is New Mexico Territory, all of it." And when Pat tells Billy that there's no place for him any longer "in this territory," that people are getting tired of his "wild" ways, Billy, feeling betrayed by this "good buddy," can't believe his ears, demands to know if Pat will "stand by them words." They almost square off at this instant, but Pat backs off, insisting it's not the time. So Billy unloads verbally: "I'll tell you what, Pat, I got more friends around here than you. You? You're just rollin' through town, you're just blowing through.

Me? I'm permanent, like the cactus." No longer is Pat identified with the country. Billy alone is. He identifies with the entire territory itself, represents it and its "uncivilized" ways, its *lex talionis,* its open range, its unlimited vistas. And he refuses to leave it, as if leaving it would be to allow it to change permanently, to slip away from the cowboys and the Indians and the Hispanic folk. The Drunk calls him "an angel," a "demi-god," the "Golden Youth." The Indians think him "one of the old gods come back again." He is a metonymy for the heroic age, about to be transformed into the banal world of bourgeois "civilization," for whom Billy is an embarrassment, bad publicity for a state intent on attracting investment. When Pat, admonishing the Kid to change with the times, predicts New Mexico will become a state, Billy exclaims, "Whoa, now, you're dancing on my grave with them big feet of yours." How prophetic.

From his first return to Fort Sumner, abandoned after Kit Carson's death and the return of the Navajos from Bosque Redondo to their traditional lands, but still a home to Hispanic tradesmen and sheepherders—and to wandering outlaws, Billy insists he will never leave again. He does so (in the film) only to travel to Lincoln to meet Governor Wallace—and then to await trial—or to travel again to Lincoln as Pat's prisoner, this time to be tried and condemned. But he keeps coming back. Because it's home and because his woman abides within it. He asks his friend who wonders why he risks returning, "Have you ever seen Celsa up some of them dusty arroyos?" On his last return he has this telling exchange with Celsa:

> *Billy:* I ain't leaving. This is where I live.
> *Celsa:* And die.
> *Billy:* No, I ain't dyin',' never.
> *Celsa:* Oh no?
> *Billy:* No.
> *Celsa: Que extraño tu eres.* You know what the Indians say about
>   you? You are one of the old gods come back again.
> *Billy:* I never went away. I've been right here all the time.
> *Celsa:* I don't want you to ever leave me—ever.
> *Billy:* All right, I won't.
> *Celsa:* Liar.
> *Billy:* I'll haunt you to the end of your days.
> *Celsa: No digas eso.*

Billy's insistence is simplicity itself. He eschews the mythologizing, but in his commonsense understanding, his boyish bravado, and his impish humor, he worries the superstitious Celsa, who sees Billy's last line as foreboding: that he will turn into a ghost.

In their last night together, Billy finds one of the dime novels concerning him, one about a widow's gold mine. Since Celsa is a widow, they have a good laugh. Billy wants to know how it turns out. Celsa says, "We live happily ever after." But Pat has gotten to her earlier, and she asks Billy if he's a bad man. Then she wonders whether he stays in Fort Sumner, despite the danger, for her. Billy insists, "You know it is." But Celsa comments, "I think you are waiting for Pat Garrett. I think that is why you stay."

There is no doubt that both Billy and Pat are caught up in a macho challenge. You can see it in Billy's body language when Pat tells him there's no place for his wildness in the territory. You can hear it in his voice: "You goin' to arrest me. You gonna try?" And you can hear it in Billy's insistence to the Drunk the night of his death: "I will not leave this country. Ever. I ain't leavin'. [. . .] Let him come if he dares. [. . .] I'm the best shot there is." This is certainly machismo. And it may be *hubris,* though Billy does not die in a gunfight where he is outdrawn. It is certainly *hamartia,* Billy's fatal error in judgment. Yet his defiance takes on a tragic glory.

Pat is the more obsessed, the one whose very manhood seems tied up in his eventual getting of Billy. As the headlines get tougher on Pat, he gets grimmer. His deputy Poe comments poignantly after Pat has killed Tom O'Folliard and now Charlie Bowdre, "Must be strange killin' your old friends." After Billy makes fools of Pat's deputies and escapes from his "jail" in the Lincoln County Courthouse, Pat's obsessiveness manifests itself in his frustrated, seemingly impotent outrage: "He can be down in hell, I'll still go down and drag him out."

Yet why do they really, fatally come together at the end? Pat is driven internally by his obsession and externally by the bad press and political pressure. Yet he painfully wishes to Poe he "could" give up the chase, and he earnestly insists to Celsa, "Celsa, I know you love him. We all do. I knew Little Casino long before I ever knew your sister or you. He's like a part of me. I want you to give him up to me. [. . .] I never wanted to hunt him down, I swear that." Yet, Pat insists, "He's bad." To Poe he maintains that Billy "plagues" him. Tears stream down his face after he kills Billy. What is the secret to this love/hate relationship?

Pat has crossed over from wildness to order, and his choice resides not only in his wife and property but his badge, a sign of his ambition: Sheriff of Lincoln County, the lawman who cleaned up after the war. Pat's ambition, his reputation is overshadowed by Billy:

> *Pat:* Then there's what the papers say: Billy the Kid done this,
> Billy the Kid done that. [. . .] It's like they're making you
> out to be some kind of hero. [. . .]
> *Billy:* And that's what's a bother to you?

The Drunk tellingly warns Joe Grant, the gunfighter who seeks out the new kid on the block, "Let us marvel, not envy." Why else would Pat drag Billy out of hell, if not to be the one to punish him, in the eyes of the press and thus the world, for making a fool of not Ollinger and Bell, the deputies Billy kills in his famous escape before hanging, but Pat Garrett? He told Billy he was liking his job "more and more" the night he captured him at Stinking Springs. And when he insists to Celsa he's just doing his duty, she sneers in his face, "Or is it your pleasure?" When he protests he didn't want to hunt Billy down, Celsa defiantly proclaims, "But you think killing him will bring you glory? [. . .] He is life. And you are death."

Ironically, Pat's envy allies him with the forces of death and corruption. In the end, he does not bring Billy to justice as he had promised, even boasted. He assassinates him. Executes him. Billy is armed only with a knife to cut himself a steak when he comes to the door of Pete Maxwell's house. The camera insists we notice that Billy is wearing no gun, and his right hand, which pushes open the door, is empty. When Poe exults that Pat outdrew Billy the Kid, Pete counters that the Kid never had a chance. Pat can say only "I killed Billy the Kid," but the audience knows that he turned that trick to account, to his fame and glory.

Why is Billy dead? Pete has berated Pat for no longer being "trusting." Has Billy trusted too much? to his skill? to his luck? He seems guilty of a *hamartia* if not *hubris* itself. Like Victorio and Geronimo, he has clung stubbornly, proudly to a lifeway, refusing to change with the times. He has underestimated—or perhaps overestimated—humans: Pat's friendship; Wallace's integrity (who told Pat Billy would never hang while he was governor and yet who never pardons him or commutes his sentence after his conviction for murdering Brady and Morton); the Hispanics' hospitality (like Pat, Celsa's father wants him to leave, for there's no place for him anymore in the territory); finally, the Drunk's monumental ingratitude. Throughout, in response to Billy's generosity in supplying him with money for drink, the Drunk praises Billy for his breeding, his aristocratic, heroic bearing and stature, his "goodness incarnate." Yet Judas-like he betrays him for a few pieces of silver—and a hard-wrung admission from Pat that "'tis a brave thing I do, [. . .] especially here where he's so loved." On this fatal night, Billy tragically overestimates his invulnerability—"I'm the best there is"—and tragically underestimates both Pat and the Drunk: Pat, because Billy miscalculates not just Pat's tenacity but his honorability, assuming Pat would meet him in a fair fight, which he could not win; the Drunk, because Billy miscalculates, has no capacity to understand, the depravity of mean spirits, their hatred of the Beautiful.

Why does the Drunk betray Billy? For the money for drinks? Of course, an alcoholic would. Because Billy insults him, calling him an old man, apparently pitying him? Yes. Yet there seems more. As he regales Billy with his "words," his only currency, his only way to repay him, Billy infers he means for the drinks. The Drunk corrects: "For giving me tragedy." He sees the irony that children play Billy the Kid in thousands of cities across the world while the real Billy sits alone, deprived of his "nimbus [. . .] of glory," waiting like a lamb for the "slaughter." And yet to be him would be much: "To be a name on the lips of men: Is anything so sweet, so brief?" And hence why glory, as Faulkner says, as Clark shows.

The Drunk argues Billy's vulnerability as the apparent sacrifice, as unable to resist his fate: "Billy, did you ever kill anybody you loved?" The point would seem to be that Billy will not be able to kill Pat, for he has only heretofore killed enemies, but Pat has killed friends. Yet when the Drunk asks, "You never tumbled a god from his temple, betrayal with a kiss?" we realize he is no longer talking about Billy but about himself, about what he longs himself to do at some level of desire: envy of Billy's "demi-god" status, his "Golden Youth"; envy like that of another dark figure for another Billy (Budd). Is it also desire of fame, "to be a name on the lips of men"? Ironically, the Drunk has no name in the film. He may lurk at the end like a parody of Judas. But nobody will ever remember him.

So what is the meaning of Billy's death, this man who represents "life"? Does he dignify his refusal to cross over? Is he a tragic sacrificial lamb that redeems society?[3] *Left-Handed Gun*'s Pat Garrett is trying to talk Billy into surrendering, thinks he has a gun when Billy whirls, thus kills him in self-defense and restores order. Peckinpah's and Gore Vidal's Garretts are assassins, no better than the ones who killed Tunstall—or who eventually kill Pat himself in the Peckinpah version. Vidal's Billy may be carried off like a crucified Christ, but only into the Hispanic church. Perhaps the Hispanic community turned him into a social *santo,* a kind of Robin Hood of the West, as Robert Utley argues anent the real Billy the Kid (200), but that's not what he represents for the contemporary audience of this film. He is not a god tumbled from his temple nor a sacrificed golden calf. He is a kid for whom the social contract has failed, for whom the old ways, the old codes seem to have worked better: revenge, yes, but friendship, loyalty, the keeping of one's word. He seems a figure for nostalgia in a world where, "Hey, this is a free country, isn't it?" as Billy says to his friends ironically when they embark on a life as outlaws, would draw cynical snickers.

Billy is profoundly hurt by both Pat and Wallace. He turns to rustling (and to drinking) almost in spite, as if to say, "Ok, you treat me like an outlaw, then I'll be an outlaw, but I ain't leavin'." So he represents (nostalgic) defiance of a supposed system of law and order that uses its courts to protect the rich (as in Dolan), that enforces the law selectively (as in who's on death row), that breaks its word (as in treaty obligations to Indians), that defiles its own principles (as in fighting immoral wars, spying and even firing on its own citizens). The defiance is nostalgic because Billy is already an anachronism in his own time, and the urbanization of America has destroyed the kind of territory he represents: wide and wild and wooly. If Billy is, as Celsa insists, "life," then it is an elusive, rebellious spirit always in danger of having boots trample on its grave. Vidal's story of Billy the Kid is a tragedy, but an ominous one, without redemption, with only the thin wisps of resistance blowing in the desert breeze.

10

"Our Pearl beyond price"

I, Pearl Hart

> It became clear to me that the world was a vicious place, and that the abused were everywhere—not just women like me, but entire races of people whose only thought was to stay alive.
>
> *I, Pearl Hart*

Jane Candia Coleman has produced another fine novel about female self-assertion in a cruel, male-dominated world: *I, Pearl Hart,* based on the true story of one of the West's bandit queens, this one who robbed a stagecoach in Arizona in 1899. Pearl asserts herself against a stifling bourgeois super-ego: "At sixteen, I was headstrong, sure of myself, impatient with the do's and don't's of what was termed 'proper behavior'" (14), "the rules and wrappings of middle-class society" (19), exemplified in her mother's perennial warning, *"You'll disgrace us all! No man will have you!"* (17), or that of the nuns at her convent school, *"Keep yourself pure. Men don't marry tarnished goods!"* (24). Interestingly, these are women who, like Kate's Wichita women, have so internalized patriarchal discipline that they become its enforcers. Out West Pearl refers to her family back East as "pale urns" (131)—not just frail china vases that will easily crack but the living dead. When Pearl decides she cannot go home again, cannot stay in stifling Ohio to raise her children in her mother's house but must return to her freedom and independence in Arizona, her mother is scandalized, and through her the superego speaks: "What will people think? [. . .] You're no lady, I'll tell you that" (82–83). "I can't help what I am," Pearl responds, "I can't be like you" (83).

Coleman takes her heroine into the depths of what the cultural critic Kristeva calls "the abject." The abject is implied here in the contrast above between purity and "tarnished goods," as well as in the image of the "pale urns." The border Pearl Hart must negotiate is not just that between East and West as symbolic of conventional versus unconventional morality. It is the border between self-assertion and abjection.

Coleman introduces us to Pearl as a battered wife. Her traveling companion holds a lantern to her face revealing a bloody, broken nose, bruises under her eyes. She can hardly move for her cracked ribs. The opening sentence reads, "The pain from my cracked ribs snaked around, coiled, struck again and again until it was all I could do not to scream" (9). The abject is personified as a python flexing, a cobra striking, attempting to kill, to drag the living self back into the matter that is its matrix. Both *matter* and *matrix,* interestingly, are terms etymologically related to *mother,* the maternal that, according to Kristeva, lurks under the suppression of the patriarchal, that threatens its patrilineal control of power and property and its order of selfhood and naming with the chaos of random and multiple and anonymous birth—and death.

Pearl runs away from her conventional upbringing with the wild Frank Hart, whose dashing gallantry soon turns to jealous beatings not just verbal but physical, from the first bruisings on her arms to his repeated hard slaps across the face. Yet, typical of battered women, she repeatedly forgives him, "following where Frank led like the beaten dog that I was—without hope, without a thought except the next meal, the next place where I could lie down and lick my wounds" (46). Finally, Frank beats her so badly she runs away. He hits her across the nose, cutting it with his ring, and the sight of the blood seems to excite him into sadistically punching, kicking, and then brutally raping her: "Maybe it was my blood, or maybe it was the sounds I was making, like a frightened rabbit" (57). Both are reduced to subhuman animals. Pearl: "I was a pile of bloody rags, an aching in the place where my heart had been. With what strength I could summon, I kicked him in the groin, not once, but twice. [. . .] I should have killed him" (57). Earlier Pearl has metaphorically referred to herself as a "savage," trying to escape Toledo for her birthplace in Ontario (20). Now she has been reduced to a real savage, lashing out to survive, in danger of being reduced further to nothing but that abject "pile of bloody rags."

Unfortunately, Pearl has not seen the last of Frank and his brutality. Pregnant from his rape, she takes him back when he finds her in Arizona. Contemplating her decision, she employs a telling metaphor: "Finally I climbed back into bed and curled up like a miserable child" (72), reduced to fetal position. Virtually immediately, Frank starts in on her again: "It would start and go on and on, a whirlpool that sucked me down and spit out the pieces" (74). Frank is dismembering her. He slaps her so hard, one piece does fall out: the baby, who she wishes would die so she could run away again. Instead, she falls in love with Little Joe. Frank pretends to love the baby too, but he nevertheless continues his practice of marital rape, resulting in another child. Only the outbreak of the Spanish-American War and Frank's subsequent enlistment save Pearl from further abjection—at least at Frank's hands.

Pearl's boss, Al Burke, tries to rape her too, until a whore named Daisy knocks him down and they both escape. Pearl escapes with a Chinese named Harry Hu, becoming his cook and waitress in a cook shack in Globe, working her hands raw but at least free from male oppression. This time it is nature, in the form of a flash flood, that washes away Harry, his shack, and all her belongings and reduces her to abjection: "Once again I was alone, penniless, and the old man I'd loved like a father for his wisdom, his kindness, his grace was gone" (109). The house of another friend, her last resort, burns down, and a telegram arrives to inform her that her mother is dying and her children are ill: "The world was a pit opening at my feet, a hole in the ground from which there was no escaping" (117). In "desperation" (119) she robs the stage, hoping to use the money to take a train back to her children.

But Pearl cannot escape "male strength, the power of pure muscle over my own wanting" (128), her own desire, from the posse that catches her, to the marshal that recaptures her after her brief escape, to the brutal prison guard at Yuma Territorial Penitentiary, Ed Simmons, who rams himself into her out of sheer meanness: "I lay there, remembering Frank and how, when he was in a rage, he would come at me, hard and quick as if I wasn't even human, thinking of a tree being chopped down in a forest, the axe biting deep, wounding to the core" (176). Pearl is transformed to wood pulp before the phallic axe. And vomiting once again discovers to her that she is pregnant with rape's child.

In Yuma Pearl becomes cellmates with a black woman named Tally and a Mexicana named Rosa. Both have also been reduced by men to abjection. Tally, whose mother was a laundress for Buffalo Soldiers, went to work for a white woman after her mother died. Lying peacefully by a stream, she was gang raped by four men, "[h]ard and quick, like they'd do to a whore, and laughing and grunting like the hogs they were. [. . .] I can still see their ugly faces. And smell 'em, too. Sweat, dirt, stinking lust" (166). Of course, like Pearl, she got pregnant, and the woman fired her as unfit to be around white babies. The baby, which she tried to get rid of but which "fastened on me like a snail in my belly" (167), was born in a barn. Despite her efforts to hate it, Tally fell in love with it. But she couldn't feed it. The sheriff refused her plea for help, and she and the baby were in danger of dying in the street. So she drowned it: "I looked down and saw the life goin' out of her, like a door closing, inch by inch, and I vowed I'd make it easy. Why should dyin' be so hard? Why should a child have to suffer, and maybe live to suffer more? So I put her in the water, gentle as I could, and watched her sink. Her face like a little flower, her arms reachin' out to me like she was sayin' . . . 'Save me!' But I had saved her" (167–68). Infanticide is the ultimate abjection for a mother: turning a bodily excretion into a corpse. When Tally is finished her narration, she curls up in fetal position, on the border between self and Other, between life and death.

Rosa was abjected by her husband Julio, who beat her for taking a lover. So she tries to kill him: "I tell him, for beating me, I will cut off his *cojones* while he watch. [. . .] His brothers, they catch me, and send me here. But not before I made many marks. Like the ones he made on me" (158). "Ugliness," "waste," "pain" are Pearl's words for all three abject lives. "Waste" suggests not only wastefulness but refuse. In Yuma Prison, the three are pieces of the detritus of civilization: born, excreted into filthy meaninglessness. The only marks they have made on the world bloody scratches and cuts, bloated corpses. Pearl revels in self-abnegation: "Pearl Hart, who'd always done the wrong thing, taken the wrong road [. . .] . I wanted to destroy the world. [. . .] My life was like one of the novels I'd read so eagerly as a girl, except there was never an end, it went on and on, each chapter worse than the one before" (129, 176, 202).

Even though she gets out of prison by threatening to expose the supervisor and the governor to the embarrassment of a pregnant prisoner, even though she is accompanied by her cell-and-soulmates, even though she is embraced by the kind Cal Jameson, who accepts both her and her child, Pearl has not escaped abjection. Simmons tracks her, tries to arrest her for violating the terms of her parole (and for writing the super about him), overpowers her with his male strength yet once more, despite her kicking and scratching:

> [I]n the end he overpowered me with a punch in the stomach and a blow to my head that knocked me to the ground where I lay half unconscious, struggling to get up and fight again.
>
> My hand closed around a rock—a poor weapon, but better than nothing. I took a ragged breath and swallowed hard to keep from vomiting, and all the beatings of my life flashed through my head: the horrors, the agony, the blood, and the crack of my bones. (216)

Coleman presents us with a fighter, one who overcomes the vomit, the blood, the cracked bones through the resilience of self-assertion. Pearl is in danger from the beginning of crossing over into the abject permanently, becoming its ultimate deposit, a corpse. Pearl repeatedly drags herself back across that border to a series of multiple selves she creates by sheer will-to-being. Even if she dies, she wants to choose the terms: "If I died of starvation, or cold, or loneliness somewhere out on the western prairie, well, at least I'd be free with no one to answer to, no hands to snap my bones like twigs" (9–10). Having suffered through the disillusioning transition from daughter to wife—*"Being a wife was worse than being a daughter,* I thought. *Your husband dictated, and you obeyed without question"* (38)—she gains impetus from the women like Annie Oakley, Helen Modjeska, Julia Ward Howe at the World's Fair in Chicago to assert herself and get a job, despite Frank's sexist objections: "With the prize of independence uppermost in my mind, I shouted at him for the first time"; when Frank demands, "Who in hell do you think you are?" Pearl declares, "I'm a person, just like you are" (52). When her first boss, the kindly Dan Sandeman, holds her jaw to force her to look at him and realize what she's doing to herself with Frank, Pearl again asserts, "'Don't . . . ,' in a voice that sounded like it came out of a ghost. Maybe it had. Maybe it came out of that other Pearl, the one he thought was there" (55). With Dan's help a new self is being born on the precarious border Pearl treads between life-affirming and life-denying modes of being. He offers to take her with him out West, where they could be a team, but "Freedom, as yet, was a frightening thing" (55).

When Pearl finally escapes from Frank and her living death with him, she luxuriates in the life-giving warmth and open spaces of Arizona: "I stood there in the warmth, in the space that seemed to go on forever, and felt I was shedding a skin, becoming a new Pearl, a woman without a past, ready to begin again. I felt it—the seed of happiness, of possibility, and I laughed out loud for the first time in what must have been years. I was home. I belonged in this place of sand, mountains, cloud shadows" (59). Reencountering Joe, her partner on the train, and giving him some money to help him prospect, for the second time Pearl has an essentially kind, well-meaning man offer to team up with her, but she refuses. Her reflection marks an important stage in her becoming: "Funny, I thought, how two such different men had been my friends, my partners. And how different they both were from Frank! With them I was like the person I wanted to be. How had Joe put it—a woman with gumption? That being the case, I needed to survive on my own. If I had a second chance at life, I needed to prove that I could live it without help" (60). Yet in the midst of this rebirth she has doubts, reservations beaten into her bones by Frank. On her arrival in Arizona, "[w]ith enough powder, I was able to disguise [my bruises] and appear almost like my old self, except that the old Pearl was gone, replaced by a woman determined to make her own way" (62). But "[t]he years spent with Frank had left scars—on my body, and inside where no one could see. He'd told me I was worthless so often that, down deep, I believed it, no matter what I'd done to prove my worth" (63). Nevertheless, her self-assertion with Burke teaches her "never to sell myself short. Miss Pearl Hart was a quick study" (67). Even when she discovers she is pregnant with Frank's rape-child, "I was happy, free to feel things, to do as I chose, not what someone else decreed" (69). Even after Frank finds her and threatens like the whirlpool to suck her down and spit out the pieces, Pearl asserts, "But only if I let it" (74). And even after the birth of Frank's second rape-child, she has enough gumption to prepare to escape again: "I was still young enough to believe I could cast off selves and live as I chose. Such arrogance I had! Well, I'm glad of it. Without that arrogance and that flame for living, I might not have survived the next five years" (79).

Spared from running away again by Frank's enlisting in the Rough Riders, Pearl prays a bullet will remove him from her life, deposits her kids with her mother, and goes back to work singing. In Ohio she reflects, "I hardly recognized myself as I stood there in almost the same spot where I had waited with Frank the night we ran away. Who had I been then? Who was I now? I was twenty-eight years old and had lived through what seemed like a hundred lives, variations of someone named Pearl, a woman whose depths and motivations I still didn't understand" (81). Rejecting her Eastern self, differentiating herself from her mother, she returns to the Valverde Saloon in Phoenix. But her career is cut short by Burke's attempted rape. So Pearl must adopt yet another self as cook for Harry, then as a prospector with Joe, then as a janitor for a woman named Lottie who runs a boarding house—all the while "fighting for myself and my life" (111). Meanwhile, she rejects Cal's offer of help, with its implication of commitment between them: "It was one of those turning points. If I'd said yes, everything might have been different. But I was proud. And cautious, not wanting to be in his, or any man's debt, wary of being owned" (103).

Pearl backslides from these assertions, however, into a self-definition as "criminal" (123) even as she desperately reaches for freedom for herself and her kids after the robbery, even as, captive, she slips toward abnegation and abjection: "[M]yself, Pearl Hart, who'd always done the wrong thing" (129). Escaped momentarily, she again asserts her self: "From here on, I vowed that I'd place my trust only in myself and never in a man" (134).

Recaptured in Deming, she despairs: "I'd been caught again, and this time I knew in my bones I'd not get free" (135). In those cracked and beaten bones.

Pearl's finest moment of self-assertion occurs in her eloquent, proto-feminist self-defense before the jury:

> "I didn't want this trial," I told them. "I didn't want to be judged by a court full of men, according to laws made by men. The law says, 'a jury of one's peers,' but you're not my peers. You're men, and you rule by the laws you make without even thinking about women. [. . .] You wouldn't be here today without women. You were all born of a woman, nurtured, taught, loved by a woman. [. . .] Think about your mothers before you condemn me. Think about me, separated from my children. Think about the fairness of your laws. Women sent to jail for adultery while the men go free. Women blamed for the fact that their husbands beat them. Women who abandon their children because they can't care for them. This is justice? [. . .] No gentlemen, it is *not* justice. There won't be any justice until women are given a say in the making of laws to protect themselves." (137–38)

Mirabile dictu, she is acquitted. Obviously, her plea to this jury of men struck a chord, and Pearl exults, "Free! I was free to go!" (139). But the judge isn't pleased, thinks she unduly influenced the jury, so he has her arrested for the theft of the stagecoach driver's pistol: "This was what happened to a woman simply trying to save herself! 'I can't be tried again. It's against the law. The law you men made'" (139), she desperately pleads with the sheriff. But since the pistol was not mentioned in the other trial, she is not subject to double jeopardy, and this time she is found guilty and sentenced to five years in Yuma Prison: "When the sentence came down, I wept. They might as well have hanged me. Yuma Prison was two steps lower than hell" (140).

No matter how low into this hell of abjection Pearl falls, however, she never quits. Despite the fact that she feels her "humanity had been left at the prison gate" (143), Pearl's final, heroic self-assertion occurs after she has been raped and impregnated by another male pig. Seizing the power of the pen, usually a male province, Pearl writes letters to the governor and supervisor. To her demands that not only she but her two female cellmates be freed, the super is only too happy to be shut of women prisoners because they're nothing but trouble, "[a]s you have proved" (184). Pearl recoils on him, talks back to him, this man with power, as she had begun to do with Frank:

His tone was insulting. "Mister Brown," I said, "I have behaved myself from the moment I entered this place. What happened was not my fault, but the fault of your administration."

Then I took Tally's and Rosa's hands and swept out the door with as much arrogance as I could muster. (184)

Even when free, even as Dan implicitly offers himself to her, Pearl suffers an identity insecurity that causes vertigo: "The question was, what did I want now? And who was I? Life had forced me into playing so many parts that, standing there in the station in Yuma, I felt like a spinning top, whirling out of control and waiting for a hand to stop me" (189). That vertiginous whirlpool again. But she does not want Dan. She tells Dan she's pregnant, and like a man, he insults her. Rosa defends her, tells how Simmons raped her, and asserts her own brand of arrogance: "[Y]ou sit there and speak to her like she's trash. You dare to make fun" (191). Dan's unthinking, insensitive joking threatens Pearl again with abjection, with being converted downward to "trash."

It is not Dan, however, but Cal who begins to break through Pearl's self-abnegation: "You don't know anything about who I am or what I've done. You're in love with some person who isn't there" (209). Cal respects her toughness and independence, yet he stubbornly insists on planning the wedding. Even after Pearl's wedding and bedding with Cal, though, Simmons turns up as the last avatar in a string of violent males who threaten Pearl with abjection. One last time she asserts: "I pushed myself up on all fours, blinking to clear my sight" (216).

"I'll do it myself," Pearl says repeatedly throughout the novel. Coleman seems to assert for women the possibility of attaining bourgeois self-reliance, even the heroic stature of leaving one's mark on history—in this case as a proto-feminist maverick on the border of abjection. But finally, the novel does not assert bourgeois individualism, rugged individualism for Western women too. Pearl does not do it herself. As a battered Pearl struggles to stand up and face an opponent for whom she is no match, Simmons is not struck in the head by her rock but is shot by Tally. And despite Pearl's protesting that not another man would ever touch her, on her wedding night, pregnant as she is, she drowns in "sheer joy" with Cal Jameson (213). Women have helped her, men have helped her. Ultimately, the triumph against abjection is collective.

Pearl connects obviously with the sisterhood of her cellmates and with a series of gentle, mostly well-intentioned males: Joe, Dan, Harry, Cal. It is her friendship with Harry Hu that allows her to make that same lateral move of cross-identification Washington Wyatt and the Buffalo Soldiers make. Pearl experiences empathy with an oppressed minority, and the movement is collective as well as individual. Harry tells Pearl of his own persecution as a Chinaman: "How well I understood! As we sat on the wagon seat, piecing together our stories, it became clear to me that the world was a vicious place, and that the abused were everywhere—not just women like me, but entire races of people whose only thought was to stay alive. And if it was unorthodox, even illegal, for a white woman to work side by side with a Chinese, too bad! I'd take the chance and worry about the consequences later" (91). In a territory where interracial relationships were *verboten,* Pearl defies convention in a solidarity of the oppressed.

Pearl's collective identification reaches beyond the oppressed in the present. Visiting Cal's and eventually her home for the first time, Pearl puts her hand on some old ruins and ruminates: "I thought of those who had loved and died there and left a mark. Perhaps letters would be all that I left" (104–5)—that is, the letters she might exchange with Cal while he's in Mexico. Near her nadir, Pearl, prospecting with Joe, again takes comfort, consolation from the past, this time of the earth itself: "[T]here seemed to me to be hope in the fact that the earth lay unchanged, had been as it was for thousands of years. I couldn't know what lay buried in the hollows and cañons of the mountains, or in Joe's tiny plot of earth, but I could keep on, as I'd been doing most of my life, looking to the future, fighting for myself and my life" (111). During her meditations on the banks of the Mississippi in New Orleans, Pearl describes the awesome power of the Old Man: "'I can take you back,' it murmured from behind the restraining levee. 'Anytime I want, I can take you back'" (32).

Individual human existence is dwarfed by such images. Coleman concludes with another. Pearl and Tally are returning from dropping Simmons's body into a bottomless cave (shades of Clark's Harley Dexter):

> As we crossed the creek and came into the yard, we were surrounded by a cloud of butterflies, their orange and black wings swirling like a tapestry—or a blessing. They had miles to go before they reached their resting place, a long, hard journey with many falling by the way. Was it luck that got them through or determination?
>
> I didn't know, simply wished them well as I climbed the steps to the porch and entered the little house, my journey's end, my home. (218–19)

Pearl's ambivalence implies that her own successful quest for identity and home combines a measure of both luck and determination. But Coleman's metaphors suggest further that the vastnesses of time and space are traversed by a species: butterflies, humans.

Pearl's greatest insight into the collective to which she belongs comes the night she performs in Tombstone after her release from Yuma. The audience response places her celebrity status in perspective: "It was as if I belonged to them, as if they were proud of what I'd done, and they'd boast about me later to their friends. It was as if they'd all ridden alongside that afternoon in Cane Springs Cañon, urging me on, shouting encouragement. Sentimental? Perhaps. And violent, too, longing for the thrill of the chase, the success of the underdog. And in that moment, I understood and became one of them as, indeed, I had been all along" (196). It was, after all, a jury of her peers that acquitted her.

The abject, whether portrayed as Dark Mother or the Old Man, can take us back any time it wants to. Pearl's triumph is not that of transcendent individual. If she is a pearl of great price, an allusion to Christ's parable, she is "*[o]ur* Pearl beyond price" (130, emphasis mine), as the prisoners at Yuma mockingly insist. It is not sacred but folk wisdom that prevails. Pearl is *our* collective symbol of human possibility, what Faulkner eulogized as *endurance*. And her value is measured by her struggle to stay on our side of the border.

PART III

SOUTH OF THE BORDER

While the bulk of my chosen/discovered historical novels and films set in the early Southwest north of the border take place before the turn of the century, those set in the early Southwest south of the border take place at and after the turn of the century. They all have as their backdrop the imminent or actual Mexican Revolution. And though in my opinion there has been no adequate treatment of Pancho Villa, in either fiction or film that I know of (he is almost always treated patronizingly as an overgrown child), his revolutionary endeavor and fervor provide the context for at least five of the six works to which I now turn.

Enslavement of Africans is a story well known. Enslavement of Indians less so. But it was carried on systematically in Nueva España and Mexico for three centuries, and as the historian Jack Forbes noted nearly half a century ago, virtually every outbreak of Indian hostility during those centuries may be traced to Hispanic slave raids (s.v. "slave-raiding" and "slavery"). Montserrat Fontes's *Dreams of the Centaur* opens as a novel about rivalry and revenge but becomes a novel about racial and class identity as Porfirio Díaz's Mexican government systematically pursues its infamous enslavement and dispossession of the Yoemem, the Yaquis—a genocidal oppression that was one of the causes of the Mexican Revolution.

In *The Wild Bunch* we cross the border with a bunch of aging desperadoes, fleeing bounty hunters and seeking new markets for their skills. Finally trapped between a meaningless dwindling out of existence or making a final gesture of solidarity with an idealized Mexican peasantry in revolt, they choose the gesture and die in a blaze, writing their last act tragic. Miles Calendar, the John Wayne character in *Last Reveille,* violates his own cardinal principle of non-involvement and loses the son he never had while chasing Villa with Pershing south into Mexico. Beginning in the sierras south of the border, Mariano Azuela's Demetrio of *Los de abajo* leads his countrymen into the heart of the Mexican Revolution, only to retreat disillusioned by the fiasco it has become and in which he is complicit. In the midst of the same political revolution, Laura Esquivel's Tita of *Como agua para chocolate* rebels against her mother and family tradition, also at great price, until her final hymeneal conflagration.

Finally, all three of Carlos Fuentes's protagonists in *Gringo viejo* converge in a quest for identity (a "luchando de ser") in a world of dreams and mirrors in the midst of the Mexican Revolution. All three discover that the border inside oneself is the toughest to cross. Yet they have an implicit pact ("un trueque") that whichever of them survives will preserve the others in her memory.

11

LATERAL CROSSING

DREAMS OF THE CENTAUR

> A voice vibrates through me. "Return to your country. Be priests of this vision, and you will be men of action, be men who move without doubt to turn Sonora into a land of generosity. Tell them what you saw here. When they enslave men there, they enslave us here. Tell them. That is why you have been saved. Be drops of water that penetrate and soften the land. Leave prints for others to follow."
>
> Monserrat Fontes, *Dreams of the Centaur*

In the recent film *The Mask of Zorro* there occurs a remarkable visual event. An American audience witnesses a truth that has been occluded from its consciousness: the enslavement of Indians to work the mines of Mexico. Three centuries of such enslavement is a history not well known, even denied. In the spring of 1998 (just before the Zorro film was released), on Arizona State University's American Indian listserv a scholar protested that, since slavery was officially outlawed by the Spanish crown, it could not have existed.

In her remarkable novel, *Dreams of the Centaur,* Montserrat Fontes tells part of this history, the enslavement of the Yaquis at the turn into the twentieth century.[1] Hector Durcal, intellectual younger brother of the protagonist Alejo Durcal, voices the shock of those who would deny such enslavement if they could: "Slavery is against our Constitution. To sell a human being is treason" (267). Like the other Durcals, however, Hector sees the evidence, condemns Porfirio Díaz, infamous president of Mexico for most of the later nineteenth century until overthrown during 1913, and agrees that the story must be told. Indeed, the Yaqui word *etehoi* means stories, which have enormous importance in oral cultures, for they represent memories that constitute a people's history: "Tellings. *Etehoi* is how

Yaquis record events" (300). Fontes brings us voices designed not just to obliterate forgetfulness or denial but, as this chapter's epigraph puts it eloquently, to "penetrate and soften the land"—of Sonora and, by extension, of the Americas—leaving "prints for others to follow." The proximate, harder result would be the Mexican Revolution; the distant, softer result would be the raising of consciousness of North Americans as we enter the new millennium with the prospect of continued (economic) colonization, imperialism, and, yes, slavery and even genocide. The holocaust of Yaquis the novel describes reminds us of other, more recent holocausts, including those of Indians in Central America. Yet *Dreams of the Centaur* leaves prints: hints and dreams of a *mestizaje,* to use Anzaldúa's apt term, that represents successful crossings.

Dreams of the Centaur begins with a *corrido* that tricks us into thinking this is a typical borderlands novel about rivals and revenge, about a horse, a card game, and a shot from a fatal gun. In 1882 José Durcal has a dream that the Sonoran ranch he has built with his own hands will be passed on to his sons, that his name will live on. But in the early 1890s he and his *hacendado* friend, Esteban Escobar, contend over a magnificent black stallion named El Moro, whom Esteban has unfairly bought out from underneath José's desire and whom José has won back in a poker game. Potent on the back of his stallion, José is known as El Centauro, as he increases his ranch and his influence in the community especially by means of a breeding business involving both Moro and the aptly named "Sueño," his prize bull. Overreaching, perhaps, José wins rich river-bottom land in another poker game with Esteban, and is found dead. Esteban maintains he shot his friend by accident, but José's wife and sons know it was murder. They just cannot prove it against the powerful Escobars. Oppressed until they cannot stand it, both Durcal's wife and his oldest son severally plan their revenge. Indeed, presciently José has primed his oldest: "Swear to me that if I fall, you will complete my dream. [. . .] If I die [. . .] or if something happens to me, swear to keep the Durcal name alive. Make the Durcal ranch a wheel that turns by itself" (37). Alejo shoots his godfather Esteban in the face. Thinking the judge will grant leniency in such a case of honor, the family and the community are surprised when Alejo gets twenty years in the dreaded pit-prisons of Mexico. Thanks to his mother's interest, he is allowed to join the army. He endures hardships, escapes, and ends up happy on a ranch in Arizona, complete with his adolescent love interest, Ana María, rejected wife of the lawyer who arranges everything.

A typical romance, a *Bildungsroman.* But intertwined from the beginning is another story, that of the Yaquis. On the opening page, José chases a Yaqui girl. He allows Yaquis to work his ranch, despite the fact that his wife Felipa hates them, for they killed her mother in a raid. The Yaquis have never sworn allegiance to Mexico, and José secretly admires their resistance leader, Cajeme, who is finally caught, paraded, and executed. José warns that Díaz is selling Mexico out to American and other foreign speculators at a cost to midlevel men like himself and especially to the Yaquis. Esteban Escobar's friend, the American speculator Billy Cameron, responds to José's anger over this exploitation with the classic Lockean argument for the appropriation of Indian land: "[T]he fact is, Yaquis are not developing what they have" (51).[2]

Alejo Durcal, who has an intimate and at times clairvoyant relationship with his mother, Felipa, "[o]n the subject of Yaquis, [. . .] was torn between his adoration of Felipa and respect for José" (58). But like Ike McCaslin, Alejo has an Indian for a surrogate father, the Yaqui Tacho, who teaches him how to make and use a bow and arrow, regales him with stories of the making of a Yaqui warrior (who was as ferocious and formidable as an Apache), and eventually trains him to break Moro to accept him as, implicitly, the new El Centauro after José is murdered. This last training constitutes his entry into manhood.

The Durcal boys' aunt, Tía Mercedes, cautions them against avenging their father, and her warning uncannily places the Durcals in a space between—a space Alejo especially must learn to negotiate. She tells them they are powerless against the Escobars, who are well connected all the way to the Capitol: "'Look at what they do to the Indians! Their families can't bury them until the bodies have rotted.' 'Tía, we're not Indians!' [. . .] 'You're not Escobars!'" (90).

The question of just who he is becomes paramount for Alejo. Just sixteen years old when he avenges his father, riding Moro into the café where Esteban drinks and shooting his *padrino* in the face, Alejo embarks on a remarkable journey. He attempts to justify his vengeance to his mother by arguing that he has avenged the Durcal name, saved "Father's dream—that our name would live" (137). Felipa responds cynically, "Bah! He took that name because he had none of his own" (137). The narrator explains that "he had taken the name Durcal from a newspaper in Sinaloa, because 'it sounded strong'" (137). Thus Alejo is deprived of the essence a name is supposed to bestow. He plans to turn himself in, to take responsibility for what he has done. Felipa wants him to run away, to avoid the "paredón" (137), the wall against which he will most likely be executed by firing squad.[3]

Instead, Alejo is sentenced to the dreaded *bartolinas*. He is first incarcerated in the caves rather than the pits, and here he makes an extraordinary acquaintance that continues to destabilize his sense of who he is. The boy in the cave next to his carries his father's and his and his brothers' birthmark. Charco, a kind of *enfant sauvage,* is his bastard half-brother, the offspring of José's fling with the Yaqui girl. "The boy claimed to have lived everywhere. Under a table, in a stable, in Mayo and Yaqui villages, with Mexicans and gringos. He didn't know if he was Mexican or Indian and he was glad," because, Charco explains to Alejo, "in Sonora everyone shoots someone, sooner or later. Like you. Best if people don't know what you are" (155). Yet Charco ineluctably resembles his father, as everyone notes eventually. Like Alejo, Charco too is caught between identities, between cultures. He just doesn't know it yet, for Alejo does not reveal to him his Durcal heritage until they have returned to their father's ranch after their ordeal.

Alejo himself, however, searches for meaning in this uncanny encounter: "How could two of José Durcal's sons end up side by side in these bartolinas? Surely that meant something" (162). The meaning only gradually unfolds, creates itself out of their bonding. Charco is tortured for information concerning the whereabouts of the Yaquis. Alejo is pressured to spy on Charco. Both end up in the pits for their resistance, where they enter into each other's spirits in order to remain sane. They endure by means not of any European religion or philosophy but Indian spiritualism, the Huichol prayer with which their one kindly keeper leaves them: Alejo narrates, "We prayed until we met in the empty wooden bucket outside the pits. At first we only saw each other's eyes. Next our faces" (188). Released from the pits and inducted into the army, as they marched to Guaymas, "Charco and I sent each other ánimo and because of that, we did not die" (189).

As is evident by these recent quotations, Fontes makes a daring switch in narration. Part 2 of the novel switches into first person so we can get into the head of Alejo during his crossing from one consciousness to another. He experiences a painful identity crisis fomented by his increasing awareness of complicity. In order to escape the pits, he must surrender his identity as Alejo Durcal, assuming the new surname, Robles, his mother's maiden name and the one arranged by the lawyer Castillo. Alejo feels he is *"losing something"* (181) in giving up the name for which he killed Esteban. When Capitán Carrasco, the commandant of the prison, calls out Alejo's new name to induct him, Alejo nearly faints: "I was more than naked, I was stripped of flesh and memory" (189). In taking on a new identity, he obtains a new "memory," indeed, one that he must struggle to keep alive, to share, to tell as *etehoi.*

He first experiences shame at his complicity now, as a soldier, in the persecution of the Yaquis, whom the army rounds up for shipment to Mexico City and beyond. Alejo wishes the silent Yaqui prisoners would curse him: "I would welcome their curses. It matters not that Charco and I were forced to do this. It matters that we did" (185). He takes refuge in a kind of schizophrenia, in his new identity as Alejo Robles, for, he says to himself, Alejo Durcal would never have participated, as he did, in the atrocities against the Yaquis, including raping the women. He continues his schizophrenic reflection: "Alejo Durcal would have remained loyal to the Yaqui. He would have remembered the Yaqui legend Tacho taught him. According to this legend the little girl, the prophet Yomumuli, translated the words from the talking tree. Those words warned of the coming of the white man and the railroad. Sadly, Durcal would have seen the dark part he played in that legend, a legend that saw the Yaquis expelled from their own land" (197). Alejo sees his dark self as an agent of the white man and his destructive domination, foretold in the legend from the talking tree.

Talking trees and crosses will play an important part later in the novel. Meanwhile, as Alejo, Charco, and their band of *bartolinas* soldiers escort Yaquis on a forced march from the sea to the railroad depot in Tepic, they are caught in a ravine in a flash flood, and Alejo and Charco seize the moment for their escape. But Charco cannot abandon the women and children and returns to save them: "Ashamed, I see my part in this terrible cruelty" (201), for Charco has torn away "the curtain" that has blinded Alejo to his complicity, that has separated his schizophrenic selves: "I ask God, what blood runs through my veins? [. . .] While Charco argues–chest out, eyes burning—I see a true son of José Durcal, known as a defender of Yaquis. But am I the son of José Durcal? Not when I fear death more than how I manage to live through this. What will we do to these people? Why don't I know? Why haven't I asked?" (202). How he manages to live through his ordeal involves his own as well as the Yaquis' dehumanization: he becomes a raping dominant male.

Witnessing the loading onto trains of the "enemies of the state" (207), Mexicans like himself whose only crime is speaking out or writing against the injustice and who are being sent to sugar plantations where they will be worked to death; witnessing the loading also of the Yaqui boys, ripped from their mothers to be taken to Mexico City and "sold to labor contractors" as slaves; arriving in Yucatán where those labor contractors will work those Yaqui boys to death on henequen plantations, Alejo slips to his nadir:

My mother's face returns and I see my life with fresh eyes. I see no future for myself and my past is blurred. [. . .]

It's possible to feel death.

I felt mine when I delivered Yaquis to men who speak the language I speak.

I turned over Sonora men and women I have known all my life to men who paid sixty-five pesos a head for them.

Sixty-five.

My father had tried to make me curious about my country and failed. Now I'd crossed my homeland, ocean to ocean, and my country poisons me. (208, 215)[4]

Alejo's nadir is not his abjection in the *bartolinas,* then. It is his consciousness of being thus poisoned. What especially poisons Alejo is that his country is contaminated, polluted by an injustice so inhumane as to betray not just its ideals but its ruling-class ideology of benevolent paternalism. Thus Alejo confronts the problem of evil, muttering a Jobish complaint: "God, why do you let this continue?" (200). Nevertheless, Alejo's reflections are shorn of faith in traditional European theodicy. They are existential, an argument of absurdist logic:

Saltillo [the most indomitable of the *bartolinas* soldiers] says there's always a worse place than the one you're in. And if we imagine such a place, then our place isn't so bad. That is of little comfort. Why must we choose between bad and worse? Who sets up the choices?

My instinct tells me that if we can imagine a worse place, we'll make sure someone ends up there. That must be how evil places get started. That's how Yaquis got chained—someone thought of a worse situation than his own, then he created it. (198–99)

No deity, benevolent or malevolent, sets up such choices. Humans, capable of incremental degradation, do.

Alejo begins to be presented with his own choices. He and Charco befriend the patrician sergeant, Gustavo. In Mexico City, Gustavo brings friends he had met in Europe, members of his *hacendado* class, to gawk at "your famous wild Yaquis" from Sonora (210), as if they were nothing more than curious animals in a zoo. When Charco pisses on the ladies' skirts, the patricians demand Charco be punished. Gustavo controls their rage, dismisses them, and returns laughing. Alejo approves of the gesture of solidarity: "I liked that he had protected Charco instead of siding with people of his class" (210).

Charco is half Yaqui and a *peon* and identifies easily with the Yaquis in their desperate plight. Alejo, from an aspiring ranchero class, and Gustavo, from an established landed class, have a much more difficult crossing, but increasingly they too identify until the crucial moment when they are ordered by an overseer on a henequen plantation in Yucatán, whither they have been brought because they know something about ranching, to teach the overseer how to brand Yaquis so he may reclaim them when they run away to other plantations.[5] Predictably, Charco refuses and is whipped. But Alejo too refuses and is whipped. What enables him to endure is another out-of-body identification, this time with a naked Yaqui man hobbled for branding. Gustavo agrees to do the branding, but only to gain time. Alejo brands the overseer instead. When Charco trips him up, Alejo then smashes his head in and frees the hobbled Yaquis.

Alejo has crossed laterally into solidarity with the oppressed Yaquis, Yaquis oppressed by him, his people, his government: "*We did this*" (227). His new identification is underscored by the Mayan Anginas, who has actually engineered Alejo's experience so he might return to Sonora and tell the truth to the Yaquis, to Mexico. Anginas says of the Yaqui with whom Alejo has bonded, named Juan, and Alejo himself, "You come from the same land. Different cribs, same land, but here, you're the same" (247): both Sonoran, separated by class, now yoked by the experience of oppression, by empathy.

Anginas was a Talking Cross, a member of the Mayan resistance, whose ability to talk was nearly stifled forever by his being made to swallow coals as punishment. Now he makes these Sonorans experience the full horror of Yucatán so they will be "priests of this vision" and therefore "men of action," men "who move without doubt to turn Sonora into a land of generosity": "That is why you have been saved" (250). In a way, Alejo, Charco, and Gustavo have become the new Talking Crosses.

Crosses mean sacrifice, however. The three (plus Juan) survive the chaos they have unleashed on the plantation by being buried beneath a heap of corpses, another descent into abjection. They return from the dead, as it were. But we take no refuge in Christian meaning. The symbolism is transformed back into Mayan pagan. Fed liquor to facilitate endurance of being transported in a wagon of corpses, Alejo has a hallucinatory vision of a great flowering *flamboyan* tree. Alejo reaches for the flowers, but they're too high, yet the tree tells him to climb: "The rest follow and soon our heads are surrounded by flowers that form a net of joy that cradles me. [. . .] I cry and laugh until I'm empty and weak with a sweet tiredness I've yearned for all my life. [. . .] A voice. 'Take the word of the ceiba, the *yaxché*, the tree of life through which all creatures live. The harmony of its smallest leaf contains the harmony of the heavens. Submit to the *yaxché* and your *kinán* will heal the cruelty of your land'" (251). The "net of joy" is their solidarity. The ascent they make is up the Bacatete Mountains, up Mazocoba Peak, last refuge of the Sonoran Yaquis before they are slaughtered by the Mexican army, the remaining Yaquis being enslaved or escaping to Arizona.

Aided by Anginas to escape Yucatán and by Gustavo's *hacendado* father to return to Sonora, Alejo and the others learn that there is a new, unofficial governmental policy: "The popular saying about Sonora is 'New century, new land. Forget coexistence'" (258). Word is out that there will be a massive government effort against the Yaquis. Alejo, Charco, and Gustavo, equipped by Castillo with the means to go to Arizona themselves, declare that they will keep their word to the Mayan resistance and inform the Yaqui chiefs of what fate awaits them if they do not make peace. They follow Juan to Mazocoba, but it is too late. The slaughter is imminent. They choose to join the Yaquis atop the mountain: "We belong on the right side. That's up there," announces Alejo for all of them (282). But the Yaquis have been betrayed by one of their own.[6] The army knows their secret routes to the top, their escape route off the back of the mountain. As the narrator puts it, speaking in her own voice in this part 3, "A world is ending" (287). Coexistence has been terminated.

Coexistence survives on a different level, however: *mestizaje,* Anzaldúa's term for a new, multicultural consciousness. It takes the form of the dream of the new centaur, the transformed Alejo, whose dream changes, expands that of his father:

> What was Father's dream? That the name Durcal live after him through his sons and the ranch?
> Small dream.
> Well, thinks Alejo, I will change El Centauro Durcal's dream. Father said, "A man must make good dreams—if not, he is capable of the worst." I say a dream should be bigger than one man's ranch or one man's land. I killed more than Esteban when I fired that gun. I killed Father's old dream too. No, made it bigger—to include everyone. And I need not step through his ghost to live my dream. I will stand on his shoulders to carve my own dreams. (275–76)

The killing of his father's dream is not Oedipal; he needs not "step through his ghost," through some symbolic parricide. Alejo can succeed his father not through supplanting him but through expanding his father's vision laterally:

> Fondly, he looks at Charco, Gustavo, and Juan and remembers the *flamboyan* tree in Yucatán. They too abandoned their personal dreams.
>
> Anginas changed us, he thinks, united our *kinán*. (276)

This *kinán*, this positive energy, gives force to solidarity, gives it healing power. Its inclusivity is what's important. Alejo survives the battle, survives the loss of a leg, replaces it with wood from a tree—as if it were *yaxché*, the "tree of life." In the end, as he approaches his new home in Arizona, as he purchases from the Nimipu, the "real people" from the north, the spotted horses (*peluse*) with which he will begin his breeding farm like his father's (334), his dream is inclusive. He explains it to a reluctant Felipa: "Please. See the good fortune in all this. We survived. The *peluse*, the Nimipu, the Yaquis, Charco, me. People tried to kill us and couldn't. We're all joined somehow. I don't have the words, but I see the picture clearly in my head. It matters that I work with those who struggled. It unites our *kinán* into a circle" (337). Alejo is priest of a new vision of solidarity of the oppressed, a vision with leavening power to raise the consciousness of those—perhaps unwittingly—complicit in the oppression. Their *mestizaje* offers pagan redemption, leaving prints for others to follow. It is appropriate for the stallion, both Moro and Alejo, to be reunited with his mare of choice at the end, for this is romance, a novel where good triumphs—or at least transforms. Charco says they were "meant to fight" with the Yaquis (269). In the end, they will meaning onto their stories, their lives. It is the rhetoric of desire. Unlike Faulkner, Fontes grants her characters efficacy.

Alejo is not the only major protagonist in *Dreams of the Centaur* to be transformed into a maverick on the border. This is a novel written by a woman, and Fontes frames it with a woman's consciousness, Felipa's. At the beginning Felipa is a devotee of the Virgin of Guadalupe—and a Yaqui hater. The first major change in this young bride of El Centauro is that she escapes the usual sacrificial sexual role of Mexican wife and experiences female desire—and orgasm. This awakening is symbolic of a larger awakening—of Felipa's enormous energy, her *kinán*, if you will, and also of her consciousness.

Felipa's *crise de conscience* occurs when, like the she-bear searching for her cub suggested in Alejo's youthful lamentation at his father's bring-

ing home a stuffed bearcub, she responds to her son's plea as he leaves for
the Bacatetes that she come find him after the battle. She rescues her wounded
son from among the corpses of old men, women, and children, slaughtered
as they tried to escape the carnage. She ministers to him in her wagon through
the night, till the light dawns, both literally and metaphorically:

> First light shows Felipa the battle's tally. Walking toward
> her must be a thousand people. In torn bloody rags, faces sooty,
> burned lips blistered, cut, they move in slow, heavy silence.
> Outraged, Felipa demands, "Dónde estás, Virgen Santa?"
> She shakes a fist at the sky. [. . .] Holy Mother, doesn't this
> silence wring your soul? (293)

She witnesses Mexican families, arriving in their buckboards, buying surviving Yaqui children for domestic slaves: "Numb, Felipa can't believe
what she sees" (294). She too finds European theodicy lacking, and she
ceases praying to her beloved Virgin.

Instead, Felipa takes matters into her own hands. She rescues the captured Charco too. They get the wounded Alejo to a small ranch, where she
herself amputates his lower left leg, supervises his healing, and simply
wills him back to life. Charco explains to Alejo, who is feeling sorry for
himself, "'You lived because of your mother's rage,' he says. 'I saw the
rage in her eyes as she fought off death. Her passion saved you. And this is
right, for that's what we are.' He slaps his chest with the palms of his hands.
'The flesh of our mothers'" (321–22).

Felipa also changes gradually here in this small ranch house, where
the Peñas, Manuel and Carmen, relinquish their bedroom to Alejo, sleep in
the wagon, and assist in every way they can. Felipa admires the quiet, strong
Carmen, who is Indian. Typically for not just Felipa's higher class but for
aspiring *mestizos,* Manuel's family "rejected his Indian wife" (328). Felipa
admires their love amid sparseness, their ability to know "when you have
enough" (328). Moreover, "[s]he has seen Alejo eye Carmen, and Felipa
admits she's wished he would find a good Indian woman like her" but she
realizes she is stereotyping (328). She vows to let her sons marry whom
they will, then realizes even that is a gesture. She is undergoing an important process of self-knowledge here:

> Empty gesture, she thinks, unable to wed her vow to pas-
> sion. Vows can't change this ugly rejection of people like me
> and those whom José called Mexico's primera gente. José was a

better person. [. . .] People like me made the Martinos [the overseers] who scarred Alejo. People like me allow the Mazocobas that maimed my son.

She remembers it was Carmen who spoke up and asked her to bring her son to the ranch. Manuel, the mestizo who is most like herself, was ready to turn her away. (328–29)

The upper class, the *primera gente,* is not morally superior. José, in his tolerance of and even admiration for Yaquis, was morally superior to them, to her. Furthermore, her supposedly unmixed caste of Hispanos is actually morally reprehensible for its inhumane practices of slavery and genocide.

This remarkable transformation takes place as she lies in the road to Arizona reflecting, indulging her sexual desires. She remains a vital woman, the only person besides José and Alejo who can ride Moro. She is an empowered woman. She effects their successful crossing of the border, as she crosses internal borders of her own. Felipa concedes to herself that Alejo and Charco "aren't wrong to want to end the evil in their country" (333). Felipa sees things differently, philosophically: "On some days the clouds separate, creating a broad aisle for the sun's setting. This gives the desert plain a uniform hue, turning it into an endless mantle, a cloak spread over the earth. Where is she on this vast cloth? At the end of the material, where edges fray into nothingness? She does not feel ragged" (333–34). Gone is Catholic ontology. She belongs to a universe of becoming, and she is not frightened.

Felipa, at first resistant, comes to accept Alejo's new dream. And she accepts Charco as the virtual reincarnation of José. Upon his quick return from Tucson with two Yaqui families, "Felipa looked at the boy's handsome face. José and his Yaquis. Again" (343). What is more, despite her jealousy of Charco's Yaqui mother, she comes to accept her husband's bastard as her own son, embracing him as "hijo" (349), the last word of the novel. Fittingly, the novel ends with Felipa independently beginning her four hundred mile trek back to Alamos, driving her wagon alone, with faith not in Christianity but in something like Charco's vision, where we are part of "something bigger" (347), where "[e]verything already happened, right, hijo?" (349)—the *mestizaje* version of Hegel's alpha and omega of Becoming.

However much we romanticize the primitive, we cannot—Fontes and her sympathetic, *fin de siècle* readers—indulge ourselves in a vision that is not *mestizaje,* not creolized, somehow pure, *indio.* Fontes knows this. Thus at the end she focuses on Charco's identity. If he is just the flesh of his mother, his identity is fluid: "He didn't know if he was Mexican or Indian and he was glad" (155). But Charco is the inescapable spitting image of his father; he carries his birthmark, "the sign of conquerors" (22)—the ineluctable sign of Hispanic forbears, of Conquistadores, of European heritage.

When Alejo informs Charco of his heritage, he denies: "Charco lashes, 'I'm no one's brother! And I don't belong here. I'm only here because I'm the son of Moro and a mare.' He stops; voice low, he adds, 'I don't belong anywhere on earth, and I never have—that I remember'" (347). Felipa asks how much he remembers. He doesn't remember his mother, thinks she was hanged by Mexican soldiers and that he was sold first to Mexicans, then to Americans, for whom he worked until he found the Yeomem.

> "But *before* that, I belonged to something big—like that sky up there, only bigger. It was huge, and I knew that though it was big to me, it was part of something bigger. No matter what happens, I don't fear death, because when I die, I'll go back *there*."
>
> Tears roll back into Felipa's hair. "Meanwhile, Charco," she says, remembering that Charco can't be more than fifteen years old, "come to your father's ranch, because on earth, that's where you belong. That's what's right."
>
> "Señora," Charco murmurs. (347)

We all are children of the cosmos. But we have specific histories, which cannot be denied. Charco's murmur marks his submission, his acceptance of being his father's son as well as his mother's: Mexican as well as Yaqui, joined not just to the oppressed but to the oppressors.

Crossing the border to Arizona emphasizes the arrival in a new world, a new space, but with its ineluctable links to the old. Charco's mixed identity seems to be a synecdoche for a potent *mestizaje* these three mavericks now share. No people can lay claim to being the "real people." At best we can aspire for a solidarity that enables potential drops of water to penetrate and soften this hard land. Felipa parts saying to Charco, "Tu casa está en Alamos" (349). Just as the Yaquis have a traditional "homeland" (passim), so do we all. Fontes's final hope seems to be the message of the *flamboyan*: "Submit to the *yaxché* and your *kinán* will heal the cruelty of your land."

12

THE IMPOSSIBLE CROSSING

THE WILD BUNCH

> También yo estoy en la region perdida,
> ¡Oh cielo santo! Y sin poder volar.
>
> from "La Golondrina" in *The Wild Bunch*

Aging outlaws cross the border into Mexico, fleeing a botched robbery of a railroad depot and a posse of bounty hunters led by a former member of their gang. Like McCarthy's kid in 1878, they would seem to be superannuated warriors indeed here in circa 1913. Like *The Magnificent Seven* or *Butch Cassidy and the Sundance Kid,* other 1960s Western films with a similar theme, *The Wild Bunch* would seem to be more elegiac than tragic, more about the end of an era than its heyday.[1] After the discovery that their robbery, having cost them several men, nets them only worthless washers, Pike Bishop, leader of the Wild Bunch, muses prophetically, "We got to start thinking beyond our guns: those days are closin' fast." Yet the Bunch never crosses over into some promised land beyond the gun. Pike never gets to "back off" as he says he would like to. He never buys a ranch with a sweat house. And not just because those who live by the sword must die by the sword. Because violence seems endemic to the human race, and crossing over out of it seems impossible. The Bunch nevertheless chooses to define themselves by means of their last, suicidal gesture: they write their last act tragic.

Sam Peckinpah's film is justly revered as having changed the American Western film forever, forcing us to confront the violence sanitized in earlier Westerns.[2] The opening and closing action scenes are famous for filmic techniques that emphasize that violence: slow motion, close-ups of exploding bodies, the sounds of bullets ripping into human flesh. Like *Blood Meridian, The Wild Bunch* is a dark parody of earlier Westerns, an antiheroic Western. One might argue (as has Mitchell) that it is a satire on the genre, a satire on gratuitous violence, a satire on violent machismo and meaningless male bonding. There is some truth in this reading, but I am not entirely convinced.

The machismo and the bonding are indeed satirized through tough-guy posturing, whoring, drinking, and raucous laughing. As the Bunch holds up the railroad depot, Pike grimly orders, "If they move, kill 'em." The Bunch is at each other's throats when they discover they've been tricked by Deke Thornton and his hired guns for the railroad. Their hands are at their guns throughout the scene, from Pike's angry assertion, "I either lead this Bunch or end it—right now," to his seething, "Go for it! Fall apart." Bothered by old wounds so that he sometimes can barely ride, Pike nevertheless gets in the face of the Gorch brothers in defense of the even older Freddie Sykes. Pike holds a detachment of *Federales* at bay by threatening to blow up not just the guns he has stolen for them but the Bunch itself. And of course, the remnant of the Bunch, walking four abreast to confront the vile Generalísimo Mapache (the "Rat") and demand the release of their tortured Mexican partner Angel, presents an archetypal image of the Western, repeated so signally in *Tombstone:* gunmen as avengers, as vigilante agents of ultimate justice. And the ultimate machismo trip seems to be the adrenaline rush. If the Bunch tries to raid an American arms shipment, "They'll be waiting for us," Dutch warns. Squaring his jaw, Pike grunts, "I wouldn't have it any other way," and Dutch settles himself down for a nice sleep around the campfire repeating Pike's line. What a way to go.

What releases the tension of the scene after the holdup is a reference to whoring. Lyle Gorch remains angry, still complains of their failure, of Pike's failure as a leader. Pike fires back, "You spent all your time and money running whores in Hondo while I spent my stake setting it up," then as he draws from the ubiquitous whiskey bottle, he softens: "Hell, I should've been running whores instead of stealing army horses." The Gorch brothers brag about how, while Pike was planning, they were doing whores in tandem. They crack up. The laughter is infectious. Dutch Engstrom, Pike's closest campadre, laughs. Sykes laughs. Angel, the hot-tempered Mexicano who has most quickly drawn his gun, laughs. Pike himself finally laughs, and the scene dissolves in a wild laughter that dissolves many more scenes. Indeed, Peckinpah closes the film with inserts of these same faces laughing again—from the dead—as the lone Wild Bunch survivors, Sykes and the reclaimed Thornton, ride off with indigenous guerrillas to play out the rest of their lives as gunmen.

Both laughter and drink are satirized as macho forms of negotiation.

They help bond the Bunch together, overcoming potentially fatal differences. Before the Bunch enters the stronghold of Aguaverde, they slowly, deliberately pass around a bottle of whiskey, setting it up so that Angel will drain its last swallow and pour out the dregs before Lyle Gorch gets any. In another scene of apparently gratuitous shenanigans, Tector Gorch chucks a passel of lit dynamite in front of Sykes while he squats, trying literally to scare the shit out of him. Yet both of these instances are still forms of aggression: the Bunch against one of the Gorches, the Gorches against one of the Bunch. The negotiation is tenuous, the laughter hollow. And drinking in the desert sun is both stupid and dangerous. But boys will be boys, and these men in some important sense are still juveniles, superannuated boys: reckless, irresponsible, lethal.

Whoring ostensibly provides relief from tension too, as the Gorches frolic through Aguaverde with several whores, shooting holes in barrels so they can shower in wine, rub-a-dubbing in a tub together. Of course, right before the climactic shootout, the Bunch must whore one last time (though Dutch defers, waits outside whittling!). All of this macho activity is done to such excess that one must infer satirical parody, as if Peckinpah had read Leslie Fiedler and anticipated Eve Kosofsky Sedgwick: that the stereotypical Western features homosocial—if not implicit homoerotic—male bonding to the exclusion of meaningful relationships with women or children or society. Guns are substitutes for phalluses. Violence is erotic. And gunmen never stay. Like Shane or Sykes and Thornton, they ride on. Or like McCarthy's kid and Billy the Kid and the rest of the Bunch, they die. As Peckinpah's penetrating bullets seem to emphasize, violence is rape.

The code of the Bunch—the code of the West, loyalty, fidelity to the Bunch—would seem to be the one positive among all the machismo, the one positive aspect of male bonding. When old man Sykes starts an avalanche of bodies down a dune, Tector Gorch threatens to get rid of him. Pike responds angrily, "You're not getting rid of anybody. We're gonna stick together, just like it used to be. When you side with a man, you stay with him! And if you can't do that, you're like some animal. You're finished. We're finished, all of us!" This code would seem to supply the later unspoken motivation for the Bunch's walking into the jaws of death to free Angel despite overwhelming odds. Pike merely glowers at the Gorch brothers at the whore house and barks grimly, "Let's go." The Gorch brothers look at each other, then Lyle sets his jaw as well: "Why not?" Outside, Dutch simply grins with pleasure as the others emerge determined. They all know what it is about.

"They know what this is all about," Thornton rails at his "gutter trash" bounty hunters, for these men he is stuck with do not. They are nothing more than scavengers, stripping the bodies of the citizens caught in the crossfire at Starbuck. Thornton demands better men from Harrigan, his railroad boss, but Harrigan orders Thornton to work with what he has and get the job done in thirty days or go back to Yuma, Pearl Hart's dread territorial—now state—prison. "We're after *men*," Thornton completes his admonition. "And I wish to God I was with them." Because the Bunch are *real* men, is the implication, who know that sticking together, standing up together, even to the point of dying together, is what "this" is all about: the chase, the game of life itself. The Bunch are warriors, like the Samurai ronin after whom are modeled the Magnificent Seven.

Of course, like the Seven, there are really only two or three who are philosophical enough to understand what is happening to their world: Pike, Dutch, perhaps Sykes, certainly Thornton. Technology, for one thing, as represented by Mapache's automobile; the rumored aeroplane that may be used in this war along the border; the machine gun itself, which changed the nature of warfare sooner and more decisively than the aeroplane; hand grenades, the new pocket ordnance. The presence of the German advisors to Huerta's counterrevolutionary government, for which Mapache fights, as well as the shadow-presence of Black Jack Pershing (called so because he headed Buffalo Soldiers in Montana), reminds the audience of the *real* war impending in Europe, whose millions of casualties will make the carnage at the end of this film seem insignificant by comparison, the bravado of the Wild Bunch that of a bunch of gnats. In an important sense, the march of the Bunch into the valley of death at the end is absurd. They do not achieve their primary objective: Angel's throat is slit by the sadistic Mapache before the Bunch kills anyone. They shoot Mapache in revenge. There is a moment of stasis while they giggle at each other. Then it is they who begin the sustained fusillade, as if to say, what the hell, let's do it. Pike starts with the German advisor because he hates him, but not for any ideological reason.

Yet does not their dying with Angel and for their code infuse at least their deaths with meaning? Dutch makes a curious point. When he curses Thornton for getting Sykes, Pike defends him: "What would you do in his place. He gave his word." Pike understands that Thornton got out of Yuma only because he pledged to track his old gang. Moreover, we know from a flashback, which apparently Pike does not share with Dutch as they are talking around the campfire on their escape across the border, that Pike feels guilty his carelessness as leader landed Thornton in the hands of the law. So Pike cannot bring himself to blame Thornton for taking his chance to escape a hellhole, and he invokes the code of word-as-bond to excuse him. Dutch introduces a new element into their ethic:

> *Dutch:* Gave his word to a *railroad*!
> *Pike:* It's his *word*!
> *Dutch:* That ain't what counts. It's who you give it *to*!

To whom *should* one give his word? When the town fathers of Starbuck complain bitterly to Harrigan about the carnage on their streets, Harrigan shouts back, "We represent the law!" But Thornton knows that the law is a mask to hide the violence of the hegemonic, of those in power: "Tell me, Mr. Harrigan, how does it feel? Getting paid for it? Getting paid to sit back and hire your killings with the law's arms around you? How does it feel to be so goddamned right?" The railroad represents the ineluctable march of industrial power, cloaked in the ideology of Manifest Destiny and sanctioned through the unholy alliance between business and government. The force is amoral, Harrigan would seem to say in his cynical response to Deke's query about how it feels: "Good."

So to whom of value worth dying for do Pike and Dutch give their word? The worthless Gorches? Angel, who since his discovery that his *novia* (sweetheart, fiancée) has gone willingly with Mapache has been warned by Pike to either let his vengeance go or leave the Bunch, and whose reckless shooting of her earns him the undying wrath of Mapache? Or whose conflicting loyalty to his people, especially to *los indígenas* and their revolutionary struggle, endangers the Bunch itself as they steal guns from Pershing to sell to the *Federales*? Sykes has warned him about conflicting loyalties: "Listen, you ride the trail, the village don't count. If it does, you jest don't go along." Indeed, Dutch abandons Angel to Mapache when he is betrayed by his *novia*'s own mother for sequestering one case of rifles for the revolutionaries. He reports to Pike that Angel "played his string right out" to the very end, meaning both that he kept his loyalty to the Bunch by not confessing that they were complicit in his theft and also that his string of luck has run out. Even though the Gorches are disgusted that the "girl's mama" would turn him in like "Judas," and even though Sykes has apparently told Dutch they ought to go in after Angel, the Bunch are pragmatic enough to know that they cannot defeat overwhelming odds. They may "hate to see" Angel dragged behind Mapache's car like some diminished Patroklos; Pike may even try to buy Angel back, but when Mapache's henchmen advise them to lose their concerns in booze and whores, Pike responds, "Why not?"

What redeems the Bunch from meaninglessness is not the tarnished code of word-as-bond. That code may be what motivates the Gorches and Dutch. But it is not finally what motivates Pike to fight and die for Angel. What motivates him is the young peasant woman, herself scarcely more than a girl, with whom he has exchanged glances ever since the Bunch's arrival in Aguaverde and who at the end services his sexual needs in the presence of her infant child. The camera focuses long and hard on Pike's face as he intently observes the woman and the child, as he gives her extra gold (doubt-less, all he has). He determines to go for Angel because his own loyalties have become not confused but compounded: he fights Mapache for Angel and his people, in lateral solidarity with the oppressed *people* of Mexico.

In order to interpret Pike's motivation, we must remember the key scene in Angel's village into which he takes the Bunch to introduce them to his people: "I have invited you to my village, to my home." The Gorches may lust after Angel's female relatives, but our first glimpse of them shows a little girl teaching them cat's cradle—as if these Herculean warriors have accepted momentarily the distaff. Despite the fact that there is tragedy in the village—the *Federales* have attacked, several villagers have been killed, Angel's father has died bravely, and Angel's *novia* has left with Mapache— the scene is so idyllic, full of young lovers dancing and singing, that Pike comments, especially about the momentarily tamed Gorches, "Hard to be-lieve." The wise old man of the village, Don José, philosophizes in re-sponse, "Not so hard: we all dream of being a child again—even the worst of us. Perhaps the worst most of all." Pike takes "the worst" to imply the old man understands "what we are"—that is, thieves, gunmen. But the ex-change implies that Pike, at least, the aging gunman, desperately longs to recover lost innocence, lost possibilities. He has reminisced with Dutch about the woman he loved once, whose husband shot them both, killing her, then escaped. Rejuvenated, if not restored to innocence, Pike and the Bunch leave the village, being serenaded like heroes to the tune of "La Golondrina" ("The Swallow," a traditional Mexican folk song, whose theme is something like the swallows coming back to San Capistrano). It is not an accident that the survivors Thornton and Sykes, accompanied by the moun-tain Indians, who have received the weapons from Angel and who have shot the bounty hunters, ride back into the village at the end to the strains of "La Golondrina."

In the sweat house Angel has protested vigorously that he refuses to steal guns "for that devil to rob and kill my people again." Dutch notes that Angel did not mind killing the people of Starbuck. Angel retorts, "They were not my people. I care about my people and my village. . . . Would you give guns to someone to kill your father or your mother or your brother?" The screenplay, written by Walon Green and Peckinpah, describes Angel as "a good-looking, bilingual, Mexican boy in his middle 20's who has seen so much blood and violence and cruelty under Díaz that he rebelled—but his rebellion was not with Villa or Obregón, his was a one man revolution against them all. He believes in his family, his village and the inherent dignity of man (some men at least)" (2). So Angel's loyalties are limited. He is not a romantic revolutionary fighting for the oppressed peoples of the world. His loyalties are local. And his reasons for not wanting to deliver arms to the "pendejo general" are complicated by jealousy and vengeance—for his father, for his *novia.*

Nevertheless, the film romanticizes Angel's *people.* The innocent pleasures of their village are contrasted implicitly with the sadistic pleasures of Starbuck, where children torture insects as the Wild Bunch carries out its botched robbery. Moreover, the European mix in their *mestizaje* is deemphasized, so that the "people" who come for the guns Angel describes thus: "They are part of the village but not from it. They are *puro* Indian, and these mountains belong to them." They are Indians who have learned the tactics of guerrilla warfare from "a thousand years" of fighting "'paches," Sykes says. They appear out of nowhere for the guns. One of them appears out of nowhere, machete in hand, to protect the wounded Sykes from Thornton and his men. Having killed the bounty hunters, they ride in with Sykes at the end. Joined by Thornton, they ride off together. The future of Mexico is theirs. Differentiating the Bunch from Mapache and his *Federales* oppressors, Dutch insists earlier, "We ain't nothin' like him. We don't hang nobody. I hope some day these people here kick him and the rest of that scum like him right into their graves." Angel comments softly, with determination, "We will, if it takes forever."

So it is as if Pike takes Dutch's point about the object of loyalty to heart. His loyalty to Angel, which might not by itself be strong enough to cause him to risk his life to rescue him, becomes compounded by a new loyalty—to *la causa,* the cause of the Mexican people, defined as the peasantry, *los indígenas,* as close to *puros indios,* to *la raza* as possible for a 1960s ideology of solidarity with the oppressed pure peoples of the (fourth) world. At the end of the film Sykes says to Thornton, "Well, me and the boys here, we got some work to do." The "boys" are *la gente.* The work is *la revolución.* Sykes comments, "It ain't like it used to be, but it'll do." The remnant of the Bunch have found new meaning by becoming soldiers of fortune. Perhaps they will be officers in the revolutionary army. Pike has predicted of such a people's army, "If they ever get armed, with good leaders, this whole country'll go up in smoke." Significantly, Don José accompanies this troop at the end. He is certainly a wise leader. Sykes and Thornton can help. Villa in the north and Zapata in the south are emerging. Can freedom be far behind?

Of course, such freedom is deferred in Mexico, the audience knows. Huerta yields to Carranza, who yields to Obregón, who yields, in effect, to the PRI (Institutional Revolutionary Party). Zapata is assassinated; Villa is assassinated; one Cárdenas was not enough, nor, it appears likely, will be the second. But Peckinpah does not gesture toward this future. His film implicitly hints at the future of American adventurers, tragically discovering they are fighting on the wrong side, that the Vietcong represent the indigenous freedom movement. That Mapache is Big Minh, perhaps, and Villa Ho Chi Minh.[3]

Peckinpah's emergent ideology undercuts itself, however. The reason for the deferral of revolutionary victory is human nature itself. Angel is betrayed by his *novia* Teresa's mother, a very *india* looking peasant woman from his village. Pike is shot in the back by one of Mapache's whores, reminding us that we cannot sentimentalize Teresa and her sisters, for they too will do anything to flee "hambre"—famine, to gain security, to survive. And Pike is finished off by a mere boy in uniform, shooting him in the back with a childlike grin on his face, as if avenging the Mapache he worships earlier and seeking the cachet that he is now a real man. Women in uniforms are shown nursing their babies too. Laughing children follow the sick pageantry of Angel's being dragged through the streets. The sadism of the children in Starbuck is not endemic to Eurocentric culture; it is endemic to the human race.

The scorpions overcome by ants in the children's sport at the beginning may symbolize warriors being overcome by the unworthy simply because of their greater numbers. Thus the Wild Bunch fall prey to too many bullets fired by the likes of Mapache and his thugs. Yet they have struck a blow for the Revolution, taking out Mapache's entire troop. On the other hand, the ants' stinging to death of the scorpions, who sting to death as many as they can with their superior firepower, may mean the triumph of the common people over bullying oppressors. Again, the vignette may simply remind us, as we saw in *Blood Meridian* and *Tombstone,* that nature is red in tooth and claw; that violence is endemic to all animals, including the featherless biped; that it is indeed necessary for survival; that civilizations are built upon it and sustained by it.

"Armed, with good leaders," Pike has predicted. Angel pleads, "With guns my people could fight." The implication is that revolutionaries without guns are like ants without stings. The film implies that it is necessary to kill in order to be free, in order not to be killed. And technology has upped the stakes. Villa has artillery that scatters Mapache's men. The machine gun is an equalizer. The car presents the possibility of mechanized warfare, the aeroplane an even higher form. The film invites contemporary speculation: if the scorpions on the planet have nuclear arms, why not the ants? Maybe Pike is not such an anachronism after all. Didn't Kennedy say of the Russians in Cuba, "If they move, kill 'em"? The only difference would seem to be the size of the gun. Machismo in perpetuo. Not even the sentimental strains of the closing serenade can obliterate it. For the content works against the lugubrious music:

> ¿Adonde irá, veloz y fatigada,
> La golondrina que de aquí se vá?
> ¿Adonde irá?
> Buscando abrigo y no lo encontrará,
> ¡Oh cielo santo! Y sin poder volar.

The *niña* who sings the song fears for the swallow who is leaving, for it shall find no shelter and, indeed, is unable to fly, is swift but spent. So are at least the superannuated warriors. We reminisce that this song was sung as a kind of swan-song to the departing Bunch headed toward Aguaverde. Now we are teased into applying the song to Deke and Sykes, who can stay in Angel's village, making their "nido" there, "la estación pasar"—to pass the season in a safe nest. But we know they really cannot. That they will leave with the *indios* to fight as soldiers of fortune. And the last lines of the song seem to glance forward to the fate of the Revolution and these revolutionaries:

> También yo estoy en la region perdida,
> ¡Oh cielo santo! Y sin poder volar.

"I too am lost in this land, oh holy heaven, without the power to fly." It is as if the final fate of the Wild Bunch is subsumed into the lament of Mexico herself, deliverance deferred.

Sykes has warned us, however, against dividing up the world into us and them: "'They?' Who the hell is 'they'?" The machismo of the Bunch is not categorically different from that of the railroad posse or that of the *Federales*. Maybe, the film seems to suggest at a deep level, the only thing that can finally obliterate oppressive machismo is a total conflagration, just as, like perverse gods, the children at the beginning finally burn their entire theater of scorpions and ants.

And yet there is something fine in the Bunch's gesture for Angel and his people. If it is suicidal, it is a choice of identity in the teeth of death: across the blank pages of perhaps an absurd existence they wrote their last act as a sacrifice in the service of a code of solidarity not just with each other but with the oppressed. They alter their story from satire to tragedy.

13

"Circles upon Circles"

Last Reveille

> Prentice had the impression of circles within circles, and it seemed they never stopped. He just wanted to break through them, get away, deny them, but he knew he never would.
>
> *Last Reveille*

Having established a reputation more recently as an author of thrillers, David Morrell perhaps anachronistically calls his cherished 1977 novel *Last Reveille* an "historical thriller" (xviii). Thrilling indeed are the battle sequences, particularly the descriptions of some of the last mounted pistol charges in the history of the U.S. Cavalry. But Morrell's novel is more than just a thriller. It is a *Bildungsroman* about a new recruit in Pershing's outfit poised in Columbus, New Mexico, at the time of Pancho Villa's infamous raid (March 9, 1916). This young soldier, aptly named Prentice, seeks to learn the wisdom of the big, barrel-chested Miles Calendar, who, as his name implies, has been around—a wizened old maverick scout not unlike Al Sieber. Reluctant at first, Calendar takes the kid on. Together they cross into Mexico as part of Pershing's expeditionary force in search of Villa and his dwindling army. Prentice crosses into Calendar's arena and its warrior craft. But he is finally horrified by what he learns—about Calendar, about himself, about the world. Not surprisingly for the creator of Rambo, Morrell's post-Vietnam *Last Reveille* concerns what hath war-as-hell wrought.

Prentice is attracted to Calendar because the latter saved his life during Villa's raid. But he is also attracted because Calendar provides Prentice with a male role model, a surrogate, substitute father for the one he has left behind. The very night of the raid the new recruit lies dreaming of running up a hill toward his father who keeps receding until he is in a "grave" of rocks trying to "burst through" (11). Gradually we learn that his father was accidentally buried under a wagonload of rocks; that after his wife, Prentice's mother, died, he had increasingly lost purpose, had increasingly been drunk. So the accident was a virtual suicide. Afterward, Prentice loses the family farm. He reflects on why he volunteered for the army: "Mostly, he suspected, he just wanted to be as far away from the sort of life his father had led as possible" (177). The detail perhaps most revelatory of Prentice's relationship with Calendar is that on the latter's birthday, the former presents him with the very watch his father had given to him.

For his part, Calendar would reject Prentice as pupil because it violates his cardinal rule of non-involvement: "[O]nce you commit yourself to somebody you start looking out for them almost as much as you do for yourself, and that's how a man gets killed" (73). He changes his mind, nevertheless, when his only quasi-friend in the Thirteenth tells Calendar about Pershing's loneliness after a San Francisco fire has killed most of his immediate family. Calendar gets a look on his face similar to one when he watches this friend, the major, kiss wife and kids good bye before heading into Mexico. The implication is that Calendar too feels the lack of lineage: lonely himself, he wants to leave a legacy to a surrogate son.

Calendar himself is without legacy, without lineage. We learn in a retrospective he narrates to Prentice that his legacy was burned to the ground in Sherman's March. His kin were brutally killed, his sister after a gang rape. Having wept over the bodies of his mother and father and over their ruined farm, he pursued the perpetrators only to lose them in the chaos—and nearly lose himself to hypothermia. So he became a survivor, finding his own surrogate father in the Union army (one Captain Ryerson), then abandoning the South—to which he feels no allegiance (like the Blairs, his family owned no slaves)—to follow this father-figure west into the Indian Wars. Killing the great Plains chieftain, Broken Nose, during what seemed a hopeless battle, Calendar took no solace, for Ryerson died. Once again Calendar wept over a fallen father, cradling him in his arms.

So the relationship between Prentice and Calendar satisfies deep needs of each. Calendar finally admits to Prentice that at one time he'd had a wife and son (the son not his by birth), but they had left him. And Prentice finally tells Calendar the truth about his father. This mutual revelation occurs after Calendar's drunk on his sixty-fifth birthday has disgusted Prentice—because it obviously reminds him of his father. To complete the shattering of Prentice's metaphoric icon, Calendar falls and breaks the watch. Yet this birthday is related to a major motif of the novel, the passing of the torch. Calendar has also agreed to teach Prentice what he knows because he is aware of his aging, as he acknowledges explicitly on his sixty-fifth birthday, when he must realistically take stock of the longevity of his lifeway: "It's like I can't overlook it anymore. I'm getting older" (178). Prentice appeals: "You're the last. [. . .] This is all a dress rehearsal for when we go overseas [into World War I], and once we do, your kind of life is over, everything you know is useless. [. . .] What I'm offering is a chance to pass it on" (72–73). Calendar's sixty-fifth birthday and its aftermath provide an apparent climax of the relationship between these two, one of self-awareness and honesty. Calendar suggests that, since Prentice wanted someone (a father) he could "respect" and Calendar himself wanted someone (a son) "devoted" to him and since both are disappointed, they simply learn to accept each other for what each is and be "friends" (207). We seem to have arrived at resolution: "Now that he understood why he and the old man had acted as they had, he found that he was free of turmoil. He felt that he had grown somewhat, had adjusted to his needs and insecurities" (212).

This is a false climax, however, and a spurious resolution, for the novel is about more than male bonding in an equitable relationship. Nor is it just another war novel where buddies die in each other's arms transcending the horrors of war. There is no transcendence here. For, Morrell's novel insists, the horrors of war cannot be blinked by heroic romance.

Last Reveille teases us readers with another false lead, a pseudo-transcendence through transcendental meditation. Calendar narrates another significant adventure. In the late 1870s—fifty years too late, as he wryly notes—Calendar decided to take up trapping, to be a latter-day mountain man in Wyoming. His solitary *agon* with winter almost drove him crazy, gibbering to himself (as McCarthy might phrase it). Miraculously, he sublated into incredible tranquillity, serenity: "It was just that things somehow reduced themselves, got simpler. I'd proved that I didn't need the comforts. Now I didn't even need people. I found that for days on end it was enough for me just to sit by the fire, legs crossed, nothing in my head, seeing nothing, thinking nothing, hearing a kind of single tone that sounded on and on, and it was lovely. I never felt more relaxed or pure" (184–85). He had achieved the meditative desideratum of emptying his mind—from care, from strife, but above all, from desire. Like any master of meditation—from Plato's Philosopher King to Lao Tzu to Buddha himself—Calendar did not want to let his mind be filled again with the detritus of desire, but the spring thaw reinstilled in him a hankering for company. Yet when he finally descended from the mountains, he eschewed the chatter of daily news, for "[i]t didn't mean a thing" (185). Then he realized it was his birth-

day and at first wanted to go celebrate. But instead he retreated to his loneliness, reassumed the meditative position, and lo, the tone and serenity
returned momentarily: "[A]nd the town was there below me but I didn't
know it. Or much care" (187).

Scarily, however, we witness such serenity, such purity again only in
the heat of battle, when Prentice, transformed into a veritable automaton of
a warrior, a fighting machine, sees himself and his fellow warriors, friend
and foe alike, "all together, bright and pure and clear" (239). A moment of
lucidity breaks refulgent into the madness: "Just for a moment a section of
himself detached and looked at him, and he thought he had lost his mind."
The horror that dawns staggering his mind is that he is "loving it."

This horror has been latent all along, especially in Calendar's attitude
toward Indians in general and the Thirteenth's Apache scout in particular.
Calendar refuses to use Indian scouts to track Villa and his raiders after
Columbus. Then when the Apache scout refuses to absent himself one
evening around the campfire, Calendar nearly kills him. He tries to explain
to his apprentice: "Look, forty years ago I went up against them. I didn't do
it halfway. I convinced myself that they were the lowest meanest creatures
on God's great earth, and I set out to kill every one of them I could. I hated
everything about them. The very mention of them set me raging. And I
didn't forget all that and suddenly shake hands with them just because the
shooting stopped. [. . .] You start treating somebody you're up against like
he's human, you're as good as dead" (157–58). War necessitates the denial
of the humanity of the enemy. Calendar has learned as much from Sherman,
who refused to do things halfway: "The purpose of the march was to teach
the South a lesson and a lesson half-taught wasn't learned. They had to do
it all the way" (106–7). Anything less is to treat war as a "game" (158), as
Prince André memorably explains to Pierre in *War and Peace.* Can
Clausewitz be far behind? Morrell's epigraph is from Sherman himself:
"War is cruelty, and you cannot refine it." Not all the Geneva Conventions
can change this tiger's stripes—or "refine" its predatory nature, its inherent
"cruelty."

Prentice is not sure he can ever make the choice to be a total warrior.
He has faced its first horror—the burning of corpses after Villa's raid—
"fighting not to think" (33). Calendar opines only time will tell whether
Prentice will be able to stand it all, be the complete warrior. Time does tell
when, after a skirmish with *villistas,* Prentice administers the *tiro de gracia*
to four fallen. He is at once repulsed and attracted by the spectacle of blown
bone and brains. He is morally outraged by Calendar's torturing of two
villistas because he apparently likes it. Yet Prentice's outrage is finally re-

vealed to be self-obfuscation. Ironically, he is so angry with Calendar, he could "smash his brains and scatter them" (222)! He reveals, if only, to himself, that the problem is not Calendar, it is all of them. He sees himself implicated at the deepest level. He finally admits to himself, "He'd taken pleasure" (229). His admission, resisted by means of his anger against Calendar, unleashes the floodgates of consciousness:

> Then the spell had broken, and he had seen the heads that he had blown apart, the slashes on the men whom Calendar had tortured, smelled the stench of open bodies, and he'd understood. Now he couldn't bear himself, couldn't bear the old man, any of them, or the thing he was a part of, any of it, and he wanted it to end. He tried to find the blame and couldn't. They were down here for a reason, but then Villa had his reasons too. Calendar had his reasons. So did everyone. Prentice had the impression of circles within circles, and it seemed they never stopped. He just wanted to break through them, get away, deny them, but he knew he never would. That finally was what did it. That he knew he'd never break away, that as long as there were people there'd be reasons for killing, and all he wanted was to be alone. (229)

Now he understands that he is complicit in the eroticism of war. All warriors are. The "circles within circles" are interimplications. None of us can escape, none of us ever will, for we will always find "reasons for killing"— and for enjoying it. Prentice sees Mexico as "godforsaken" (228)—and finally understands the meaning of the word: it's not just Mexico. His desire to escape, to "deny" is an attempt to parry the inevitable truth, that the species, the planet is "godforsaken."

Thus Prentice at the end surrenders to the inevitability. He kills and kills, "loving it" yet seeing himself as mad for doing so. Calendar, not fully understanding Prentice's *crise de conscience,* tries desperately to save him. When he fails, not even his own reckless pursuit of death as he chases the *Federales* who have blown Prentice's brains out can free Calendar from his grief, as yet a third time in his life he cradles a loved one and weeps over his corpse, pathetically muttering that he was not a "good enough" teacher (243), for Prentice never did get that backup gun Calendar was always harping on him about. And it cost him his life—and Calendar his legacy, his lineage.

Calendar's last appearance as a "speck" on a ridge pursuing *villistas* three years later constitutes a final image of his desperation. He crosses over into no final, fulfilled fatherhood, no final serenity. Instead of the Zen detachment from the desire for meaning he embodies the final, utter meaninglessness of war—and perhaps, since we cannot escape its interimplicating circles, of human existence itself. No McCarthyite posthole digger here, with his divine sparks. "Godforsaken."

14

Monsters from Below

Los de abajo

En su impasible rostro brillan la ingenuidad del
niño y la amoralidad del chacal.

Los de abajo

Mariano Azuela's classic novel about the Mexican Revolution features a
band of mavericks who drift into and along with the Revolution without
any clear sense of purpose. Along the way they encounter and temporarily
incorporate into their midst two or three prominent ideologues who seem
to provide them with the appropriate rhetoric to manifest their real purpose. Unfortunately, instead of crossing from innocence to an experience
that achieves the sublime of sacrifice, redemption, freedom, the band comes
from already tainted origins and crosses over, if into anything, then the
monstrous. The words of revolutionary ideology eventually fail to gild the
cause, and the band drifts into nothingness.

The novel opens with a scene of oppression. *Federales* approach the home
of Demetrio Macías to punish him, we learn later, for an insult to Don
Mónico, the *cacique* of the nearby village of Moyahua. Demetrio hides. A
lieutenant demands sex from his wife. Demetrio rescues her, but doesn't
kill the *Federales*. Instead he advises his wife to go with their son to his
father's house, while he goes off to join other *serranos*, mountain folk,
resisters. Because the *Federales* kill Demetrio's dog, threaten his wife, not
to mention his life, we are encouraged to read the lieutenant's characterization of Demetrio, albeit he speaks from fear, as unironically appropriate:
"[Y]o respeto a los valientes de veras" (1.1; translated as "I respect real
men").[1]

As he leaves in the night, Demetrio watches his house burn, and he
knows now that he is a fugitive and must stay on the run. Like a modern

mountain Roland/Orlando, he blows his horn to summon his men, and they heroically decimate the pursuing *Federales* with their legendary marksmanship. The band carries the wounded Demetrio to a village, where the inhabitants bless them as heroes even as they lament their lot anent the *Federales:*

> ¡Dios los bendiga! ¡Dios los ayude y los lleve por buen camino! . . . Ahora van ustedes; mañana correremos también nosotros, huyendo de la leva, perseguidos por estos condenados del gobierno, que nos han declarado guerra a muerte a todos los pobres; que nos roban nuestros puercos, nuestras gallinas y hasta el maicito que tenemos para comer; que queman nuestras casas y se llevan nuestras mujeres, y que, por fin, donde dan con uno, allí lo acaban como si fuera perro del mal. (1.4)

> (God bless you! May he help you and keep you on the right path! You're on the run now; tomorrow we'll be running too, fleeing from the recruiters [the draft], hounded by those government bastards [accursed]. They've declared war to the death on the poor; they steal our pigs, our hens, and even the little bit of corn we've saved to eat; they burn our houses and carry off our women; and, in the end, wherever they catch up with us, right there they finish us off as if we were rabid dogs.)

We seem to have our bearings: we are in a world of injustice, where conscientious humans have heard the complaints of the poor; where the rich have declared war on them, and the common people are rising up to defend them.

So we are not surprised when Luis Cervantes arrives, having been converted to the revolutionary cause and proclaiming, "[P]ersigo los mismos ideales y defiendo la misma causa que ustedes defienden" (1.5; "I pursue the same ideals and defend the same cause that you do"). But we are pulled up short as the exchange continues:

> Demetrio sonrió:
> —¿Pos cuál causa defendemos nosotros? . . .
> Luis Cervantes, desconcertado, no encontró qué contestar.

> (Demetrio smiled. "So tell me, what cause is it we're defending?"
> Luis Cervantes, flustered, couldn't find the words to respond.)

The word "words" has been added by the translator to make sense out of the Spanish abbreviated construction, but it is an appropriate addition. For Luis overcomes his momentary speechlessness to provide Demetrio and his band with the words to invest their cause. He has come to raise their consciousness to interpret the significance of that cause. It is the greatest of all causes. It is the cause of justice, as Luis proclaims even in the teeth of potential execution by Demetrio, who suspects him of being a spy:

> La revolución beneficia al pobre, al ignorante, al que toda su vida ha sido esclavo, a los infelices que ni siquiera saben que si lo son es porque el rico convierte en oro las lágrimas, el sudor y la sangre de los pobres. [. . .] Yo he querido pelear por la causa santa de los desventurados. (1.7)

> (The revolution is for the poor, the ignorant, those who've been slaves all their lives, poor wretches who don't even know that if they're poor it's because the rich convert their tears and sweat and blood into gold. [. . .] I wanted to join the sacred cause of the downtrodden [I wanted to fight for the holy cause of the unfortunate].)

As the Battle of Zacatecas approaches, Demetrio explains to Luis his unideological reasons for signing up: that he was ready to start spring plowing when the trouble with Don Mónico occurred; that the trouble occurred in a drunken situation that was filled with macho pride but not much more, one of those situations where one has to demonstrate one's worth: "¡Claro, hombre, usté no tiene la sangre de horchata, usté lleva el alma en el cuerpo, a usté le da coraje, y se levanta y les dice su justo precio!" (1.13; "Hey, friend, that's blood running through your veins, not soda pop, and you've got your soul right there in your body, where it belongs, and you get a little mad, so you stand up and tell them exactly who you are!" [more literally, "You don't have rice-water in your blood, you bear a soul in your body, somebody makes you mad, and you stand up and tell them your exact worth"]). Yet Luis can hear in this humble rhetoric the culturally ingrained values of Hispanic society. This is a vulgar expression of the ancient ideology of the caballero, the knight, the warrior. Luis needs merely to tease out of Demetrio the latent ideology of the hero.

So what happened with Don Mónico? Hardly anything, just a little spit in the beard for meddling ("Una escupida en las barbas por entrometido"),

and he got a troop of *Federales* to run Demetrio down as a Maderista. But
Demetrio had friends to protect him, and when they had killed someone or
ran afoul of the law, others joined him, obviously for similarly non-ideo-
logical reasons. Almost in an apology, Demetrio concludes, "[H]acemos la
lucha como podemos" ("[W]e're carrying on the fight as best we can"), but
when the war is over, he will want nothing more than to go back home: "No
quiero yo otra cosa, sino que me dejen en paz para volver a mí casa" ("That's
exactly what I want, to be left alone [left in peace] to return to my home").
So Luis intervenes, tries to raise Demetrio's consciousness to the real cause
of the revolution. What he articulates is a kind of iron law of oligarchy, that
if the Demetrios of the revolution go home, then just another oligarchy will
be in control of the government, the country. Luis waxes rhapsodic, again
transforming the petty, the selfish into ideals:

> Mentira que usted ande por aquí por don Mónico, el cacique;
> usted se ha levantado contra el caciquismo que asola toda la
> nación. Somos elementos de un gran movimiento social que tiene
> que concluir por el engrandecimiento de nuestra patria. Somos
> instrumentos del destino para reivindicación de los sagrados
> derechos del pueblo. No peleamos por derrocar a un asesino
> miserable, sino contra la tiranía misma. Eso es lo que se llama
> luchar por principios, tener ideales. Por ellos luchan Villa, Natera,
> Carranza; por ellos estamos luchando nosotros. (1.13)

> (It's not true [you lie] that you're here just because of your run-
> in with Don Mónico, that cacique. You've taken up arms against
> [you have raised yourself against], the very idea of *caciquismo*
> which is destroying this nation. We are part of a great social
> movement whose goal is to make our country great. We are in-
> struments destined to revindicate the sacred rights of the people.
> We aren't fighting to overthrow some wretched assassin, but
> against the very idea of tyranny. That's what's called fighting
> for principles, having ideals. That's why Villa, Natera, and
> Carranza are fighting; that's why we're fighting.)

Agents of a grand movement for social justice and the sacred rights of the
people! These are fighting words—words worth fighting for.

After Luis's abrupt departure from the campaign to pursue his interests and career in the United States, his function is assumed by the poet
Valderrama, who employs the same kind of uplifting rhetoric to recall

Demetrio to the cause. Offended by the lack of welcome and food from the same kind of villagers who once serenaded them out of town, Demetrio demands that those hiding from them be summoned forcefully before him. Valderrama protests vehemently:

> —¡Cómo! . . . ¿Qué dice? —exclamó Valderrama sorprendido—
> ¿A los serranos? [. . .] ¿A los hermanos nuestros[. . .] ? [. . .]
> —Los serranos —le dijo con énfasis y solemnidad—son carne de nuestra carne y huesos de nuestros huesos . . . "Os ex osibus meis et caro de carne mea" . . . Los serranos están hechos de nuestra madera . . . De esta madera firme con la que se fabrican los héroes . . . (3.1)

> ("What do you mean? What are you saying?" exclaimed Valderrama, surprised. "These mountain folks? [. . .] Our brothers [. . .] ! [. . .]
> "These mountain people," he said solemnly and emphatically, "are flesh of our flesh and bone of our bone . . . *os ex osibus meis et caro de carne mea.* . . . These mountain people are carved from the same timber we are . . . from the stout timber heroes are made of.")

Sounding like John Horse in *Buffalo Soldiers,* Valderrama insists on brotherhood, on class solidarity against the common enemy. Or like Ike McCaslin, he insists that the revolutionaries among the common folk are uniquely good:

> —¡Juchipila, cuna de la Revolución de 1910, tierra bendita, tierra regada con sangre de mártires, con sangre de soñadores . . . de los únicos buenos! (3.4)

> (Juchipila, cradle of the revolution of 1910, blessed land, land soaked with the blood of martyrs, the blood of dreamers . . . the only good ones!)

These are Angel's mountain folk. They are the Salt of the Earth.

From the beginning of the novel, however, our expectations of an heroic tale are undercut. The grandiose rhetoric of the ideologues is undercut. The ideology of a just war, of a justified revolution for social justice is under-

cut. At every turn. These turns, tropes are Azuela's most effective tech-
nique. When his wife asks Demetrio why he did not kill the *Federales* who
assaulted her and insulted him, he responds not with an explanation of
noble restraint but with vulgar cliché: "¡Seguro que no les tocaba todavía!"
(1.1; "I guess their time hadn't come yet"). Is Luis's ideological rhetoric
not undercut by the story of how he came to be a revolutionary? Apparently
he had not uttered revolutionary sentiments as he told Demetrio but fulmi-
nated in editorials against the revolutionaries as bandits. He might have
been forced into service, but it was as a relatively privileged sublieutenant
of cavalry. He ran and hid at the first fighting. He looked so ridiculous
when his colonel found him, that the other men laughed and saved him
from execution. But he is placed on kitchen duty. And this grievous insult
("[l]a injuria gravísima" [1.6]) caused him to turn his coat. Suddenly he
adopts the rhetoric of the Revolution:

> Los dolores y las miserias de los desheredados alcanzan a
> conmoverlo; su causa es la causa sublime del pueblo subyugado
> que clama justicia, sólo justicia. Intima con el humilde soldado
> y, ¡qué más!, una acémila muerta de fatiga en una tormentosa
> jornada le hace derramar lágrimas de compasión.

> (The sorrows and misfortunes of the downtrodden [disinherited,
> dispossessed] start to affect him now; his cause is the sublime
> cause of a subjugated people clamoring for justice, only justice.
> He begins to identify with the humble soldier and—what do
> you know!—a mule fallen dead from fatigue during a day's
> march in a rainstorm elicits tears of compassion from him.)

The detail of the mule is Azuela's coup de grace to Luis's idealism.

From this moment on we suspect Luis's rhetoric, looking for Azuela's
framing device of undercutting. For example, Luis reflects on his captors'
failure to live up to the romantic image of revolutionary rhetoric. They
are a ragtag bunch, not the well-paid followers of Villa at all. Thus, Luis
muses,

> ¿Sería verdad lo que la prensa del gobierno y él mismo habían
> asegurado, que los llamados revolucionarios no eran sino
> bandidos agrupados ahora con un magnífico pretexto para saciar
> su sed de oro y de sangre? ¿Sería, pues, todo mentira lo que de
> ellos contaban los simpatizadores de la revolución? (1.8)

(Could it be true what the government-controlled press and he himself had charged, that the so-called revolutionaries were no more than bandits joined together now with a splendid excuse to satiate their thirst for gold and blood? Then was everything the apologists for [sympathizers with] the revolution claimed just a lie?)

Whatever, rumor has it that Huerta's relatives are leaving, so the revolutionaries are going to win, and one had better be on the winning side! At his core, Luis is not an idealist. He is just a wordsmith. After all, his name is Cervantes. And we are in the presence of satire.

After Luis's grandest pronouncement about their role in securing human rights, Demetrio calls for two more beers! After his ringing toast,

> por el triunfo de nuestra causa, que es el triunfo sublime de la Justicia; porque pronto veamos realizados los ideales de redención de este nuestro pueblo sufrido y noble, y sean ahora los mismos hombres que han regado con su propia sangre la tierra los que cosechen los frutos que legítimamente les pertenecen, (1.18)

> (to the triumph of our cause, which is the sublime triumph of justice; may we soon see the realization of the ideals of redemption of this noble and long-suffering land of ours, and may those who have nourished the land with their own blood reap the fruits which are theirs by right,)

Luis is undercut again by Natera's harsh gaze at this chatterbox ("el parlanchín"), as he turns his back to him.

The last example of Luis's rhetoric is deliciously framed:

> [N]osotros no nos hemos levantado en armas para que un tal Carranza o un tal Villa lleguen a presidentes de la República; nosotros peleamos en defensa de los sagrados derechos del pueblo, pisoteados por el vil cacique. (2.6)

> (We didn't go to war so some Carranza or Villa could end up being president of the republic; we're fighting for the sacred rights of the people, which have been trampled by the vicious cacique.)

Offering Demetrio gold he has found in a sacked hacienda, offering him
the opportunity to go to the United States and set themselves up on what
they've already looted, Luis employs this rhetoric of human rights to justify their getting theirs since the leaders surely will, with impunity.

Valderrama's rhetoric is undercut as well by the narrator himself. After Valderrama's ostentatious display of rhetoric from the Vulgate's Latin
(*os ex osibus meis et caro de carne mea*), Azuela, asking in his own voice,
undercuts Valderrama's rhetoric:

> ¿Valderrama, vagabundo, loco y un poco poeta, sabía lo que
> decía? (3.1)

> (Did Valderrama, a crazy vagabond and something of a poet,
> know what he was saying?)

He answers his own question by the fine, poignant description that follows:

> Cuando los soldados llegaron a una ranchería y se arremolinaron
> con desesperación en torno de casas y jacales vacíos, sin
> encontrar una tortilla dura, ni un chile podrido, ni unos granos
> de sal para ponerle a la tan aborrecida carne fresca de res, ellos,
> los hermanos pacíficos, desde sus escondites, impasibles los unos
> con la impasibilidad pétrea de los ídolos aztecas, más humanos
> los otros, con una sórdida sonrisa en sus labios untados y ayunos
> de barba, veían cómo aquellos hombres feroces, que un mes
> antes hicieran retemblar de espanto sus míseros y apartados
> solares, ahora salían de sus chozas, donde las hornillas estaban
> apagadas y las tinajas secas, abatidos, con la cabeza caída y
> humillados como perros a quienes se arroja de su propia casa a
> puntapiés.

> (When the soldiers came to a small settlement and desperately
> charged [literally, milled around, a wonderful image] through
> the houses and empty huts, without finding a stale tortilla, a
> rotten chili pepper, or even a few grains of salt to sprinkle on the
> despised dried beef, their brothers who had not gone to war
> [peaceful brothers], some as impassive as the stone faces of the
> Aztec idols, others more human, with sordid smiles on their
> greasy lips and beardless faces, looked out now from their hid-
> ing places as those fierce men, who just a month earlier had

made their miserable, isolated homes tremble with fright, walked dejectedly [embattled] from those huts with cold ovens and dry cisterns, their heads hanging down [and humiliated] like dogs who've been kicked out of their own houses.)

So much for the *serranos'* independence. So much for solidarity with these brothers. So much for any romanticized linkage with their Aztec past. Their stoniness is that of the starving. Their smiles are sordid. Azuela makes us wonder what to be more human means.

Valderrama's sublime praise of the martyrs of Juchipila, those who are, among men, "los únicos buenos," is undercut by an ex-*Federal* now riding with the band, who comments cynically, "Porque no tuvieron tiempo de ser malos" (3.4; "[B]ecause they never got the chance [time] to be bad!"). After the news of Villa's disastrous defeat at Celaya, Valderrama boasts more bravado:

> —¿Villa? . . . ¿Obregón? . . . ¿Carranza? . . . ¡X . . . Y . . . Z . . . !
> ¿Qué se me da a mí? . . . ¡Amo la Revolución como amo al volcán que irrumpe! ¡Al volcán porque es volcán; a la Revolución porque es Revolución! . . . Pero las piedras que quedan arriba o abajo, después del cataclismo, ¿qué me importan a mí? . . . (3.2)

> ("Villa? . . . Obregón? . . . Carranza? . . . X . . . Y . . . Z! What do I care? . . . I love the revolution the same way I love a volcano that's erupting! The volcano because it's a volcano; the revolution because it's the revolution! . . . But why should I care which stones stay on top or which ones get buried [are on the bottom, *abajo* being an important word and concept] after the cataclysm? . . . ")

This is an interesting image, a wild kind of identifying with the forces of cataclysmic change in the cosmos, as if Valderrama, like all true romantics—and perhaps a little like McCarthy's judge, would ride the whirlwind. But the moment Valderrama hears Demetrio's pessimism about the war effort, he strangely, summarily disappears. No Byronic hero he.

Valderrama and Luis both, then, like rats desert a sinking ship. No true idealists, they throw for the main chance. Luis's letter to Venancio from El Paso gives the reader a shock because it strips bare any illusions we might still have. Luis invites the barber to join him in a venture only because Venancio has capital to invest in the proposed Mexican restaurant. As if to emphasize Luis's ultimate banality, Azuela has him suggest to

Venancio that he bring his guitar-playing skills and put them in the service of the Salvation Army!

Luis's disturbing letter also reveals that Demetrio's band has begun not just to be destroyed by outside forces but to destroy itself from within. Pancracio and Manteca have killed each other in a knife fight, and Margarito, the blond *güero,* has committed suicide. This physical self-destruction, however, is a symbolic manifestation of a moral corruption that grows in the band like a cancer. Their ability to kill without feeling is evident early in their threats to Luis. Azuela cloaks their sadism toward him in folk humor, but it is sadism nonetheless when they bring a "priest" to him for his last "confession" in order to discover whether he's an assassin. In an early image Azuela captures the schizophrenic blend of lovable folk and deadly savage that characterizes the members of the band. Amid the slaughtered *Federales* atop the church roof, Anastasio Montañés, holding his bloodied knife, stands wearied, "en su impasible rostro brillan la ingenuidad del niño y la amoralidad del chacal" (1.17; "his impassive face [. . .] shining as innocently as a child's, with the amorality of a jackal" [the translation loses the parallel structure of the original: in his impassive face shine the ingenuousness of a child and the amorality of a jackal]).

The viciousness suggested by the ugly metaphor of jackal is present within them, within all men by implication. It surfaces occasionally on those Sundays when the peasants come to town for mass, some shopping, a few drinks and somebody pushes too many buttons and out comes a knife or a pistol and someone is killed. But here in war it is unleashed. The band kills relentlessly in battle. They get drunk and kill during their celebrations—sometimes a prostitute, sometimes a villager, sometimes a captive. Demetrio tries to rape Luis's young virgin he has appropriated for himself, beating everyone who tries to stop him. But of course, she is no virgin, for Manteca and Meco have passed her around before Luis buys her from them. Demetrio's revenge on Don Mónico by burning his hacienda is a condign punishment that we can understand, perhaps, but then Pancracio assassinates a dandy just because his figure offends him. On the way to Jalisco, Quail and others kill a priest by hanging him only in order to rob him, and Manteca, revelling in the spoils, swears, "¡Ya sabe uno por qué arriesga el cuero!" (2.9; "Finally a guy knows what the fuck [why] he's risking his hide for!"). Margarito is sadistically cruel to a *Federal* prisoner, dragging him along behind his horse, but when Camila complains to Demetrio, Demetrio just shrugs it off. When Demetrio does take pity on a poor widower and orders Margarito not to take from but give back to him, Margarito plays sadistic mind games with the widower then beats him with the flat of his sword. This is the same Margarito who, the night Demetrio tries to rape Luis's little girl and La Pintada locks her in a room for safe-keeping, has stolen the key and lain with her disgustingly. In Lagos, Margarito recklessly shows off his skill with a pistol by first shooting a shot glass off the head of a young boy, then trying to duplicate the feat during a whirling fast draw— only to blow the boy's ear off. When the bartender at the cantina demands payment for the band's destruction, Margarito knocks all the bottles off the shelves and tells him to charge "tu padre Villa" (2.13; "big Daddy Villa"). Margarito's suicide is a moral emblem not of his amorality but his immorality.

In their wanton destruction of property and life the band has crossed over the line. Luis's theory of the iron law of oligarchy applies even to Demetrio's band. They become that which they set out to destroy. Their invasion of houses resembles the *Federales*' invasion of Demetrio's house. His burning of Don Mónico's house resembles the *Federales*' burning of his. The rape of the little girl is no different from the threatened rape of Demetrio's wife. The plunder, the stealing, the desecration of fine art are all acts that, as Luis warns, disparage them and disparage their cause ("eso nos desprestigia, [. . .] desprestigia nuestra causa" [2.2]). La Pintada, the female warrior who has latched onto Demetrio as the budding general after his success at Zacatecas, redirects his paces from a hotel toward a rich man's house. Their victory has given them the right to comandeer lodgings wherever they want: "Entonces ¿pa quén jue [*sic*] la revolución? ¿Pa los catrines? Si ahora nosotros vamos a ser los meros catrines" (2.2; "Otherwise, what was the revolution for? For the fat cats? Hell no, now we're the fat cats!" [more accurately, Then for whom was the revolution? For the fat cats? Well, now we are going to be the very fat cats ourselves]).

Riding with the band for the while they are with Natera's army is another philosopher, another adept at words, the cynic Alberto Solís. He articulates the darker side of the band's crossing, the dark side of their deeds:

> Amigo mío: hay hechos y hay hombres que no son sino pura hiel . . . Y esa hiel va cayendo gota a gota en el alma, y todo lo amarga, todo lo envenena. Entusiasmo, esperanzas, ideales, alegrías . . . , ¡nada! Luego no le queda más: o se convierte usted en un bandido igual a ellos, o desaparece de la escena, escondiénose tras las murallas de un egoísmo impenetrable y feroz. (1.18)

> (My friend: there are deeds and there are men who are nothing but bile. . . . And that bile starts falling drop by drop into your

soul, turning everything bitter, poisoning everything. Enthusiasm, hopes, ideals, joys . . . nothing! Then there's nothing left: either you become a bandit just like them, or you vanish from the scene, hiding behind the walls of a fierce and impenetrable selfishness.)

Has Alberto himself become a poisoned bandit? Astonished by Alberto's comment, Luis wonders what could have so disillusioned him. Alberto's answer provides perhaps the novel's most remarkable rhetoric:

Insignificancias, naderías: gestos inadvertidos para los más; la vida instantánea de una línea que se contrae, de unos ojos que brillan, de unos labios que se pliegan; el significado fugaz de una frase que se pierde. Pero hechos, gestos y expresiones que, agrupados en su lógica y natural expresión, constituyen e integran una mueca pavorosa y grotesca a la vez de una raza . . . ¡De una raza irredenta!

(Trifles, little things: facial expressions unnoticed by almost everyone; a wrinkle appearing for an instant, then contracting, a gleam in someone's eyes, pursed lips; the fleeting meaning of a muttered phrase. But events, facial expressions and movements which, taken together in their logical and natural context, constitute and make up a whole race's mask, frightful and grotesque at the same time . . . the mask of a race that is utterly unredeemable!)

This verbal painting of a mask for the Mexican people is haunting, uncanny, nightmarish. The condemnation is devastating. Azuela adds to it in Alberto's reflections on the Battle of Zacatecas, won by Demetrio's band's reckless courage in a momentary, random relaxation of vigilance by the *Federales* and followed by looting of the rotting bodies by the women of the city (shades of the bounty hunters in *The Wild Bunch*):

—¡Qué hermosa es la Revolución, aun en su misma barbarie!—pronunció Solís conmovido. Luego, en voz baja y con vaga melancolía:
—Lástima que lo que falta no sea igual. Hay que esperar un poco. A que no haya combatientes, a que no se oigan más disparos que los de las turbas entregadas a las delicias del saqueo; a que resplandezca diáfana, como una gota de agua, la psicología de nuestra raza, condensada en dos palabras: ¡robar, matar! . . .

¡Qué chasco, amigo mío, si los que venimos a ofrecer todo
nuestro entusiasmo, nuestra misma vida por derribar a un miserable asesino, resultásemos los obreros de un enorme pedestal
donde pudieran levantarse cien o doscientos mil monstruos de la
misma especie! . . . ¡Pueblo sin ideales, pueblo de tiranos! . . .
¡Lástima de sangre! (1.21)

("How beautiful the revolution is, even in its savagery!" pro-
claimed Solís with emotion. Then, suddenly melancholy, he said
in a low voice:
"A pity that what's coming next won't be so beautiful. We
won't have long to wait. Just until there are no more combatants, until the only gunfire you hear is that coming from the
mobs indulging themselves in the pleasures of pillaging; until
the psychology of our race shines forth in resplendent clarity,
like a drop of water, condensed in two words: *rob* and *kill*. . . .
How frustrating [what a trick] it would be if we who've come to
offer all our enthusiasm, our very lives to overthrow a murderous
tyrant [wretched assassin (picking up Luis's earlier phrase)], turned
out to be the architects of a pedestal enormous enough to hold a
couple hundred thousand monsters of the same species! . . . A
people without ideals, a land of tyrants! . . . All that blood shed
in vain [shame of blood]!")

We of course wish to deflect Alberto's characterization. We thought these
were the champions of social justice. And we might just dismiss Alberto's
words as the mere rhetoric of nihilism. For him the symbol of the Revolution is the smoke from gunfire mingling with the dust of collapsing houses
"que fraternalmente ascendían, se abrazaban, se confundían y se borraban
en la nada" ("fraternally, embracing, merging together and then vanishing
into nothingness"). But Alberto's rhetoric is echoed by that of the narrator
himself, who comments,

Pero los hechos vistos y vividos no valían nada. Había que oír la
narración de sus proezas portentosas, donde, a renglón seguido
de un acto de sorprendente magnanimidad, venía la hazaña más
bestial. (1.20)

(Just seeing and experiencing the events didn't mean much. You
had to hear the stories of their portentous deeds, where right

after the description of a surprisingly magnanimous deed would come the meanest and most bestial act.)

Peaks of heroism followed by pits of bestiality! And the narrator describes Demetrio's band riding against a background as stark and void as McCarthy's landscapes:

> Vanse destacando las cordilleras como monstruos alagartados, de angulosa vertebradura; cerros que parecen testas de colosales ídolos aztecas, caras de gigantes, muecas pavorosas y grotescas, que ora hacen sonreír, ora dejan un vago terror, algo como presentimiento de misterio. (2.5)

> (Gradually the spiny vertebrae of the mountains rise into view like huge lizards; crags shaped like colossal Aztec idols, faces of giants leering out grotesquely, provoking smiles, or a vague terror, like a mysterious foreboding.)

These grotesque leers forebode no friendly cosmos but rather cosmic disaster. Azuela's riders look like Earp's apocalyptic immortals or Glanton's demonic hunters:

> El torbellino del polvo, prolongado a buen trecho a lo largo de la carretera, rompíase bruscamente en masas difusas y violentas, y se destacaban pechos hinchados, crines revueltas, narices trémulas, ojos ovoides, impetuosos, patas abiertas y como encogidas al impulso de la carrera. Los hombres, de rostro de bronce y dientes de marfil, ojos flameantes, blandían los rifles o los cruzaban sobre las cabezas de las monturas. (2.9)

> (The whirlwind of dust, covering a long stretch of the road, would suddenly break into diffuse, violent masses, and then you could see the panting chests, wind-tossed manes, trembling nostrils, and wild, almond-shaped eyes, hooves extending and contracting to the rhythm of the gallop, and men with bronze faces, ivory teeth, and flashing eyes, rifles brandished aloft or slung across the saddles.)

Out of Job's whirlwind, as it were, burst these violent masses who have taken on a timeless quality, an eschatological momentum. Azuela relates them to all other bands of warriors in human history who ride relentlessly across its pages:

> En su alma rebulle el alma de las viejas tribus nómadas. Nada importa saber adónde van y de dónde vienen; lo necesario es caminar, caminar siempre, no estacionarse jamás; ser dueños del valle, de las planicies, de la sierra y de todo lo que la vista abarca. (3.7)

> (The spirit of ancient nomadic tribes stirs within them. It doesn't matter whether they know where they're going or where they come from; their only compulsion is to ride, to keep riding always, never to stop; to be masters of the valley, of the high plain, of the sierra, and of everything that their eyes encompass [the view embraces].)

This passage occurs the morning of their last ride. Perhaps the lack of conscious motivation reflects merely on them. But the association of them with eons of nomadic tribes suggests that such warriors will ride violently for no cause but for the freedom of the ride: freedom from responsibility (they rarely go home and then only to leave again), but what's worse, freedom from cause, from meaning. Meaning is something added by the philosophers or by the *serranos* themselves around the campfire in their "narración de sus proezas portentosas," which they embellish with "mucho color" (2.1). A perfect example of such embellishment are all the stories about Villa, his achievements, his glories, his airplanes—when none of the band has ever really seen him:

> Villa es el indomable señor de la sierra, la eterna víctima de todos los gobiernos, que lo persiguen como una fiera; Villa es la reencarnación de la vieja leyenda: el bandido-providencia, que pasa por el mundo con la antorcha luminosa de un ideal: ¡robar a los ricos para hacer ricos a los pobres! Y los pobres le forjan una leyenda que el tiempo se encargará de embellecer para que viva de generación en generación. (1.20)

> (Villa is the invincible lord of the sierra, the eternal victim of all governments, who pursue him like a wild beast. Villa is the reincarnation of the ancient legend: the bandit named Providence who goes through the world carrying the luminous torch of an

ideal: stealing from the rich to give to the poor [to rob the rich in order to make rich the poor]! And the poor shape a legend around him that time will embellish [will take charge of embellishing] so it can live on generation after generation.)

Yet after Celaya, Villa is "un dios caído" ("a fallen god"), and fallen gods are "nada" (3.2; "nothing"). At the core of the legend now is nothingness. So mere words can inflate or deflate a legend. The implication is that meaning is mere words.

The terrible corollary is that the momentum of the band is unconscious, lethal, monstrous. Anastasio wants to know why they must keep fighting, and Demetrio doesn't know, but some passing soldiers answer his question:

> Porque si uno trae un fusil en las manos y las cartucheras llenas de tiros, seguramente que es para pelear. ¿Contra quién? ¿En favor de quiénes? ¡Eso nunca le ha importado a nadie! (3.1)

> (Because if you've got a rifle in your hands and plenty of shells in your cartridge belt, surely it's for the purpose of fighting. Against whom? For whom? That had [has] never mattered to anyone!)

Alberto has said that one gets caught up in the Revolution as a leaf gets caught up in a hurricane. When his men ask why they continue, Demetrio reminds them of the peón they saw one day who, though he constantly curses his boss and his sour luck, nevertheless continues to work from dawn till dusk. But Demetrio's words take on darker connotations: "Y así estamos nosotros: a reniega y reniega y a mátenos y mátenos" (3.4; "And that's the way we are: constantly griping [but with the stronger sense of renouncing and renouncing] and constantly busting our butts [literally, killing ourselves and killing ourselves]"). *Renegar* traditionally has strong connotations of apostasy, of denying one's faith. Have Demetrio and his men renounced their faith, the ideals of the Revolution they could never articulate themselves, they perhaps never did believe in? Or is theirs an unconscious denial of the meaning of existence?

Demetrio's wife asks plaintively and poignantly,

> —¿Por qué pelean ya, Demetrio?
> Demetrio, las cejas muy juntas, toma distraído una piedrecita

y la arroja al fondo del cañon. Se mantiene pensativo viendo el
desfiladero, y dice:
    —Mira esa piedra cómo ya no se pára . . . (3.6)

("Why are you all still fighting, Demetrio?"
Demetrio, frowning deeply [knitting his brows], absent-
mindedly picks up a small stone and throws it down into the canyon. He stands there for a moment, staring pensively into the abyss.
Then he says: "Look at that stone, how it never stops . . . ")

His and his band's momentum is cosmic, like gravity's. Increasingly for
them and for Demetrio in particular, the pull comes from the reality principle. Ever since La Pintada has stabbed to death Demetrio's mistress
Camila, he has sung a song about stabbing to death, and he seems pursued
by recurrent melancholy, by a shadow. The song is about the absence of
purpose, of meaning:

> *En la medianía del cuerpo*
> *una daga me metió*
> *sin saber por qué*
> *ni por qué sé yo . . .*
> *Él sí lo sabía*
> *pero yo no . . . (2.13)*

> (*Right here in my side* [In the middle of my body]
> *He stuck his sharp knife;* [A dagger entered me]
> *He didn't know why* [Without knowing why]
> *And neither did I . . .*
> *Maybe he knew,* [He Himself surely knew—the translator's "maybe"
>   is impertinent, and I am trying to capture both senses of *sí*]
> *But not I . . .* [95])

The capital *e* in "*Él*"—in the absence of other initial capitals except the
first—signals that the *he* in this line is *He*, God. Even if this is Christ speaking in the poem, it is an existential Christ, who knows not why His Father
has forsaken him. That is, God knows, but His knowledge, His meaning,
His purpose are all unavailable to us. Demetrio knows no more as he feels
the dagger of death working in his side.
    The shadow looming over Demetrio deepens with the news of Villa's
signal defeat, as a dark cloud passes before Demetrio's eyes. With a cock-

fight in the background that results in "un charco de sangre" (3.3; "a pool of blood") Demetrio calls repeatedly for Valderrama to sing him a song, "El enterrador," or "The Gravedigger," literally he who inters, places in the earth. One of Demetrio's last encounters is with a spiteful old woman who rails at their worthless paper money, which obviously no one can cash, no one can eat. The Medusa look on her face is one of absolute abjection that says, "[Y]a durmió en el petate del muerto para no morirse de un susto" (3.5; *"You can't frighten someone who's already lain with the dead"* [She hasn't slept on the pallet of the dead to die from fright]).

The memorable description of Demetrio's death is the grand finale to this rhetoric of nihilism.[2] Ironically, he and his men have traded places with the *Federales* in the canyon at the beginning. Ironically, he and his men, great marksmen as they are, those who are left, are no match for the omnivorous machine gun. Demetrio himself watches his last men fall around him, then seeks cover, and keeps firing and firing, until:

> Y al pie de una resquebrajadura enorme y suntuosa como pórtico de vieja catedral, Demetrio Macías, con los ojos fijos para siempre, sigue apuntando con el cañón de su fusil . . . (3.7)

> (And at the foot of an enormous chasm gaping open as sumptuously [a chasm enormous and sumptuous, like] as the portico of an old cathedral, Demetrio Macías, his eyes fixed in an eternal stare [forever], keeps on aiming down the barrel of his rifle . . .)

The wide-angle lens focuses on one of the Southwest's magnificent canyons, a geological formation older than the human race. If it is as enormous and as sumptuous as the portico of an old cathedral, it marks a cosmos whose god is dead and gone. Demetrio's fixation is petrified for all time. In his bloodthirsty, aimless, meaningless journey he has crossed from the organic to the inorganic. An earlier comment by the narrator makes a fitting epitaph to Demetrio:

> Y en la tristeza y desolación del pueblo, mientras cantan las mujeres en el templo, los pajarillos no cesan de piar en las arboledas, ni el canto de las currucas deja de oírse en las ramas secas de naranjos. (3.5)

> (And amid the sadness and desolation of the town, while the women sing in the temple, there's no end to the chirping of

the sparrows in the trees [groves], or to the song of the linnets in
the dead [dried] branches of the orange trees.)

The novel closes with the suggestion that life may continue on this planet,
but the human race may not be part of its future. It may annihilate itself. Or
worse, it may never find the words to endow itself with any real meaning.
Not all of its rhetorics, its ideologies may be up to the task. Meanwhile, we
will continue to kill ourselves over the old ideologies, the ancient idols and
cathedrals. Oligarchy will keep its iron law. And peasants will continue to
lead the life that only those pursuing false grails can ignore:

> ¿Quien se acordaba [. . .] del mísero jacal, donde se vive como
> esclavo, siempre bajo la vigilancia del amo o del hosco y sañudo
> mayordomo, con la obligación imprescindible de estar de pie
> antes de salir el sol, con la pala y la canasta, o la mancera y el
> olate, para ganarse la olla de atole y el plato de frijoles del día?
> (1.15)

> (Who cared now [who remembers] [. . .] about the wretched
> hut where you lived like slaves, always spied on by the owner
> [always under the vigilance of the master] or some brutal [sul-
> len], angry foreman [majordomo], under the relentless [indis-
> pensable] obligation to be on your feet before the sun comes up,
> with your shovel and basket, or plow handle and ox-goad, just
> to earn your daily bowl of corn mash and a plate of beans?)

Demetrio's men can forget these cares as they ride under a magnificent sun
experiencing the expansiveness of the country—under the illusion of freedom. They can ignore their transition from mavericks to monsters. But not
forever. And they can ignore their failure to really change anything. But
Azuela assures that the reader cannot.

15

THE FEMINIZING OF FREEDOM AND FULFILLMENT

COMO AGUA PARA CHOCOLATE

> ¡Me creo lo que soy! Una persona que tiene todo el
> derecho a vivir la vida como mejor le plazca.
>
> *Como agua para chocolate*

In the midst of the male violence of the Mexican Revolution triumphs the rebellious adulterous love of Tita De la Garza for Pedro Muzquiz, the man her mother, Mama Elena, gave to her sister, Rosaura, in Laura Esquivel's *Como agua para chocolate.* This is a novel (and a film, directed by Esquivel's husband, Alfonso Arau) about defiance of convention and freedom through self-determination. But it is also a story about the naturalness (and related-ness) of food and sex, both of which are essential for the feeding and fertil-izing of the body, the soul, the earth. Tita is a maverick, a rebel against convention, and though she is reduced to abjection, she achieves fulfill-ment through female agency and turns her story from tragedy to comic romance.

The main action of the novel is set during the Revolution. "La lucha revolucionaria amenazaba con acarrear hambre y muerte por doquier" (81; "[T]he revolutionary struggle threatened to haul in its wake famine and death everywhere" [78]).[1] Near the Texas border Pancho Villa wages war, a reality of hangings, shootings, dismemberments, decapitations and literal heart-rendings, supposedly carried out by Villa himself: "Pancho Villa le llevaban los corazones sangrantes de sus enemigos para que se los comiera" (69; "Pancho Villa carried off the bleeding hearts of his enemies in order to devour them" [66]). But the world inside the De la Garza hacienda is in its way no less violent, for Mama Elena devours Tita's heart. Tita's story, like the Revolution, is about individual rights even of the lowly.

Born into this vale of tears is a traditional Christian metaphor. In her version of magical realism Esquivel puckishly materializes the metaphor: "Tita fue literalmente empujada a este mundo por un torrente impresionante de lágrimas que se desbordaron sobre la mesa y el piso de la cocina" (4; "Tita was literally pressed into this world by an impressive torrent of tears that overflowed onto the table and the floor of the kitchen" [4]).[2] Tita seems destined to a life of sorrow. The novel's first chapter is entitled "Enero" for January, and Tita is preparing Christmas sausage rolls as a special treat for her sixteenth birthday. Throughout the novel phallic rolls, sausages, and chiles are signs of Tita's—and others'—repressed sexuality. Despite the family tradition, enforced by Mama Elena, that the youngest daughter must not marry but care for her mother till she dies, Tita's sexuality has been aroused by Pedro, who the previous Christmas has declared his undying love. Pedro and his father have come to ask for Tita's hand, but Mama substitutes her oldest daughter, Rosaura. The news desolates Tita, and she goes to bed without eating even one Christmas roll—apparently forever denied the fulfilling phallus.[3]

Mama's suppression of Tita's desire has a chilling effect that Esquivel also literalizes, materializes into a growing chill within her: "una álgida sensación dolorosa" (18), a "molesto frío" (18), "uno frío infinito" (14; "an icy cold, sorrowful, sensation"; a "disturbing cold"; "an infinite coldness" [17, 14]). This last description relates her coldness to a cosmic chill. The narrator says if black holes had been discovered, that would have been the perfect metaphor for what Tita felt in her chest. Her feeling of emptiness is related to a cosmic collapsing in upon oneself, an infinite abject.

Mama further humiliates and abjects Tita by making her work on the wedding feast, preparing capons and meringue for the cake. Two hundred roosters must be castrated and fattened. Tita feels like screaming at her mother that they had chosen the wrong one to castrate, that it should have been she, then at least there would have been some justification for denying her marriage and substituting Rosaura by the side of her lover. When Tita bungles her first castration, her mother senses her defiance and slaps her so hard she sends her sprawling beside the rooster, who has died of his botched operation! A meal created out of sorrow, the wedding feast results in a grotesque communal vomiting. Not only Tita's sorrow affects especially the wedding cake and its icing, but also the sorrow of Nacha, whose own love was also frustrated by the superego: after finishing the meringue for Tita while experiencing her great lack, the black hole in her, Nacha dies holding a picture of her forbidden lover. It is as if the cultural ideology had communicated its negativity into the nubial food and made it life-denying instead of life-affirming: a coitus interruptus caused by those who would forbid, castrate.

Later the narrator will use the appropriate phrase "la mujer castrante" (139; "the castrating woman" [135]) for Mama Elena. She not only castrates, she kills slowly. As Tita wrings the necks of quail for another special meal, she realizes that she has learned from her mother to kill fast to reduce suffering. Except in her case, whom Mama has been killing "poco a poquito" (48; "bit by bit" [45]) without giving her the "golpe final" (48; "coup de grace" [45]).

Esquivel renders her best depiction of Mama Elena as superego when Mama confronts the *villista* captain to save her ranch:

> Realmente era difícil sostener la mirada de Mamá Elena, hasta para un capitán. Tenía algo que atemorizaba. El efecto que provocaba en quienes la recibían era de un temor indescriptible: se sentían enjuiciados y sentenciados por faltas cometidas. Caía uno preso de un miedo pueril a la autoridad materna. (90–91)

> (In reality it was difficult to sustain the gaze of Mama Elena, even for a captain. It held something that intimidated. The effect it provoked in those who were its recipients was a kind of indescribable fear: they felt prosecuted and sentenced for offenses committed. He [the captain] fell prisoner to a puerile fear of maternal authority. [86])

Ironically, of course, this captain is the *villista* with whom Gertrudis, Tita's passionate sister, has run away, escaping her mother's repressive gaze. Throughout, Mama's gaze withers, causing sterility. Not even the rebel officer can escape it.

Mama's chilling gaze is juxtaposed to the heat-engendering gaze of Pedro, who brings Tita's passion to the boiling point, like water for chocolate, time and again. He has married Rosaura only to stay close to Tita, though he is frustrated that their encounters are so furtive and brief because of Mama's gaze of surveillance. Yet the chemistry between them operates willy-nilly on themselves and those around them. In March, the month after the wedding, in a blatant display of affection Pedro presents Tita with roses. The indignant mother orders her to destroy them, but instead she makes an aphrodisiacal dish of quail in a rose-petal sauce containing blood from scratches the roses make in her flesh. Their sensuality flows into the guests and sends Gertrudis running naked in the fields to be picked up by a *villista* officer, who makes love to her on his galloping horse. The guests have consumed all but the last chile in walnut sauce, which Tita lusts after for it "contiene en su interior todos los secretos del amor" (57; "contains inside all the secrets of love" [55]). One sweltering summer night Pedro secretly embraces Tita and touches her hand to his tumescent chile, "un tizón encendido, que palpitaba bajo la ropa" (99; "a burning coal that palpitates underneath his clothes" [94]). Tita's pubescent sexual desire has been ineluctably aroused and seeks fulfillment.

Preparing the feast for Pedro and Rosaura's new son Roberto's baptism, Tita grinds seeds, her nubile breasts swinging freely, and Pedro witnesses them. Tita straightens with pride. Without touching them, Pedro transforms Tita's breasts "de castos a voluptuosos" (67; "from chaste to voluptuous" [65]). Then as if in direct consequence of that gaze, because Rosaura cannot feed Roberto and he is in danger of starving, by extraordinary chemistry Tita lactates and feeds him unbeknownst to all but Pedro. "Tita era en ese momento la misma Ceres personificada, la diosa de la alimentación en pleno" (77; "At this moment Tita resembles Ceres herself personified, goddess of bountiful nutrition" [75]). Opposed to her mother, Tita is allied with the forces of nutrition and fertility.

But Mama is vigilant, suspects something between Pedro and Tita, and decides to send Pedro and his family to live with cousins in San Antonio. Thus she deprives Tita of the source of her warmth, of her surrogate wifehood and motherhood, of her nutritive role. Hiding in the cellar during the *villista* foraging raid, Tita "inconscientemente tenía la esperanza de que al salir la encontraría muerta" (93; "unconsciously harbors the hope that when she gets out she would encounter her mother dead" [89]). She clings to life and warmth in the pathetic nursing of the sole surviving pigeon, because "sólo de esta manera la vida tenía cierto sentido" (93; "only in this manner does life hold a kind of sense" [89]). In her description of Mama's ability to cut up a watermelon, we get the full sense of Tita's growing despair:

> Indudablemente, tratándose de partir, desmantelar, desmembrar, desolar, destetar, desjarretar, desbaratar o desmadrar algo, Mamá Elena era una maestra. (97)

> (Indubitably, concerning dividing, dismantling, dismembering, desolating, dis-teating, dis-hocking, undoing, or dis-mothering something, Mama Elena was a master. [93])

Esquivel conveys not only a sense of cannibalistic dismembering of a human body but also a double entendre of abandoning a child ("desmadrar") as well as depriving it of its capacity to suckle, to mother ("destetar"). Consequently, "desolar"—to make desolate—conveys in Esquivel's symbolic tapestry the etymological connotation of depriving the earth of the sun—and thus drying it up, like Tita's milk. Or, for that matter, Mama Elena's.

The castrating woman as a figure for the superego has interesting implications. Like Big Nose Kate's sister or Pearl Hart's mother, Mama Elena has so internalized patriarchal discipline of women's sexuality that she becomes the enforcer of a code that once made her, like Tita now, a victim, a martyr. For her own parents had forbidden her marriage to a mulatto son of an American black who had escaped persecution during the Civil War (shades of John Horse). The novel withholds this information until after the death of Mama when Tita looks through her keepsakes and finds letters and photos that reveal the aborted love affair. The film reveals it earlier, having Mama in a moment of longing stare at her lover's photos in her locket and box. We also learn earlier that the reason for Tita's father's fatal heart attack after her birth is the discovery that Mama not only had an affair, but that it was not terminated with her forced marriage to him but produced his second daughter, Gertrudis. Ironically, Papa's death upon learning of his suspected impaternity causes Mama's milk to dry up, and the film especially suggests that Mama's vindictiveness stems from her own suppressed sensuality. After the episode with the quail and the chiles—and Gertrudis's absconding—the film pictures Mama, who has just burned Gertrudis's birth certificate in a particularly violent act of disowning, staring disconsolately at a hidden picture of her love child, whose rebelliousness is inherited from her apparently stoic mother. Declaring, in answer to the priest's fears that sending Pedro away during the Revolution is dangerous, that "Los hombres no son tan importantes para vivir [. . .] [n]i la revolución es tan peligrosa como la pintan" (82; "men are not all that important in order for them to live, [. . .] nor the revolution so dangerous as one paints it [79]), Mama Elena paradoxically appends to her declaration the folk joke,"¡Peor es un chile y el agua lejos!" (82; "[W]orse is a chile and water absent" [79]). Worse than an absent man is a limp dildo. The film emphasizes the bawdry by the resultant burst of laughter, including Mama's.

The film also interpolates a wonderful scene that flashes through the mind of the thoroughly abject Tita while kindly Dr. John Brown ministers to her after Mama's physical assault leaves her in a fetal position naked and catatonic. Through the metaphor of matches (literalized through Esquivel's magical realism) John describes the wondrous igniting of the quantum of passion each contains and the terrible consequences of losing one's opportunity for love. For the breath of a lover is what nourishes the soul. Deprived of fire, the soul leaves the body and goes searching, "ignorante de que sólo el cuerpo que ha dejado inerme, lleno de frío, es el único que podría dárselo" (116–17; "unaware that only the body, which it has left defenseless, full of coldness, is the unique thing that can produce it [the fire, the food]" [112]). As John utters these words, Tita has a vision of her mother walking hand in hand with her lover along the tracks—from the wrong side of which he hails. It is an uncanny moment of sympathy between Tita and Mama—and perhaps better than the novel prepares us for Tita's recovery and return to her mother's side. The novel makes Tita's return far more difficult, for Tita must nurse a hateful, spiteful shrew who eventually dies from her own paranoia—and too much ipecac to protect her against Tita's imagined poisoning. But in both novel and film Tita's genuine weeping at Mama's grave occurs for the same reason: Tita weeps, "[p]ero no por la mujer castrante que la había reprimido toda la vida, sino por ese ser que había vivido un amor frustrado. Y juró ante su tumba que ella nunca renunciaría al amor" (139; "but not for the castrating mother who had repressed her all of her life, rather for this being who had experienced a frustrated love. And she swears on her grave that she would never renounce love" [135]).

Tita has descended to the abject nadir and survived with a will-to-being, figured in crossing: she crosses the Rio Grande to heal in John's house, where she has a vision that enables her to transcend hatred for her mother and cross back over into Mexico to care for this woman who has all but killed her.

Tita and Mama are never reconciled, however. The bonds between mother and daughter have been permanently broken. In a sense they have been broken because Tita has from the beginning refused to allow Mama's gaze to kill the life, the warmth within her. To herself at first she defies Mama's rules, especially the stifling and illogical family prohibition on the youngest daughter's getting married: Then who's going to take care of her in her old age? One of her challenges, with her mother and later with Rosaura, who replaces Mama as family superego (and whom the film portrays brilliantly as looking more and more like her mother, even to the hairstyle), is "¿Se había tomado alguna vez en cuenta la opinion de las hijas afectadas? (10; "[w]hether at any time the opinion of the affected daughters had ever been taken into account?" [10]). She defiantly refuses to allow the neighbors to script for her "el papel de perdedora" (35; "the role of the loser" [35]). Her using the rose petals in the recipe for quail is an

act of what Mama calls "la rebeldía" (11; "rebelliousness" [11]). The rebelliousness of her very thoughts brings slaps, her glances at Pedro bring
separation. Yet Tita persists, even as she loses strength. Remembering her
touch of Pedro, Tita feels Mama's penetrating gaze and drops the chorizo
sausage she is molding (as if she held Pedro's phallus in her hands). Finally, desperately, after the death of Roberto because he had been deprived
of her teat—"todo lo que comía le caía mal ¡y pos si petatió!" (99; "whatever he ate, it ill befell him, and so he died" [95])—Tita articulates her
defiance to her mother's face. Tearing the sausages, she exclaims, "¡Mire
lo que hago con sus órdenes! ¡Ya me cansé! ¡Ya me cansé de obedecerla!"
(100; "See what I do with your orders? I'm tired of it! I'm tired of obeying
you" [96]). This defiance brings Mama's most castrating physical blow
yet: she breaks Tita's nose with a wooden spoon. But she hasn't yet broken
Tita's spirit, who screams back, "¡Usted es la culpable de la muerte de
Roberto!" (100; "You are the culprit in the death of Roberto" [96]).

Exhausted, Tita retreats to the empty dovecote, where she slips into a
near-fatal fetal abjection. Even under Dr. Brown's loving care, Tita "no
quería pensar en tomar una determinación" (109; "doesn't want to think
about making a decision" [105]); she refuses to speak "[p]orque no quiero"
(119; "because she doesn't want to" [114–15]). Yet by writing these words
on John's wall, Tita takes "el primo paso hacia la libertad" (119; "her first
step toward recovery, toward freedom" [115]). A female Bartleby, she prefers not to, but that very communication defies nihilism. For the first time
in her life, Tita, when she returns home to care for her mother, returns gaze
for gaze: "Y por primera vez Tita le sostuvo firmemente la mirada y Mamá
Elena retiró la suya. Había en la mirada de Tita una luz extraña" (130;
"And for the first time Tita sustained firmly the gaze and Mama Elena
withdrew hers. There was in the gaze of Tita a strange light" [126]). The
ambiguity here suggests that Tita both held her own gaze and sustained that
of her vindictive mother until Mama lowered it.

Yet in the novel the narrator opines that the only way for Tita ever to
be really free is for her mother to die, for Tita again feels the superego's
chill, which threatens to extinguish the warmth regenerated in her by the
doctor. Mama does die, and Tita and Pedro finally consummate their frustrated love in Mama's own special shed. Sparks fly, literally, and Chencha
convinces Rosaura that Mama's ghost lives in the little shed. Esquivel presents a delightful thumbing of the nose at the absent superego: "¡Si la pobre
Mamá Elena supiera que aún después de muerta su presencia seguía
causando temor y que ese miedo a encontrarse con ella les proporcionaba a
Tita y a Pedro la oportunidad ideal para profanar impunemente su lugar

preferido, al revolcarse voluptuosamente sobre la cama de Gertrudis, se volvería a morir cien veces" (160; "If poor Mama Elena had known that even after her death her presence would continue to cause trepidation and that this fear of encountering her would provide the ideal opportunity for Pedro and Tita to profane with impunity her preferred place and to frolic voluptuously on Gertrudis's bed, she would have replayed her death a hundred times" [156]). But Tita herself knows that freedom and self-determination do not come so easily, for "son pocos los que pasándose de listos logran realizar sus deseos a costa de lo que sea, y que obtener el derecho de determinar su propia vida le iba a costar más trabajo del que se imaginaba" (168; "few are those who, surpassing the clever, achieve the fulfillment of their desires at whatever cost; to obtain the right of self-determination was going to cost her more than she imagined" [164]). The price to Become, in Tita's case, is Being Itself.

Indeed, even Mama's ghost haunts Tita for her shameless adultery with Pedro, much more for the shameless pregnancy that results. Tita wishes for Gertrudis's moral support—that sister who threw inhibition to the wind, even lived in a brothel for a while, and now finds fulfillment not only in her lost loving captain but in the Revolution itself. As if in answer to Tita's wishes, Gertrudis returns, like her lover now a general in Villa's army. Ordering around her troops, she is a model of achieved agency. And she helps Tita break through the essentialism of her mother's—and her culture's—ideology. Tita has not been able to tell Rosaura, the new superego, the truth about her relationship with Pedro and its consequences. Gerturdis exclaims, "¡La verdad! ¡La verdad! Mira Tita, la mera verdad es que la verdad no existe, depende del punto de vista de cada quien" (190; "The truth! The truth! Look, Tita, the mere truth is that truth doesn't exist; it depends on the point of view of each and everyone" [184]). From one point of view Rosaura was wrong to steal Tita's lover. But Gertrudis's outburst conveys more than relativism: it conveys the death of traditional ontology. Truth preexists no more than essence. Truth is existential choice.

Armed with this de-essentializing of the ontology upon which the cultural superego is based (the naturalized system of patriarchal genealogy and the religious rhetoric imported to sustain it), Tita can now confront her mother's ghost and lay it to rest. It is the climax of her story. Maintaining that she has, by becoming Pedro's lover and getting pregnant, done no more than her mother, Tita can defy her mother's threat of damnation and declare herself:

> —¡Cállate la boca! ¿Pues qué te crees que eres?
> —¡Me creo lo que soy! Una persona que tiene todo el

derecho a vivir la vida como mejor le plazca. Déjeme de una
vez por todas, ¡ya no la soporto! Es más, ¡la odio, siempre la
odié!" (200)

("Shut your mouth! Just who do you think you are?"
"I know who I am. A person who has the absolute right to
live life how it best pleases her. Leave me once and for all. I
cannot stand it anymore! What's more, I hate you, I have always
hated you!" [194])

These "palabras mágicas" (200; "magical words" [194]) make Mama Elena,
as representative of the cultural superego, disappear forever. But not before
her last vindictive act, one more of envy than spite, the disfigurement of
Tita's lover. She diminishes to a little spark but before disappearing forever
sets Pedro afire and burns him badly.

Magical words alone do not save Tita and Pedro, then, any more than
Tita's few words scrawled in phosphorus across John's wall have saved
her. Tita's recovery and eventual liberation occur also because Mama Elena's
false, stifling, killing motherhood is balanced by that of surrogate mothers,
mestizas or *indias* curanderas who heal Tita, who minister to her, who come
to her aid with not Western allopathic but native, homeopathic remedies:
not just Chencha's ox-tail soup but those of the ghost of John's Kikapu
grandmother, "Luz de amanecer" ("Morning Light") and the ghost of Nacha,
Tita's nurse. Whenever Tita has needed help, she has prayed to Nacha, who
helped her birth Roberto, and who now comes to help her prepare an un-
guent for Pedro's burns, a remedy Nacha has learned from Morning Light.
The film nicely highlights this countermotherhood by having the
countermothers appear in Pedro's room to advise Tita.

These figures also symbolize a counterculture, one Tita learns from
Nacha in the kitchen, one she teaches her niece Esperanza in the same
kitchen. Esquivel underscores its radical difference from Eurocentric culture through her depiction of John Brown's family's mockery of and rejection of Morning Light, whom his grandfather had captured from among the
Kikapus and brought home to be his wife; who miraculously cured John's
great-grandfather when conventional medicine revealed its own inad-
equacy—and barbarism in the practice of bleeding:

Este era sólo un pequeño ejemplo de la gran diferencia de
opiniones y conceptos que existían entre estos representantes
de dos culturas tan diferentes y que hacía imposible que entre

los Brown surgiera el deseo de un acercamiento a las costumbres
y tradiciones de 'Luz de amanecer.' (112)

(This was only a small example of the large difference of opin-
ions and concepts which exist between these representatives of
two cultures so different and which made it impossible that
among the Browns would arise the desire for a reconciliation
with the customs and traditions of Morning Light. [108])

There are two conclusions to this story, both representing an important crossing. John Brown's affection for Tita has reengendered warmth,
but it is not the fire she feels for Pedro. She agrees to marry John, but first
the false pregnancy intervenes, then Tita's own wrenching doubts, about
whether to seek security with John, especially in the light of Pedro's growing jealousy after his burns and Rosaura's insistence that whatever passes
between Tita and Pedro be kept a secret for reputation's sake. Esquivel
concludes the penultimate chapter with Tita poised to make the most important decision of her life, "su decisión, la definitiva, la que determinaría
todo su futuro" (225; "*her* decision, the definitive one, which will determine her entire future" [emphasis mine, 219]).

The final chapter, for which the recipe is those delightfully erotic
chiles in walnut sauce, opens on a wedding that reader and viewer alike
take to be Tita's with John. Instead, the wedding is between John's son
Alex and Tita's niece Esperanza. Esperanza is a kind of replacement child
for Roberto, and Tita becomes a surrogate mother for her too, passing on to
her the secrets of the kitchen, of the indigenous counterculture. But
Esperanza has also attended the Eurocentric schools. In herself she represents the hope her name means in at least two ways: she is a living reconciliation between the customs and traditions of two opposing cultures, and
she embodies Tita's defiance of stultifying tradition within her own, for she
too refuses to sacrifice her happiness to attend her mother as the last daughter.
Rosaura's continuation of the life-denying, absurd tradition, which John
appropriately calls "una tontería" (80; "a stupidity" [77]), loses out to Tita's
new life-affirming tradition, literally that which she hands down to
Esperanza. Rosaura's foul breath and flatulence, which eventually kill her,
embody, materialize her and her mother's negativity. The chiles symbolize
the positive world vibrations of sex and love. Esperanza's marriage to Alex
also represents a blending of two cultures, Anglo and Mexicano, producing
mestizaje, the cultural mixedness Anzaldúa celebrates, which overcomes
stagnant, sterile opposition. A doctor like his father, trained in Western

allopathic medicine and about to get a Ph.D. in medical research at Harvard, Alex, who will undoubtedly research Morning Light's wonderful remedies, in himself represents a blending, a crossing of cultures.

The second ending presents Tita's final crossing over from repression to fulfillment: "La verdad, a estas alturas a Tita también le importaba un comino lo que la gente pensara al hacer pública la relación amorosa que existía entre Pedro y ella" (237; "In truth, at this point it no longer mattered to Tita a pinch what people might ponder at the publication of the amorous relationship that existed between Pedro and her" [231]). The chiles act as an aphrodisiac. Everyone couples all over the place. And Tita and Pedro enter Mama's special place, lit up in the film by Nacha, and share an orgasm so profound it affects the cosmos. The "miradas libidinosas" (242; "libidinous looks of the people" [236]) signify unleashed fertility. When the narrator says, "Ese día hubo más creatividad que nunca en la historia de la humanidad" (243; "This day possessed more creativity than ever in the history of humanity" [237]), she underscores the total reaffirmation of food, sex, life, fertility.

Pedro dies at the moment of monumental climax, and Tita does not want to be left alone, so she consumes candles until she reaches that tunnel John learned about from Morning Light, the entrance to our origins, and walks off hand-in-hand with Pedro "hacia el edén perdido" (246; "into Paradise Lost" (240]). If she had died at the moment Pedro brought her to *la petite mort,* she might have seemed an adjuct to him. Esquivel makes her the master of her own destiny. She finally surrenders Being.

Pedro bequeathes the world his daughter. Tita bequeathes that daughter Tita's life-giving, life-affirming secrets, "esta historia de amor enterrada" (247; "this history/story of interred love" [241]). Interred after their death beneath the ash heap caused by the enormous conflagration of the entire ranch under Tita's enormous quilt, but also interred during Tita's lifetime as suppressed desire. Tita and her love "quien seguirá viviendo mientras haya alguien que cocine sus recetas" (247; "will go on living as long as someone [currently, the narrator, Esperanza's daughter] cooks her recipes" [241]). In other words, the transcendence at the end of the book is not traditional, neo-Platonic Christianity. However much the tunnel seems a Platonic or Wordsworthian way back to where we came from, "el camino que olvidamos al momento de nacer y que nos llama a reencontrar nuestro perdido origen divino" (117; "the way which we forgot at the moment of our birth, and which summons us to reencounter our lost divine origin" [113]), it represents a material transcendence. Thus in the film the tunnel resembles the sun, the origin of life. Transcendence is not that of the soul escaping the prison of this world, of the body. In the film the naked, sexual bodies of Tita and Pedro are silhouetted in a last embrace. The body is still necessary, the recipes, the food. Transcendence, as in Gabriel García Márquez and Isabel Allende, is generational, as the film visualizes through the presence of the ghosts of Tita and Esperanza behind the narrator as she concludes her story by closing the book of recipes. Tita's final crossing is the interring of both body and spirit into the refertilization of the land: "Dicen que bajo las cenizas floreció todo tipo de vida, convirtiendo ese terreno en el más fértil de la región" (247; "They say that underneath the ashes flourished every type of life, converting this land into the most fertile of the region" [241]). For Tita, that is the ultimate fulfillment and freedom—an inheritable liberation linked to the potential achievement of the Revolution. After all, the chiles in walnut sauce Tita serves at her last feast are decked out in red, white, and green.[4]

Tita's potential tragedy, then, has been transformed into a secular magical romance. And a comic romance at that, for Esquivel's style continuously pulls us back from the sentimental to a realism that is both magical in the sense of fantastic but also Rabelasian, Cervantean, celebratory of what the great Russian critic, Mikhail Bakhtin, calls "the lower bodily stratum." Esquivel's humor is positively "carnivalesque." It never lets us forget the body: its sublimities and its grotesqueries—and above all, its need for food.

16

MIRRORS, DREAMS, AND MEMORY

GRINGO VIEJO

Fueron capturados por el laberinto de espejos. . . .
Uno de los soldados de Arroyo adelantó un brazo hacia el espejo.
—Mira, eres tú.
Y el compañero señaló hacia el reflejo del otro.
—Soy yo.
—Somos nosotros.

(They were caught in the labyrinth of mirrors. . . .
One of Arroyo's soldiers held an arm toward the mirror. "Look, it's you."
And his companion pointed toward the reflection in the other mirror. "It's me."
"It's us.")

Carlos Fuentes, *Gringo viejo*

Carlos Fuentes's *Gringo viejo* is a house of mirrors in which characters not only see themselves but blend in with others. It is a house in which mirrors blend with dreams, into which others enter almost at will. It is a house constructed by memory of such existential crossings—a memory that preserves the times, the fragmented consciousnesses of others, in a negotiation of borders between and within selves and between and within countries, namely, the United States and Mexico.

One of the most striking images at the beginning of the novel, as we witness a patrol of *villistas* exhuming the body of the Old Gringo, is of this border as "la herida que al norte se abría como el río mismo desde los cañones despeñados" (16; "the wound that to the north opened like the Rio Grande itself rushing down from steep canyons" [8]).[1] The novel tells of an old gringo and a young gringa who cross that wound into Mexico and of the revolutionary general they encounter, who invades and changes their lives even as they do his. Each has his or her own wound of divided consciousness.

In a delightful spoof, unfortunately omitted from the English version, Fuentes turns the traditional "Nota del Autor" at the end into a note not on himself but on the Old Gringo, historically authenticating, as it were, the basis of his character at last. Fuentes informs us that the North American writer Ambrose Bierce—"misántropo, periodista [journalist] [. . .] y autor" (189)—not wanting to die of old age or some debilitating disease, said goodbye to friends and crossed the border into Mexico to provoke his own death, preferably "ante un paredón mexicano" (that is, before the wall used for execution by firing squad). Fuentes quotes Bierce as inscribing a postcard, "Ah [. . .] ser un gringo en México; eso es eutanasia" ("Ah [. . .] to be a gringo in Mexico: that is euthanasia"). Bierce entered Mexico in November 1913 and never returned.[2] "El resto es ficción," Fuentes's fiction, this novel, narrated ostensibly by an omniscient third person but perhaps really by a voice within the consciousness, the memory of the aging gringa, Harriet Winslow, who sits alone in her Washington, D.C., apartment and remembers her momentous crossing.

The Old Gringo has come to die, yet strangely he has a rebirth of sorts, culminating at the moment of death in a unity of his heretofore divided consciousness. That the Old Gringo has come to die in Mexico is the constant refrain, with incremental repetition: Dying in front of a wall beats falling down stairs; I want to be a good-looking corpse; I seek the gift of nothingness; please grant me the coup de grace. Beyond the bravado lies loss and lament: "Él no le dijo que había venido aquí a morirse porque todo lo que amó se murió antes que él" (43; "He did not tell her that he had come here to die because everything he loved had died before him" [37]).

But he does tell her that everything he loved not only died but that he killed it, that he drove his two sons to different forms of suicide, his wife to death after a long illness metonymic of the acrimony between them, his daughter into permanent alienation from him—and all through the bitter cynicism that was his trademark as a journalist. He condemns himself as a born cannibal, even at his mother's breast. No wonder his family feared he would devour them as well.

His relationship with his father is, if possible, even more complex. As the Old Gringo rides into his first battle with the *villistas,* he reminisces about joining the Union army just because he dreamed that his father was on the Confederate side and "[q]uería lo que soñó: el drama revolucionario del hijo contra el padre" (58; "he wanted what he dreamed: the revolutionary drama of son against father" [54]). In other words, he seeks the drama of Oedipal rebellion McCarthy insists a son should not be denied.[3] The Old Gringo rides crazily toward the ensconced *Federales,* like an "espejismo"— a mirror-mirage (59), but sees behind the Mexicans his father's ghost urging him on: "Haz tu deber, hijo" (60; "Do your duty, son").[4] Later Arroyo relates to the Old Gringo that when young, the corrupt President Pofririo Díaz was a brave revolutionary against the French. The Old Gringo responds,

> No, dijo el gringo, no lo sabía: él sólo sabía que los padres se les aparecen a los hijos de noche y a caballo, montados encima de una peña, militando en el bando contrario y pidiéndoles a los hijos:
> —Cumplan con su deber. Disparen contra los padres. (79)

> (No, the gringo said, he hadn't known. He only knew that fathers appear to their sons at night and on horseback, outlined atop a high cliff, serving in the opposing army and bidding their sons: "Carry out your duty. Fire upon your fathers." [79])

As is obvious from the mad fixation of this image, the duty the father enunciates has nothing to do with Villa or Huerta and everything to do with the Old Gringo's ability finally to lay the ghost of his father as every man must in order to be himself, free from an overwhelming superego. After the battle, whether aloud or to himself, the Old Gringo declares triumphantly, "He matado a mi padre" (60; "I have killed my father" [56]). He seems liberated, free at last—to die. Or is it to live again?

The Old Gringo's bravery does not bring back his wife and children. But even as he muses on the irony of his tracing his father's very footsteps into Mexico (during the Mexican-American War), now that he has laid his father's ghost he seems liberated enough to start falling in love with a woman young enough to be his daughter. From the moment he has seen her, despite his self-destructive purpose, he sees them both as having crossed into Mexico "luchando por ser" (41; "fighting for [their] very being" [35]). He may have thought that ultimate, frozen being would be achieved in a death sought leading a charge against the ghost of his father. But Harriet Winslow awakens in him Electral love that begins with a kiss and the penetration of her dreams by the sheer force of his "deseo" (57; his "desire" [52]). He has hoped that when he returned from the battle, "vivo o muerto, ella lo recibiera en este sueño ininterrumpido" (57; "dead or alive, she would welcome him in this uninterrupted dream" [52]) and that they might "penetrar sus sueños respectivos, compartirlos" (57; "penetrate each other's dreams, share those dreams" [52–53]):

> Hizo un esfuerzo gigantesco, como si éste pudiese ser el último acto de su vida, y en un instante soñó con los ojos abiertos y los labios apretados el sueño entero de Harriet [. . .] .
> —Estoy muy sola.
> —Puede usted tomarme cuando guste.
> —¿ . . . te viste en el espejo . . . ? (57)

> (He made a tremendous effort, as if this might be the last act of his life, and in an instant he dreamed with open eyes and clenched lips Harriet's entire dream [. . .] .
> "I am very lonely."
> "You may have me at your pleasure."
> " . . . did you look at yourself in the mirror . . . ?" [53])

These fragments from Harriet's dream will become clearer. For now, suffice it to say that they are expressions of her intimate desires, desires the Old Gringo has penetrated through an enormous act of his own desire, a will-to-being already countering his death wish. That he fails to recognize, to acknowledge the nature of his desire is perhaps underscored by the reference to Harriet's looking at herself in the mirror as the two of them entered the ballroom earlier that night: the Old Gringo did not look in the mirror either, because "sólo tuvo los ojos para miss Harriet" (44; "he had eyes only for Miss Harriet" [39]).

The night of his victory over his father, the Old Gringo watches Harriet and Arroyo together and closes his eyes in fear, for he sees them as "un hijo y una hija" (63; "a son and a daughter" [60]) and he is afraid again to get involved, to have love in his life. Yet even his metaphors and abstractions employed to distance himself from the nature of his desire ooze with sexuality: "ambos nacidos del semen de la imaginación que se llama poesía y amor" (63; "both born of the seed [semen, sperm] of the imagination called poetry and love" [60]).

The poetic form the Old Gringo's love takes is intercourse, interpenetration through dreams: "Quizás la podría visitar en sueños. Quizás la mujer que entró al salón de baile la noche anterior no se vio a sí misma, pero sí se soñó" (77; "Maybe he could visit her dreams. Maybe the woman who entered the ballroom the previous evening had not looked at herself, but had dreamed herself" [77]). After the Old Gringo's second victorious battle they meet again in a mirror in the railway car that serves as Arroyo's quarters. The Old Gringo tells Harriet, "Creo que hasta soñé contigo. Me sentí tan cerca de ti como un . . . " (99; "I think I even dreamed about [with] you. I felt as close to you as a . . . " [103]). Harriet's response is devastating: "¿Como un padre?" (99; "As a father?" [103]). He kisses her on the cheek; they embrace; her blouse is not fully buttoned. It is an erotic moment, full of possibilities. Yet abruptly there in the doorway is Arroyo, who, naked to the waist, smokes a big black cigar and watches them as they go to join the village festival. When Harriet misses the pearls she has discovered in the hacienda and is about to accuse Arroyo's people, he appears again, still half naked, strapping on twin holsters (a sign of his potency) and seizing Harriet by the wrist to show her the error of her ways: that the pearls have been used to deck the Virgin during the festival. Harriet appeals to the Old Gringo,

> pero él supo que su tiempo con esta muchacha había llegado y se había ido, aunque ella todavía tuviera tiempo de anidarse en brazos de él y quererlo como mujer o como hija, no importaba, ya era demasiado tarde: vio la cara de Arroyo, el cuerpo de Arroyo, la mano de Arroyo y se dio por vencido. Su hijo y su hija. (102)

> (but he knew his moment with this woman had come and gone; she might still have time to nestle in his arms and to love him as a wife or a daughter, it didn't matter; it was too late; he saw Arroyo's face, Arroyo's body, Arroyo's hand, and he surrendered. His son and his daughter. [106])

She would not be his lover. He relinquishes her to the role of daughter, lover to this surrogate son.

So the Old Gringo yields his quasi-incestuous desire to the quasi-incestuous desire of Tomás Arroyo. His liberation has been short-lived. If he has laid the ghost of his father, he has not laid the ghosts of his two sons, who have been denied their Oedipal struggle, and now displaced Oedipal jealousy between pseudo-father and pseudo-son interrupts the Old Gringo's new dream and spells his doom. For Arroyo has watched the Old Gringo and Harriet kiss and embrace, and now he supplants this father, this gringo.

Before the Old Gringo even knows (except perhaps in his sympathetic imagination) that Harriet has yielded to Arroyo in order to save his life, the Old Gringo sees himself and Arroyo as "enemigo[s]" (115; "enemies" [120]), as Arroyo

> se paseaba como un gallito para dar a entender que la gringa era suya, se había desquitado así de los chingados gringos, ahora Arroyo era el macho que se cogió a la gringa y lavó con una eyaculación rápida las derrotas de Chapultepec y Buenavista. (115)

> (was strutting like a cock to let him know the American woman was his, he had got the best of the fucking gringos, now he, Arroyo, the macho, had fucked the American woman and with one quick ejaculation washed away the defeats of [the Mexicans at the hands of the Americans in the Mexican-American War at] Chapultepec and Buenavista. [120])

Walking with her the morning after her night of love-making with Arroyo, the Old Gringo's fragmented consciousness comes to realize that love, without which (or at least without the imagination of which) humans cannot live, finally—for both of them, for all of us—"nos da la medida de nuestra pérdida" (134; "gives us the measure of our loss" [140]). His love for her, her love for Arroyo—both measure lost opportunities of being and becoming. He laments her loss, especially because, he tells her, she was loved without even knowing it—in the thousand fragments of his "sueños" ("dreams"), in the very "espejos" ("mirrors") through which she had entered "a un sueño olvidado" ("a forgotten dream") (135 [140–41]). The dream is forgotten now because its possibility is past, unrealized, obliterated by the Old Gringo's "verdadera violencia" (135; "real fury" [140]) at their dual betrayal of him: not only had Arroyo taken her for his vanity, she had enjoyed it.

Realizing that each had been creating the other as both a product and a project of their imaginations, that she had been the final answer to the "loco sueño del artista con la conciencia dividida" (140; "the mad dream of the artist with a split consciousness" [146]), the Old Gringo, as he gathers his thoughts at the critical instant before he will seek revenge on Arroyo, nevertheless achieves a final intercourse of consciousness with Harriet, as they walk "sacralizando estos minutos en los que ambos lograron unir su conciencia dividida en la del otro: antes de la dispersión final que adivinaban" (141; "sanctifying those minutes when they succeeded in unit-ing—each in the other's—their split consciousness, before the final disper-sion they sensed was near" [148]).

There is nothing traditionally transcendent about the Old Gringo's final consciousness, for "siempre la muerte y la ignorancia al cabo de todo, siempre la paz muda e insensible de la inexistencia y la inconsciencia al final" (144; "in the end, it's always death and unawareness, always the mute and insentient peace of nonexistence and unconsciousness" [162]). As in Faulkner's novels (especially *If I Forget Thee, Jerusalem*), memory provides the only transcendence of time. The Old Gringo achieves a final unity of consciousness, enabled by the unexpected: by Harriet Winslow, by Mexico itself, which has awakened his sensitivity to the natural world:

> Su conciencia errante, cercana a la unidad final, le dijo que
> ésta era la gran compensación por los amores perdidos porque
> mereció perderlos; México, en cambio, le había dado la
> compensación de una vida: la vida de los sentidos despertada de
> su letargo por la cercanía de la muerte, la dignidad de la
> naturaleza como la última alegría de la vida[.] (139)

> (His ranging[5] consciousness, close to final unity, told him
> that this was the great compensation for the loves he had lost
> because he deserved to lose them. Mexico had, instead, com-
> pensated him with a life: the life of his senses, awakened from
> lethargy by his proximity to death, the dignity of nature as the
> last joy of his life[.] [146])

Together, then, Harriet and Mexico have vouchsafed the Old Gringo an invaluable gift—a unified consciousness enabled by the old body itself. The Old Gringo reflects back on his crossing into Mexico and reinterprets it:

> Se sintió liberado al cruzar la frontera en Juárez, como si de
> verdad hubiera entrado a otro mundo. Ahora sí sabía que existía
> una frontera secreta dentro de cada uno y que ésta era la frontera
> más difícil de cruzar, porque cada uno espera encontrarse allí,
> solitario dentro de sí, y sólo descubre, más que nunca, que está
> en compañía de los demás.
> Dudó por un instante y luego dijo:
> —Esto es inesperado. Es atemorizante. Es doloroso. Y es
> bueno. (143)

(He had felt freed the moment he crossed the border at Juárez, as if he had walked into a different world. Now he was sure: each of us has a secret frontier within him, and that is the most difficult frontier to cross because each of us hopes to find himself alone there, but finds only that he is more than ever in the company of others.

He hesitated for an instant and then added: "This is unexpected. It's terrifying. It's painful. And it's good." [161])

The Old Gringo's final unity of consciousness, then, his final becoming, creates not the radical self of bourgeois ideology but an interimplicated self, penetrating and co-created by the consciousnesses of others, kept alive only in the memory of others who have shared one's *tiempo,* one's time.

Yet the Old Gringo's final act is violent, vengeful, parricidal. He kills Arroyo's ancestors by burning the papers that prove his people's claim to the land. Furious, Arroyo of course kills the Old Gringo in return, granting him the death he has sought. Ironically, this destruction of a sacred link to the past may itself be strangely liberating. For it not only implicates Arroyo in the Gringo's death and consequently in his own death but interimplicates his people in a consciousness that reaches beyond their comfortable confines:

> [N]unca conocimos a nadie fuera de esta comarca, no sabíamos que existía un mundo fuera de nuestros maizales, ahora conocemos a gente venida de todas partes, cantamos juntos las canciones, soñamos juntos los sueños y discutimos si éramos más felices solos en nuestros pueblos o ahora volando por aquí revueltos con tantos sueños y tantas canciones diferentes[.] (145–46)

> (We never knew anyone outside this region, we didn't know there was a world beyond our maize fields, now we know people from all parts, we sing our songs together, we dream our dreams together and argue whether we were happier isolated in our villages or now, whirling around everywhere, dizzied by so many dreams and so many different songs. [163–64])

The final "dispersion" of death for the Old Gringo means insemination: of the memory of both Harriet and the Mexican people. Moreover, the burning of the papers breaks an umbilical cord to the unrecoverable past and catapults if not Arroyo himself at least Mexico into the future.

In a fine scene very unfortunatley omitted from the translation, Pancho Villa explains to La Luna, the moon-faced mistress of Tomás Arroyo, who knew Villa when he was only a rustler named Doroteo Arango, why he has left home:

> —Usted dejó su casa. Yo dejé la mía.
> —Tú no tenías casa, Doroteo Arango.
> —Pero ahora soy Francisco Villa y los persigo a ellos por violar hermanas y asesinar padres. Nunca he hecho nada que no sea por la justicia. Ellos me quitaron mi casa. [. . .] La revolución es ahora nuestro hogar. (171)

> ("You left your house. I left mine."
> "Thou didst not have a house, Doroteo Arango."
> "But now I am Francisco Villa and I pursue those who violate sisters and assassinate fathers. Never have I done anything that was not for justice. They took my house from me. [. . .] The Revolution is now our home."[6])

Villa's response is fraught with ironies: those who violate sisters and who assassinate fathers are not *unheimlich* others; they are right here at home in Villa's own family, especially in the figure of Tomás Arroyo. Moreover, Arroyo commits the fatal mistake of trying to go home again.

After meeting the Old Gringo at the beginning of the novel, Arroyo returns to the Miranda hacienda where he was engendered and raised, a bastard of Señor Miranda himself. He burns it to the ground—except for its ballroom, its hall of mirrors. He insists that he is motivated by the cause of justice in the face of *hacendado* oppression of the *mestizos* of northern Mexico, an oppression that leaves these mixed people only three choices: disappear among the Indians, become midnight *bandidos,* or submit to a life of virtual forced labor on the haciendas. Arroyo insists he has chosen rebellion so that the next generation will not be limited to these horrible alternatives: "He regresado para que nadie en México tenga que repetir mi vida o escoger como yo tuve que escoger" (131; "I have come back so that no one ever again has [to repeat my life or to choose as I have had to] in Mexico" [137]).

Yet the general doth insist too much. His inability to burn the hall of mirrors and rejoin Villa reveals that he is trapped in his own dreams: of Oedipal assassination and Oedipal supplantation of the father in his mother's bed. After grabbing Harriet by the wrist, Arroyo drags her to the ballroom,

y detrás de una puerta de espejos salió Tomás Arroyo un niño a
bailar con su madre, su madre la esposa legítima de su padre, su
madre la señora limpia y derecha [. . .] que bailaba con su hijo
el vals *Sobre las olas* que tantas veces oyeron desde lejos, en el
caserío donde podían vedarse las miradas pero no los rumores
de la música. (106)

(and from behind a door of mirrors the boy Tomás Arroyo came
out to dance with his mother, his mother, his father's legitimate
wife, his mother, the straight and clean woman [. . .] [who]
danc[ed] with her son the waltz *Sobre las olas* that they had
heard so often far away in the big house, where they could keep
out prying eyes but could not keep in the sounds of the music.
[110])

Arroyo's desire from the time he was a young boy to legitimate his mother
and thus himself, to displace his father in the arms of his mother and dance
with her in the palatial ballroom has been fulfilled, as it were, in a waking
dream.

As Arroyo's desire for Harriet increases, however, the narrator says,
"Arroyo había abandonado a su madre decente y respetada" (109; "Arroyo
[. . .] had abandoned his decent and respectable mother [113]). But we are
denied insight into his consciousness and have only Harriet's observation:
"Harriet vio a Arroyo saliendo entre las piernas de todas las mujeres cargadas
de pesares y sombras: asombradas, apesadumbradas" (109; "Harriet saw
Arroyo pushing out from between the legs of all women burdened by cares
and shadows [astonished, nightmare-stricken]" [113]). It is a double image. Arroyo's mother will not remain fixed in his dream-fantasy as his
father's legitimate wife, dancing with her son-husband. She is all the oppressed women of Mexico, both giving birth to and copulating with Arroyo, El Libertador, the Revolution itself.

Even this last image is complicated. Arroyo tells how as a child he
was taken up to the big house by Graciano, the trusted old servant who had
access to the keys of the house so he could wind the clock, among other
things. When Graciano let Arroyo hold the keys for a minute, a minute in
which he felt he held the house and all its inhabitants in his power, Señor
Miranda seemed to sense the threat and immediately ordered Graciano to
take the keys back from the little "mocoso" (126; "[snotty] brat" [132]).
On his deathbed, Graciano transmitted to Arroyo the box with the sacred
papers in it, the land grants from the King of Spain proving the people

owned the land. Graciano, as it were, designates Arroyo the heir to his ruthless father's estate.

This story relates to the last story Arroyo tells Harriet on their night of love-making—a story we get only in Harriet's final reminscences. Arroyo begins the story announcing his father was shot trying to rape an Indian woman in Yucatán, where he was visiting an *hacendado* whose wealth came from enforced Indian labor on his maguey plantation (shades of *Dreams of the Centaur*). But as he tells the story, Arroyo's wish-fulfillment seems to penetrate. Instead of being shot, the old man is murdered, assassinated by being forced, by the Indian woman's lover, to swallow keys until he strangles to death. It is a grotesque, distorted image of Oedipal fellatio rape. The old man is then hung by his scrotum in a well until his flesh rots off his bones— imagery that recalls Arroyo's earlier narration to Harriet that he had re-fused to look into his dying father's eyes but instead had waited to see his denuded bones.

The lover is thus a twin for Arroyo, whom he hopes the Revolution will allow him to meet as north meets south. But Arroyo is also a twin for his father and the Indian woman a twin for his mother. Arroyo's grotesque image of his father wiping blood off his penis after raping the Indian woman mingles with Harriet's earlier image of Arroyo's emerging from the loins of the oppressed, for the old man was "imaginando que se estaba cogiendo en una virgen a todas las mujercs de México" (184; "imagining he was fucking, in one virgin girl, all the women of Mexico" [194]). Arroyo curses his father and wishes he had been there with the couple. His hesitation in the naming of the couple reveals his Oedipal anxiety:

> [A]h viejo cabrón, cómo lo detesto y cómo deseo haber estado allí cuando esa pareja de jóvenes, una pareja como yo y . . . y . . . carajo, no como tú, miss Harriet, maldita seas, ni como La Luna tampoco, chingada sea, la última muchacha que mi padre se cogió jamás no era como ninguna mujer que yo haya tenido nunca, chingada seas gringa, nadie como esa mujer, digo chingada seas gringa y chingada sea La Luna y chingadas sean todas las viejas que no se parecen a mi madre que es la melliza de la última mujer que mi chingado padre tuvo jamás. (184)

> ([O]h the fucking bastard, how I hate him and how I wish I had been there when this young couple, a couple like me and . . . and . . . and . . . God damn it, not you Miss Harriet, damn you, [. . .][7]

not like La Luna either, oh, damn it [may she be fucked], that last girl my father ever had is like no woman I have ever had, oh, damn you [may you be fucked], gringa, no one like that other woman, I say damn you [may you be fucked] and damn La Luna [may she be fucked] and [may they be fucked] all the other women [all the old hags] who do not resemble my own mother, who is the twin sister of the last woman my damned [fucking] father ever had. [195])

Arroyo's obscene rage at these other women, his calling all other women, including by implication all the ones he has had and the one in his current bed, "viejas," is a screen to obscure his Oedipal desire to violate, through this surrogate sister, her twin his mother, and to assassinate his father, his own double—a final desire that yields his own death wish. In shooting his rival the Old Gringo, his pseudo-father who is in the castrating act of destroying Arroyo's inheritance, his potency as the new Miranda, Arroyo displaces Oedipal assassination and brings about his own death at the hands of the avenging woman.

Arroyo has tried to go home, where he could negotiate his Oedipal crisis. But instead of finally being associated with his mother and through her with the oppressed of Mexico, he has become enchanted, as he explains to Harriet, transfixed before the castrating image of his father (the hacienda itself, its mirrors, which Fuentes describes in a telling image as "una esfera de navajas que corta por donde se la tome" [105; "a sphere of blades that cuts wherever it is grasped" (109)]). Harriet pronounces the final condemnation: he wanted his dream of avenging his mother to become a reality, but instead,

— [T]u nombre no es Arroyo como tu madre; te llamas Miranda como tu padre: sí—le dijo mientras la lluvia dispersaba las cenizas de papel—, eres su heredero resentido, disfrazado de rebelde. Pobre bastardo. Eres Tomás Miranda. (165)

("Your name isn't Arroyo, like your mother's; your name is Miranda, after your father. Yes," she said, as the rain dissolved the ashes of the papers, "you're the resentful heir, disguised as a rebel. You poor bastard. You are Tomás Miranda." [175][8])

Harriet speaks these lines as Arroyo is about to be executed by Villa. Arroyo shot the Old Gringo in the back as he was leaving the railway car with the burning papers in his hand. Harriet has told United States officials that a *villista* general has assassinated an American in Mexico and thereby created an international incident, bad press which Villa cannot afford. So he orders the Old Gringo exhumed, shot from the front by a firing squad in front of that wall after all, and as Arroyo adminsters the coup de grace on the Old Gringo, Villa has him executed as well, administering the coup de grace on Arroyo himself—a father figure punishing a wayward son: "Tomasito. [. . .] Ya sabes que tú eres como mi hijo" (167; "Tomasito [a diminutive showing affection]. [. . .] You know [thou knowest] you're [thou art] like a son to me" [177]).

Yet ironically, Villa has managed to grant Arroyo a final being, essence. As the Old Gringo had predicted, Arroyo would only escape the inevitable corruption of power by dying young. As Harriet has said, "Lo más importante de la vida de Arroyo no iba a ser cómo vivió, sino cómo murió" (114; "The most important thing in Arroyo's life would be not how he lived, but how he died" [119]). Villa has given him "la victoria del héroe" (187; "a hero's victory" [199]).

Of course, the text reminds us that the agent in Arroyo's death is not so much Villa as Harriet: "Sin embargo Harriet Winslow sabía [. . .] que no dañó a Arroyo, sino que le dio la victoria del héroe, la muerte joven" (187; "And yet Harriet Winslow knew [. . .] that she had not harmed Arroyo but given him a hero's victory: a young death" [199]). Harriet kills him partly to avenge his killing the Old Gringo, partly to avenge his showing her the possibility of being she could never become.

If like the Old Gringo Harriet Winslow has come to Mexico "luchando de ser"—wrestling for her being—like the Old Gringo and like Tomás Arroyo she has a ghost to lay. Her struggle for being involves escaping from spinsterhood in subsistence living with her mother in Washington, D.C., supported only by pension checks for her father, who disappeared in Cuba and who is presumed dead (though Harriet knows better). It involves, too, escaping from her beau, Mr. Delaney, a lobbyist in Congress, whose idea of a good time is having Harriet masturbate him through his clothes. Harriet decides to leave for a teaching job at the Miranda estate even before Delaney is indicted for fraud. But she is also running away to a dry climate from the insufferable humidity of the Potomac—and the tumescent sensuality associated with it, especially in the figure of her father's Negro mistress.

"Era una mujer que soñaba mucho" (52; "She was a woman who dreamed a lot" [48])—of her father, of his mistress, sometimes substituting herself obliquely for the mistress, as when a detached voice announces,

"Capitán Winslow, estoy muy sola y usted puede tomarme cuando guste" (55; "Captain Winslow, I am very lonely. You may have me at your pleasure" [51]). Was it Delaney or her father who appeared old and tired without his starched Arrow collar? Was it in or out of a dream? Which one said women can be only "putas o vírgenes" (55; "sluts or virgins" [51])?

Entering Mexico Harriet enters the Miranda hacienda, the ballroom with its mirrors. But perhaps she didn't look at herself in the mirrors, muses the Old Gringo, because "sí se soñó" (77; she "had dreamed herself" [77]). It is not only the Old Gringo who penetrates her dreams. The day after she arrives, after she has tried, out of a sense of duty, to put what she can in order on the ruined hacienda, she has a humid dream about when she was happiest, assuming the duty that everything depended on her:

> Pero algo faltaba en el sueño. Había algo más, sin lo cual el simple deber no bastaba. Trató de invitar a otro sueño dentro de su sueño, una luz, un patio trasero regado de pétalos de cornejo caídos, un quejido desde lo hondo de un pozo. (94)

> (But something was lacking in her dream. There was something more, something without which simple duty was not enough. She tried to invoke a different dream within her dream, a light, a back yard strewn with fallen dogwood blossoms, a moan from a black pit. [97])

The moan is the cry of sensuality, the cry of the Negro mistress from her dark pit, the cellar where she met her father. Harriet wants what the black woman experiences: passion, orgasm, her father. As she dances with Arroyo in the hall of mirrors, she fantasizes, "*[B]ailo con mi padre que regresó condecorado de Cuba*" (105; "*I am dancing with my father, just back from Cuba [a decorated hero]*" [109]). She buries her nose in his neck and "olió a sexo erizado y velludo de una negra: Capitán Winslow, estoy muy sola y usted puede tomarme cuando guste" (106; "smelled a Negress's swollen, velvety sex: Captain Winslow, I am very lonely, you may have me at your pleasure" [109–10]). Arroyo senses her incestuous desire (which only matches his) and asks cruelly, after she has given herself to him to save the Old Gringo, what she really wants, "¿Tener un padre como el gringo viejo, o ser como su padre con Arroyo?" (116; "To have a father like the old gringo, or to be like her father with Arroyo? [122]). She begs him to unsay what he has just said, for he has uncovered not just her incestuous desire but her gender duplicity: in her dreams and mirrors.

Turmoil seizes Harriet from her dream that afternoon before she can order her conscious self. One of the *soldaderas,* La Garduña, desperately needs Harriet's help to save her asphixiating baby. Harriet is half in, half out of dream, seeing herself as the child. She can only save the baby with her body, with a sympathetic abjection that leads her to suck the phlegm out of the child: "mi cuerpo dijo Harriet: cuándo bañaré mi cuerpo, cuándo lo podré lavar, vengo cargando mugre y muerte, muerte y sueño" (95; "[m]y body, Harriet thought: when shall I bathe my body, when will I be able to wash, I'm covered with filth and death, death and dream" [98]). Miraculously, the child is saved, born again. Still in a kind of dream state, Harriet thinks of spanking the child, knocking out the phlegm, but then goes on to spank sadistically:

> *Yo sentí un gusto enorme en azotarla. La salvé con cólera. Yo no tuve hijos. Pero a esta niña yo la salvé. Me cuesta descubrir el amor en lo que no me es familiar. Lo concibo y lo protejo como un gran misterio.* (97)

> (*I enjoyed spanking her. My anger saved her. I never had children. But I saved the child. It's difficult for me to find love in what I don't know. I conceive and protect love like a great mystery.* [100])

Then she thinks ahead to when she will tell Arroyo, "Yo no tendré hijos" (97; "I will never have children" [100]).

The dream-memory of the armpit and crotch smell and sperm and vaginal juices of her father and his mistress and now the near-dream experience of the child and the phlegm and the muck and the mire and the spanking and the accompanying sadistic pleasure and secret hatred of children—all represent the abject, as Kristeva describes it, and it is related to what Freud called the reality principle. It is what she can experience only through the body, as in her scream of passion, of glory at orgasm:

> [S]e vino con un gemido intolerable, un gran gemido animal que no hubiese tolerado en nadie más, un suspiro pecaminoso de placer que desafiaba a Dios, [. . .] un grito de amor que le anunció al mundo que esto era lo único que valía la pena hacer, tener, saber, nada más en este mundo, nada sino este instante entre el otro instante que nos dio vida y el instante final que nos la quitó para siempre: entre ambos momentos, déjame sólo este momento, rogó[.] (185)

(She came with an unbearable groan, a great animal moan she would have tolerated in no one, a sinful sigh of pleasure that was God-defying, [. . .] a scream of love that told the world that this was the only thing worth doing, worth having, worth knowing, nothing else in the world, nothing else but this instant between that other instant that gave us birth and that final instant that took our life away forever. Between these two moments, let me have only this moment, she prayed[.] [196])

She prays, but pro forma. For the glory she has experienced gains its great value because it is God-defying: it defies organized religion, metaphysics. It recognizes that behind the masks of heroism and glory, "cuando al cabo ambas se desenmascaraban y mostraban sus verdaderas facciones," there is only "la muerte" (170; "when [. . .] both were finally unmasked to show their true features: those of death" [180]). In the bodies of the dead soldiers, eaten by pigs, she sees Mantegna's Christ, a vision of clotted snot and matted blood and hair that showed "que la muerte no era noble sino baja, no serena sino convulsiva, no prometedora sino irrevocable e irredenta" (181; "that death was not noble but base, not serene but convulsive, not promising but irrevocable, unredeemable" [191–92]). It is the vision of Arroyo's father's bones Harriet asks him about:

¿Tú sabes cuánto tiempo toma para que [. . .] la esencia absoluta de nuestra eternidad sobre la tierra aparezca, Arroyo, cuánto tiempo, sobre todo, para que toleremos la visión no sólo de lo que hemos de ser sino de la eternidad en la tierra como es de verdad, sin cuentos de hadas, sin fe en el espíritu o esperanza de resurrección? (179)

(How long, do you know, does it take [. . .] for the sheer essence of our eternity on earth to appear, Arroyo, how long, above all, for us to tolerate the sight not only of what we shall be but of eternity on earth as it truly is, without fairy tales, without faith in the spirit or acceptance of the resurrection? [189])

What Harriet discovers through the abject component of the body, of love, of existence, then, is the oxymoron of existential metaphysics, the metaphysics of the desert:

Se encontraba en el desierto mexicano, hermano del Sáhara y del Gobi, continuación del Arizona y el Yuma, espejos del

cinturón de esplendores estériles que ciñe al globo como para
recordarle que las arenas frías, los cielos ardientes y la belleza
yerma, esperan alertas y pacientes para volver a apoderarse de
la Tierra desde su vientre mismo: el desierto. (22)

(He was deep in the Mexican desert, sister to the Sahara and the
Gobi, continuation of the Arizona and Yuma deserts, mirror of
the belt of sterile splendors girdling the globe as if to remind it
that cold sands, burning skies, and barren beauty wait patiently
and alertly to again overcome the earth from its very womb: the
desert. [15])

The desert: the ultimate abject underlying all other metaphysics. Harriet's
primal scream at the glorious, excruciating moment of *la petite mort* gains
its great value through its bodily, material link with death itself.

The novel begins and ends with the repeated statement that Harriet
would never forgive Arroyo for showing her what she could be, knowing
she would never become it, she would return home. At first we may think
the novel means that Harriet could never surrender her Protestant, puritan
self to the eroticism of La Luna, of a Mexican woman. But perhaps what
Arroyo's love and sex with Harriet have revealed is just this existential
metaphysics of nothingness beyond birth, death, the glory of passion that
cannot abide.

So why does Harriet kill Arroyo? The Old Gringo senses she has
changed forever after sex with Arroyo, after her moment of terrific orgasm:
"su hija cambió entre los brazos y entre las piernas de su hijo" (141; "his
daughter changed in the arms and between the legs of his son" [147]). He
recognizes that she contains her own fire within. So if she is changed and
fulfilled, why kill Arroyo? She does not actually pull the trigger, but she
knew the consequences when she complained to the U.S. authorities: "cuando
reclamó el cuerpo del gringo viejo a sabiendas de las consecuencias" (170;
"when she demanded the old gringo's body, knowing what the consequences
would be" [180]). She reminisces that willing his death was her only lapse
in compassion. So why?

At one point the narrator says Harriet will never forgive Arroyo because he made her admit she liked their love-making. The Old Gringo thinks
that, because she has said that Arroyo had no right to her body and that she
will make him pay, "Harriet no admitía testigos vivientes de su sensualidad
y que ella le daba al viejo el derecho de soñar con ella, pero no a Arroyo"
(142; "Harriet would [did] not allow a living testimony to her sensuality,

that she was giving the old man the right to dream about her, but not Arroyo" [149]). But he may have it wrong, for he himself was not a witness to their intimacies. After their second love-making, apparently after her cataclysmic orgasm, Fuentes describes the fire in her that lay smoldering, that was her fire, not Arroyo's, rooted in her American experience. Strangely, she pictures Arroyo in stereotypes she shared with her mother of bullfighters, opera singers with macho arrogance, an arrogance she now attacks by taking his tumescent penis in her mouth and turning the tables on him, as if she were penetrating him, could bite him off. It is an image of the desire for control, for power over him as he had had power over her. But he refuses to submit to her power, refuses to come in her mouth, and she curses him:

> [M]aldito negándose a fruncirse y declararse vencido, negándose a admitir que en la boca de la mujer él era el cautivo de la mujer, pero otra vez haciéndola sentir que antes sabría estrangularla, antes de venirse y encogerse y dejarla a ella saborear su victoria. (133)

> ([D]amn him, refusing to shrink and be beaten, refusing to acknowledge that in her mouth [in the mouth of the woman] he was her captive [the captive of the woman], but again making her feel that she would throttle first [he could strangle her] before he ever came and shrank and let her savor victory. [139])

Because she cannot subdue him, at least coequally sharing dominance, she spits him out with a guttural sound

> mientras ella gritaba ¿qué te pasa, qué te hace ser como eres, chingada verga prieta, qué te hace negarle a una mujer un momento tan terrible y poderoso como el que antes tomaste para ti? (133)

> (as she screamed what is it with you, what makes you what you are, you damned brown prick, what makes you refuse a woman a moment as free [terrifying] and powerful as the one you took before? [139])

It is this radical denial of her subjectivity, this perpetuation of her as object that Harriet cannot abide: "Y por esto Harriet Winslow nunca perdonó a Tomás Arroyo" (133; "And, for this, Harriet Winslow never forgave him"

[139]). Because he gave her an image of the subjective being she could be and then denied it her.

Furthermore, Arroyo compounded his crime: he killed the site of her precious intersubjectivity, the Old Gringo, in whose consciousness the three of them met:

> Arroyo sabía bien el nombre de la persona que reclamaba el cuerpo. La vio en sus sueños mientras arrullaba la cabeza muerta del viejo entre sus manos y lo miraba a él de pie a la salida del carro como si hubiera matado algo que le pertenecía a ella pero también a él, y ahora los dos estaban de nuevo solos, huérfanos, mirándose con odio, incapaces ya de alimentarse el uno al otro a través de una criatura viva y de colmar las ausencias angustiadas que ella sentía en ella y él en él. (165)

> (Arroyo knew full well the name of the person who was claiming the body. He saw her in his dreams, with the old man's blasted head in her arms, looking at Arroyo standing in the door of the railroad car, as if he had killed something that belonged to her, but also to him; and now they were both alone again, orphans, looking at each other with hatred, no longer capable of nourishing each other through a living creature, or of filling the tormented void that she felt in herself and he in him. [174])

Arroyo has orphaned them both—again, for each has been abandoned by a father, forsaken by a mother, if only metaphorically. Arroyo has committed a form of parricide.

Yet if the Old Gringo is right that the last frontier, the one we cross at night, brings us to the realization that we are not all alone, then he and Harriet are not orphaned in solitary confinement. If Harriet can overcome the hatred she struggles with as we witness her reminiscing at the beginning of the novel, it will be through memory, the final "hogar" (124), one to which a person can go "home" (129). Harriet can negotiate this final crossing by generating a

> nueva compasión que, precisamente en virtud de ese pecado, le fue otorgada, ella se la debía a un joven revolucionario mexicano que ofrecía vida y a un viejo escritor norteamericano que buscaba muerte: ellos le dieron existencia suficiente a su cuerpo para

vivir los años por venir, aquí en los Estados Unidos, allá en México, dondequiera[.] (170)

(new compassion granted her precisely by virtue of that sin [of causing Arroyo's death], she owed to a young Mexican revolutionary who offered life and to an old American writer who sought death: they had given her enough life to live for many years, here in the United States, there in Mexico, anywhere at all[.] [180])

The English version misses the fact that this sufficient existence has been granted to Harriet's body ("a su cuerpo"), to her material being.

Through the materiality of her memory, Harriet must try to negotiate the Border, to turn it from the wound, the "cicatriz" Inocencio still sees it as when he delivers Harriet and the coffin carrying the Old Gringo to the Border crossing (175; "scar" [185]). When the American journalist asks her if she doesn't want to see the United States civilize and democratize Mexico, she responds with verve, "No, no, yo quiero aprender a vivir con México, no quiero salvarlo" (177; "No! No! I want to learn to live with Mexico, I don't want to save it" [187]), wanting to say further,

que lo importante era vivir con México a pesar del progreso y la democracia, y que cada uno llevaba adentro su México y sus Estados Unidos, su frontera oscura y sangrante que sólo nos atrevemos a cruzar de noche: eso dijo el gringo viejo. (177)

(that what mattered was to live with Mexico in spite of progress and democracy, that each of us carries his Mexico and his United States within him, a dark and bloody frontier we dare to cross only at night: that's what the old gringo had said. [187])

She tries to yell to Inocencio and Pedrito across the river that she had accomplished Arroyo's desire: to die young and to bequeath to her *"su tiempo, mantenerlo ahora"* (177; *"his time, [in order to] safeguard it for him"* [187]). They did not hear her shout, as the bridge burst into flames (cf. the Old Gringo's initial crossing), "He estado aquí. Esta tierra ya nunca me dejará" (177; "I have been here. This land will always be a part of me [will never leave me]" [187]). She refuses to burn bridges.

All Arroyo wanted the gringos to say when they returned from Mexico was:

—He estado aquí. Esta tierra ya nunca me dejará. Eso es lo
que les pido a los dos. Palabra de honor: es lo único que quiero.
No nos olviden. Pero sobre todo, sean nuestros sin dejar de ser
ustedes, con una chingada. (108)

("I have been here. This land will always be a part of me
now." That's what I ask of them. I swear: it's the only thing I
ask. Don't forget us. But, more than anything, be us and still be
yoursel[ves] . . . and fuck it all [this time I would avoid the
literal and translate, "for chrissake"]. [113])

Be us without ceasing to be yourselves. Now that Bierce and his friends in
San Francisco have toasted the end of Manifest Destiny, it is time to turn to
this "más extraña siendo la más próxima" (176; this "strangest, because it
was the closest" [186]), most dangerous when most forgotten of borders.
The United States has killed its "pieles rojas" (77; "Redskins" [76]); it
seems to be mired eternally in its practice of genocide. Perhaps it could
learn from Mexico how to become a nation "de mitad y mitad" (77; "a half-
breed nation" [76]). These are Bierce's cynical terms; they come from his
former self. But his cynicism may bear hybrid fruit.

The novel virtually opens with the wound between the two sides of
the Border. Yet there is a tableau: an exhumation patrol pauses for a moment with a decayed corpse in their arms, and as they blindly meditate on
the moment, it is as if "los largos tiempos y los vastos espacios de un lado
y otro de la herida [. . .] venían misteriosamente a morir aquí" (16; "the
long spans and vast spaces on both sides of the wound [. . .] both seemed
[mysteriously] to die here" [8]). Both sides of the wound, then, momentarily dissolve their differences, as the patrol feels "la compasión hermana
del acto" (16; "an accompanying compassion [the brotherly compassion of
the act]" [9]). The Old Gringo had said at the beginning, as Harriet and
Arroyo remembered, the worst border is "la frontera de nuestras diferencias
con los demás, de nuestros combates con nosotros mismos" (13; "the frontier of our differences with others, of our battles with ourselves" [5]). Can
these battles be won, these differences negotiated?

The novel closes with Harriet sitting, reminiscing. Not thinking about
how Arroyo did not let her become what she might have been. But thinking
that both Arroyo and the Old Gringo got what they wanted after all, and she
blesses them both: "Ah, viejo. Ah, joven" (187; "Ah, old man. Ah, young
man" [199]). She has finally, successfully negotiated her crossing. She has
achieved a kind of closure by filling the tomb of her missing father (who is

perhaps himself still copulating with his mistress somewhere in the tropics of Cuba) with the corpse of the Old Gringo. And she has filled the gaps in her lack, as Faulkner's Addie Bundren might say, with the Old Gringo's greatest gift to her—not his body, not his *tiempo,* not his consciousness, but his words, the enabling, creating tools of the verbal artist: "Ella quizá sabía que nada es visto hasta que el escritor lo nombra. El lenguaje permite ver. Sin la palabra todos somos ciegos" (140; "Maybe she knew that nothing is seen until the writer names it. Language permits us to see. Without the word, we are all blind" [146]). This "palabra" is not the *logos* of St. John, the *verbum dei.* It is the material creative word of the poet, of Harriet shaping, bringing into being her memories—of Fuentes's "ficción." Nothing, *nada* is seen without it; without it, we are blind to the realities and possibilities of material existence. It can engender meaning, it can negotiate crossings in the very womb of the desert that inevitably will reclaim us all. In this instance, thanks to Fuentes, perhaps we readers can at least momentarily, like the gravediggers in the opening Pietà, achieve that desired state Anzaldúa describes in the second epigraph to this book's introduction: "we are on both shores at once and, at once, see through serpent and eagle eyes." It is a crossing, Fuentes insists, devoutly to be wished.[9]

EPILOGUE

CROSSING INTO FASCISM IN *BISBEE 17*

> They're not talking about Bo. In a month, two
> months, Bo will be part of a roll of copper wire, a
> shell casing, a penny. It's not so terrible. In a little
> while it will be all right.
>
> *Bisbee 17*

On July 12, 1917, the "largest posse in the history of the West," writes
Robert Houston in his fine novel, *Bisbee 17,*[1] about two thousand strong,
rounded up about two thousand mine workers and their sympathizers in
Bisbee, Arizona, herded them into a baseball stadium, weeded out those
who were not hard-core, loaded the remaining twelve hundred or so in
cattle cars and boxcars without food or water, and dropped them in the
sweltering desert of southwestern New Mexico. The miners were members
of the Industrial Workers of the World (IWW), nicknamed Wobblies, and
they had struck the copper mines in Bisbee in coordination with a copper
strike in Butte, Montana, and an attempted general strike of all workers in
America. Hundreds were rousted from their homes in the middle of the
night, their names on a blacklist provided by company surveillance. The
vigilantes were armed with rifles and machine guns, sequestered from the
United States Army in a hospital dispensary, and even "a one-pound can-
non captured from the Villistas" across the border (233). The telegraph
office was seized so no one could send news to the wire services. The roads
were sealed off. Cochise County, Arizona, larger than any state in New
England, had become a police state, headed by Sheriff Harry Wheeler, last
of the two-gun sheriffs of the West, but really controlled by Walter Douglas, copper magnate. The strike was thus broken. The Wobblies were
crippled, their headquarters in Chicago sacked. Criminal charges, for kid-
napping, among other things, were later filed against the company bosses

and the vigilante leaders, but no one was ever convicted. Civil suits were filed, but the companies settled cheaply out of court. The incident was euphemistically called "the Deportation"—that is, of U.S. citizens to another state in violation of basic constitutional rights, like freedom of speech and assembly, protection against unlawful search and seizure, guarantee of due process of law.[2]

In *Bisbee 17* Houston has invented a story to tell against the background of this history. It is the story especially of a young union organizer, Bo Whitley, originally from Bisbee, who has come home to lead the strike. It is about his relations with, among others, his estranged wife, the famous Rebel Girl Wobbly organizer, Elizabeth Gurley Flynn,[3] and one of the company bosses, John Greenway. Bo learns things about himself he would rather not know. Yet he finally consciously chooses to reject Greenway and the secret desirable object he represents and to embrace the freedom Elizabeth represents, even though it costs him his life.

Bo's surprisingly passive relinquishment to his death at the will if not the hands of the sadist Greenway constitutes an acceptance of his role in a tragic pageant. The theory of tragedy behind Bo's death is not so much Greek, though he does suffer from hubris, and not so much Christian, though he allows himself to be sacrificed, as it is existential, wherein Bo's refusal of Greenway and his choice of Elizabeth lead through loss to a paradoxical material transcendence. This is a novel about the end of the classic Southwest, about crossing over into the modern age of fascism, into the kind of us/them dichotomy that produced the Holocaust. After all, the roundup and deportation are collectively called "the cleansing" (232). Yet the fascists could not kill Bo after all.

Bo Whitley is radically ambivalent about his home town. Even though he has come down from Montana to organize the strike in Bisbee, when we first meet him he is thinking, "It's a god-awful town, a detestable place. He could never hate a human being the way he hates Bisbee" (58).[4] His father has died of "miner's consumption" and his mother of cholera (61). He had been back in 1911 to watch his mother die, but "[n]obody in Bisbee cared then that he was home. Bisbee has never given a damn about him. Not yet anyway." He swore he'd never come back, but he heard in Butte about the strike and thought about it all night: "In one way, it's like he's come back to his old man, too. In another, it's like a strike in Bisbee is his own property. Either way, Bisbee owes him something. He'll be thirty on the Fourth of July" (61). Yet Bo is already pessimistic about the strike; he tells Oscar Hamer, another organizer who has accompanied him from Montana (but who is secretly a spy for the companies), "We won't win it. [. . .] I was born here" (62). Especially when he learns that Big Bill Haywood and Mother Jones, figures of huge national prominence in the Wobblies—and in the labor movement generally since before the turn of the century—are coming in to take over, Bo decides to leave on the next ore train out. But he receives a message from "Captain" John Greenway, manager of the Calhumet and Arizona (C&A) mine, that he would like to meet with Bo, only Bo, alone, privately.

Bo now dedicates himself to the strike with the intent of winning, because "things are happening that he never let himself think about before this week. Things between him and Bisbee—and between him and Elizabeth. [. . .] Bo will be somebody in the new setup here . . . in a way the damn scissorbills [workers loyal to the company] and plutes [plutocrats] never guessed he would when he was a kid" (163–64). A prophet is not without honor . . . Bo obviously wants recognition from his home town, especially because he associates "his town" with "his devils" (167). One of those devils is his father, who was not only consumptive but a drunk—and a child molester, his own child. Through another character's narration, we overhear Bo, badly injured in a scuffle with deputies and babbling uncontrollably, reveal his dark secret:

> When his father was drunkest, he'd think he was in bed with Bo's mother. He'd start to whisper to Bo and touch him and . . . do things to him. It was pretty lurid. Now Bo's telling about his father dying of the miner's consumption. He begged Bo to hold him as he was dying. Bo says he couldn't bring himself to touch his father. He ran out of the house and never came back. And the oddest part is that somehow he muddles it all up with Bisbee, as if it were Bisbee's fault. (152)

One of the consequences of this childhood trauma is that Bo cannot abide another man's touch. When Bo left home, he worked odd jobs, including shoveling shit for the mines, and although everyone said he had talent, the talent seemed unrealizable in Bisbee, so he hit the road. The recognition he now seeks from Bisbee constitutes a reckoning with his father—and with the town fathers.

Another of Bo's "devils" is his failed marriage with Elizabeth. It seems to have failed partly because of Bo's inability to escape patriarchalism. Despite their chemistry together and their energy in the labor fights, when Elizabeth got pregnant, Bo wanted her to become a bourgeois wife, to stay home and not go to those free-speech rallies in Washington state. When she went anyway and then got arrested, even though she begged him to come to her, to comfort her, he refused in order to punish her, and she never forgave him. When he came to her home in the Bronx to get her back, she humiliated him in front of her father, saying she didn't love him anymore for he bored her.

So for Bo, winning the strike means besting his old man, breaking the deceased Whitley's hold on Bo from beyond the grave, and regaining his wife and son. He fantasizes, "Why shouldn't he have a shot at being like every other stiff with a front porch to sit on and a wife and kid to give a rat's ass what happened to him?" (164). But Bo has even higher ambitions, some of them unknown to himself. Bo angers Haywood by insisting Bisbee is his "lookout," that he's organizing it (166). He thinks to himself, "'And when Haywood's general strike goes bust, who are they going to have to come asking to hold Bisbee for 'em?' He wants to add: And who is the only one that John Greenway will talk to? Bo Whitley holds the ace, no matter what Haywood thinks. He'll use it too, damn it, if the time comes. And then it will be his decision, with nobody, not even Elizabeth, interfering. [. . .] He left this town once, whipped. He'll not do it again, not as long as he's breathing" (167–68). Bo's ambition is his hubris. It will bring about his fall.

Bo has two other antagonists in the novel, one major, one minor. The minor antagonist is Sheriff Harry Wheeler. More of a proto-yippie than a good organizer (Houston's novel looks at history through lenses ground in the sixties and early seventies), Bo delights in provoking his opponents in the strike. He, his cousin and foster father Jim Brew, the ubiquitous Hamer, and Elizabeth outrageously invade an engagement party at the center of plute culture, the Bisbee Country Club. Bo and Jim take quite a beating, and Jim—loveable, loyal, but a bit slow on the uptake—wants vengeance. So on the early morning of the Fourth of July, covered by dynamite explosions set to begin the turning of Sacramento Hill inside out into the largest open-pit mine in the world, Jim firebombs the country club, unwittingly catching a deputy and a scullery maid inside. When Bo watches the look on Wheeler's face as he is told the news, he miscalculates that all he needs to do is push him a little further and he will overreact, giving the strike renewed momentum through solidarity and needed publicity. Bo, who has spotted Wheeler slipping into his whore's crib up on the Line, supplants him in bed, not with himself, but with Art Matthews, son of the purchasing agent for Phelps-Dodge and therefore the son of a plute, the class with which Wheeler increasingly allies in the course of the novel on account of their embodiment of authority and discipline. Because he is himself attracted to Elizabeth and therefore to her cause and because he is also an admirer of Bo Whitley's athletic prowess as a youth, Art is caught slumming with the Wobs and thus provides the perfect dupe—Bo thinks the perfect target. But instead of shooting Art, whom he finds naked with his whore, Wheeler responds with controlled hatred. Hating Bo and by extension his "people," the Wobblies, as less than "human beings" (184), Wheeler cloaks himself in plute rhetoric that the strikers are un-American, guilty of "treason" (188).

Ironically, Wheeler is himself duped. He has been manipulated into deputizing a private army of vigilantes, placed to hand by the company bosses. The bosses don't want the real army, for it might protect constitutional rights. Of course, they can't say that in public, so they cloak their purposes in racist rhetoric. The closest soldiers are at Fort Huachuca. Greenway asks Wheeler, "And what kind of soldiers are they? Buffalo soldiers. Can you conceive the terrible blowup we would have on our hands if the government decided to send in buffalo soldiers to run Bisbee, Harry? Niggers, Harry. Will you turn the town over to the darkies to save it from the Wobblies?" (101). Greenway's racism has its roots in his father's Confederate past. But its acceptability to Harry and the other plutes reveals racism that transcends the South and seeps outward to include Germans, Jews, Russians, Bohunks—"foreigners" (passim). With his army behind him, Wheeler outlaws assemblies of Wobblies. The bosses order the workers back to work or they will lose not only their jobs but their pensions. Bo has merely succeeded in pushing Wheeler into the companies' traces. He has lost the Wobblies their strike; he has apparently lost Bisbee after all.

Thus Bo plays his trump card. He accepts Greenway's invitation and goes for a parley one-on-one. Greenway is Bo's major antagonist. He is called "Captain" for his days in the Rough Riders as "right hand" to Teddy Roosevelt (25), with whom he is in constant contact and who, according to Greenway and Douglas, deplores the strike. But "captain" is symbolically appropriate on several counts: Greenway was a sports captain, "just about the biggest football star Yale ever had" (25). More important, he is what Thomas Carlyle would call a *Captain of Industry.* Carlyle is one of Greenway's favorite authors, along with Nietzsche, both of whom he appears to be consulting during the strike. Carlyle's "book [. . .] about heroes" lies open on his study desk: "Captain Greenway has been reading a section of the book about natural leaders and the rights of men who are destined to rule. [. . .] The other book is by a German. [. . .] The German's name is Nietzsche"(93). One of the major theses of Carlyle's *On Heroes, Hero-Worship, and the Heroic in History* (1841), further developed in *Past and Present* (1843), is a theory of natural aristocracy, which produces leaders, heroes, whom other men need to and will follow and obey as superior, braver, wiser. He deplores mobs, anarchy, democracy. His figure for the leader is the man on horseback, who wields a beneficent whip—like Captain Greenway.

Carlyle's writings have an anti-Semitic strain, as do those of Friedrich Nietzsche, whose *Beyond Good and Evil* (1886) and *On the Genealogy of Morals* (1887) inveighed against Judeo-Christianity as an ethic of weakness in contrast to the ethos of *virtù,* where virtue is what the strong men (the gender bias is built into the etymological root of the word from Latin *vir* so that it means literally *manliness*) say it is, those heroes who by right of strength and superior qualities have the right to rule. Greenway cleverly incorporates these theories into a patriotic, Christian rhetoric, worth quoting at length so we feel the power and horror of it:

> What's involved [. . .] is Christian civilization. [. . .] Wobblies are the advance guard of the Antichrist. [. . .] Now you've seen the IWW posters, I reckon, just like I have. No God, No Master, says one of them. Now what's that if not a proclamation? Make an earthly paradise, they say. Not godly, but earthly.
>
> They're the signs of this damnable century. No God, no master! Horseshit. People have always had a God and a master. Without them, there can't be any civilization. [. . .]
>
> The men who *can,* who *know,* who are *able* to rule, are the ones who, in nature, must. Without them, there is chaos. Without them there would be no arts, no progress, no "peaceful discourse," as the saying goes. They are the men who are entitled to their reward for providing work for those who can't provide it for themselves. They are above the normal restrictions of men, but bound by even higher laws. They are us, boys. Like it or not, it's our duty.
>
> Now this IWW outfit. Who the hell are they? Drifters who don't vote. Slackers who refuse to fight for their Christian, enlightened government. People who have no families, no backgrounds, no talents, and no respect for those who do. People who recognize no authority, no goal beyond this jackleg idea of an earthly paradise. They hook up with immigrants who have none of our traditions, our language. And whose interest do they serve? Ours, or a nation's we're at war with? Their aim is to shrink the soul of man, and to replace it with one mass soul with no face.

> They're enemies, gentlemen, enemies. Plagues, blots, things
> to be exterminated—a cancer to be cut out before it consumes
> the body. It isn't too much to say that we are engaged, whether
> we like it or not, in a kind of holy war. (97–98)

This is not just the rhetoric of capitalist ideology—the leaders who are inherently superior and who provide the jobs—but it is an antidemocratic rhetoric ("People who have no families, no backgrounds, no talents, and no respect for those who do. People who recognize no authority"). The aristocrats provide the "arts," the "progress," the peaceful, enlightened discourse of civilization. The hoi polloi want to "shrink the soul of man"—read *real men*—and replace it with "one mass soul"—that is, the faceless, teeming multitudes, who should suffer and accept the march of social Darwinist history. This is also and more profoundly the rhetoric of incipient twentieth-century fascism: reducing humans to "things to be exterminated—a cancer to be cut out before it consumes the body." From the perspective of the late twentieth century, we know, unfortunately, where this rhetoric leads. Ironically, it is Greenway who appropriates the word "holocaust" to refer to the potential destruction wreaked by not his storm troopers and their machine guns but the workers and their picket signs—or at worst, like Bo's, their brass knuckles (100). Though he appropriates the language of the religious Apocalypse, Greenway views the battle in Bisbee, in the Wild West of Arizona, as the last chance for the secular heroes, the rugged individualist leaders, the captains of industry: "The world is shrinking [. . .] . This is the last place a man can breathe. Now they want to suffocate me here, too. I've been waiting for them" (108). This nameless threat is the weak, the meek who have been wrongly told they shall inherit the earth. What they need is a good cleansing.

At the crucial moment in his interaction with Bo, however, for some strange reason Greenway abandons the rhetoric of Victorian bourgeois ideology. Greenway desperately wants two things: a woman he can't have and the son she can't give him. In the vivacious, willful Bo, Greenway sees that son: "Whitley will come to me [. . .] . He will [. . .] . He's too good for that crowd. I've watched him. I could make something out of him. [. . .] I've never had a son [. . .] . I'd like a son. It's good for a house to have young men in it" (107–8). When Bo comes to see him, Greenway dismisses Bo's attempt at negotiation, because they both know you can't negotiate from a position of weakness. Instead, Greenway offers Bo a chance to be his "son"—whatever name they might choose to publicly explain their relationship (230). Greenway leads up to his offer by arguing that he's a Wobbly only because that's the best game in town for someone of his class, that he's a "born leader" (229). Sensing a vulnerability, Bo says, "Reckon you'd rather I be you, Cap'n," and that gives Greenway his entrée:

> You can't be me. You can't acquire blood and breeding any more than you can acquire red hair. [. . .] What you can do is be yourself and take what help is offered you. You don't have the instincts for selfless fanaticism, you know. That Flynn woman does. And that's why you haven't a chance with her. No, you can't be me, but you can be my great-grandfather. You can be a founder, Whitley. You can be the first step to something. That's what endures in this country. Generations. That's the future a sane man builds for, not the nonsense of a world in which people go against every trace of human nature and create bleak "earthly paradises." (229–30)

What bothers Bo is not so much Greenway's offer but his susceptibility to it. He realizes he has been breaking his neck "to prove something to this man, and those like him" (231). To prove what? That Bo is worthy to share power: "He's let himself be flattered into believing that he was important. He's believed in Greenway's power, believed that this thing he came back to Bisbee to take for himself was worth fighting for" (231). But now Bo realizes that Greenway wants to patronize him, to groom him. After all, Greenway opened their conversation by commenting on Bo's grammar: "We'll have to work on that" (226). What's worse, Bo realizes his own vulnerability to Greenway's Carlylean argument: "He wondered if Greenway knew something about him that he'd never admitted even to himself. All that talk about generations——for a moment while Greenway was talking it seemed so damn reasonable. He saw himself in a wool suit and patent-leather shoes and celluloid collar, imagined his portrait on some future grandkid's wall in a gold frame. Like that was, after all, what he figured Bisbee owed him" (255). Just as he wanted Elizabeth to be a bourgeois housewife, so also his real dream is to be not just a stiff homeowner but part of the power structure, a bourgeois, maybe even a captain of industry. That would show his father's ghost and Bisbee!

What causes Bo to strike Greenway, however, is not conscious anger at his insight into Bo's bad faith. It is that Greenway touches him. And that touch is not simply the male touch he has abhorred before from Hamer or Art Matthews. It is his father's touch: "Greenway slides his chair closer to Bo, first touches his shoulder, then runs his hand up his neck to his cheek.

'I'm offering much more than I'm asking, Whitley'" (230). Houston has inserted references to Greenway's strange smile throughout the novel. That smile has often been cast at Bo. We put the smile together with Greenway's bachelorhood, his desire to have "young men" around the house, his sadistic streak, his homosocial identification with the real men of the Rough Riders and the Captains of Industry, and we arrive at the interpretation that Greenway is gay. Of all people, because of his father's molestation of him, Bo would gay-bash.

Surprisingly, Greenway gives Bo one more chance to take his offer. Bo responds that he pities him, and Greenway's rhetoric turns strange: "Don't be so damn sanctimonious. I suppose I was wrong about you—you are acting just like that priggy bunch you associate with" (257). In other words, if Bo pities him for his secret, he is being self-righteous, a characteristic Greenway associates with Wobbly, leftist ideology. Bo, no match for Greenway's sophistication, cockily asserts that there might be lots of things Greenway's wrong about. Greenway's response is not that of the confident Carlyle or Nietzsche: "Oh, my God. Maybe I am wrong about everything—even everything I believe. Does that matter so much? Right and wrong are so bloody imprecise, Whitley. That's what drives me mad about you people. Not a one of you will ever be anything but a petty Puritan" (257).

In short, Greenway's ideological rhetoric masks his eros. Freud or Marcuse might argue that up to now Greenway's eros has been sublimated onto the building of an orderly civilization. In a moment when desire breaks through his normal restraint, Greenway reveals his own passion, a revelation that makes him vulnerable. Since hell hath no fury like a lover scorned, Greenway will not just break the power of the Wobblies. He will annihilate the man who scorned him.

Bo scorns—and pities—Greenway not just because of his homoerotic advances. A picture of his unattainable woman Greenway hangs "so that Captain Greenway looks into the woman's eyes whenever he is sitting at his writing desk" (95). When Bo sees the picture, he virtually "shudders at the blankness in the woman's eyes" (230). That blankness greatly affects Bo's response to Greenway:

> Greenway is as twisted by this place as Bo's old man was. He's pitiful, empty, nailed down by the blankness in that woman's eyes and all it stands for.
>
> Great God! There has to be more worth fighting for than that blankness! He thinks of Elizabeth's warmth against the cool

leaves on the mountain. Then his eyes move back to the face of
the woman in the portrait. Is that what Greenway can offer him?
He feels violently duped, defrauded. (231)

The blankness is associated with the ideal bourgeois woman, whom
Greenway describes as "everything woman ought to be. It's not to be
touched, but not to be lived without. It's the thing a man gives to his children, the kind of mother he creates" (230). Victorian woman, never to be
touched, deprived of passion, conduit for the transmission of power and
property, enforcer of the culture's values and of the ruling class's status. An
Anglo version of Mama Elena. Elizabeth's contrasting "warmth against
the cool leaves on the mountain" (231) refers to her naked body as she and
Bo make love amid the leaves he has strewn for her on the floor of a shed.
Her energy, her spontaneity, her joie de vivre, her uninhibited sexual passion are what Bo wants, not the sterility of the ruling class. And when
deported, he returns for it.

Bo romantically believes that the contest is now just between him and
Bisbee, him and Greenway, him and Elizabeth. But what he wants from
Bisbee, in Bisbee is not now status but merely Elizabeth and their life together. By choosing her, standing with her hand-in-hand, he completes the
rejection of Greenway and his offer. He lays all his "devils" to rest and can
live in peace. None of this is spoken. We infer it. But Bo is still no match
for sophisticated evil. Greenway has arranged every step of his return. He
arrives to rescue Elizabeth, and the spy Hamer awaits him. Bo has a knife,
but he does not use it. He relinquishes to the following feeling, which re-
curs throughout the denouement: "Somehow—again like a dream—he
knows he's supposed to be here. That this is supposed to be happening.
And that it will be all right" (278). Set up before a firing squad of Texas hit
men on a platform by the new ore crusher, Bo accepts his fate, his role:
"He's doing what he's supposed to do. What he came home to do. There's
nothing to fight, to settle, anymore" (281).

Does Bo's resignation constitute a ritual, redemptive sacrifice? Perhaps, but if so, in a strange way. Exiled from his peers, he dies alone. But
his death is not cloaked in religious rhetoric. The sense of fate is, as Houston phrased it to me in private conversation, "more archetypal."[5] That is, as
I interpret it, secular, less in Northrop Frye's sense of seasonal death and
renewal than in the root sense of secular. For Bo's rebirth and its effect will
occur only over time, perhaps centuries. As he is being hauled to the ore
crusher, Bo thinks of his assassins: "Who are these sons of bitches? Who
was Hamer? Does it matter? Does it matter who *he* is? He could be the

Mex or Bohunk or nigger that he looks like [in his disguise] and the bastards would still have to do this. Through the pain, the sense that something will be all right remains. He's glad Elizabeth isn't there. He's glad she doesn't know he fucked up again" (280–81). What is important to Bo is no longer his (bourgeois) individual triumph. This surrender of self plays out in a remarkable denouement. As his assassins quarrel among themselves how to finish this disagreeable task, the narrator takes us one last time into his head: "They're not talking about Bo. In a month, two months, Bo will be part of a roll of copper wire, a shell casing, a penny. It's not so terrible. In a little while it will be all right" (282). Bo's transcendence is material. He will be part of the most common coinage, in everybody's pocket. Like the germ of an idea. Not Bill Haywood's Marxist utopia of lunch-pail symphonies, but the thing the strikebreakers can never kill: collective resistance to capitalist exploitation. Captain Greenway may hide in those "scrub woods" at the end (282), furtively watching the execution of his estranged "son." The IWW may be crippled, and fascism will triumph with a vengeance in Italy, in Spain, in Germany, in Russia, and almost in J. Edgar Hoover and Joe McCarthy's and Richard Nixon's and Al Haig's and Oliver North's America. But as Haywood prepares for his last speech, knowing he will be arrested soon, the narrator addresses him: "And there are arrest warrants out. Not just for you but for everyone, the whole leadership, hundreds of you. There is a face behind that, too, a face you couldn't stop for before. It has tracked you from Bisbee, has multiplied a hundred thousand times, waits for you in every city" (284). Tragically, more trains than those in Bisbee await the suffering masses. And Harry Wheeler thinks he has won, has by his actions taught the world how to deal with restive resistance. Wheeler thinks he "proved that the West was alive" (286). But the only West still alive is Bill Cody's, and Wheeler's last performance is as a buffoon before the king of England. For paradoxically, the masses, represented in the novel by a union whose leadership was collective, await the new Bill Haywoods and Mother Joneses and Elizabeth Gurley Flynns to rally them.

The danger Elizabeth feels momentarily is that the spirit of resistance is "[g]one from herself, maybe from the world" (272). So desperately she hurls herself into "the future," for she understands the new stakes: "There's been a terrible and new kind of violence let loose here. It doesn't have to do with just bosses and strikebreakers anymore, but with new words, and with the workingpeople themselves. The old words, the old dream, failed here. Harry Wheeler's guns didn't" (272–73). The dream failed because even working stiffs turned on one another: "Come on, [. . .] Shoot your brothers!" shouts one worker in defiance of the vigilantes (250). The AF of L turned against the Wobblies. In the 1970s the Teamsters would turn against the United Farm Workers. What is worse, U.S. Army troops would burn out protestors in the Bonns Army Protest in 1932; National Guard troops would turn their guns against antiwar demonstrators at Kent State University who knew that the Vietnam War was fought for colonial economics. So it will take Elizabeth time. Time to rebuild grass-roots movements, and time especially to stitch together words that can countervail the Christian patriotic rhetoric: "Things that will take root, build, hold, until they're stronger than Harry Wheeler's guns" (273).

The novel does not end on this slightly upbeat note, however, and the reader might dismiss Elizabeth as a dreamy-eyed Major Barbara. Jim Brew, confused by the happenings on that fatal predawn morning of July 12, 1917, thinks the strike forced him to be somebody he's not, and he generalizes: "That's maybe the worst of this strike. Everybody is something they're not. [. . .] Nobody is who he is anymore" (237, 242). Caught up in the collective paranoia the novel opens with, characters relinquish themselves to the roles they seem to be asked to play: Wheeler to the role presented him by Walter Douglas that causes him once again signally in his life to turn his back on a community (the way he did the Apaches when he followed orders and dismissed the party come to dance for him as he went to war); Greenway to the role presented him by Carlyle (as he prods Bo with a rifle from his white mare, telling him not to count his "people"—his class—out yet [259]); Haywood to the role he thinks presented him by history but which will end in exile in Moscow; Elizabeth to the role bequeathed her by Mother Jones as the seamstress of the new radical garment. Losing oneself in such roles can be dangerous because their ideologies can be dehumanizing, even Elizabeth's if it slips into self-righteousness and the potential totalitarianism of those Bolsheviks about to come to power.

In contrast to such identity surrendering role playing, Houston presents us with an interesting minor character in the novel, Lem Shattuck, the independent mine owner who has worked his way up into it through gambling (much as the Earps obtained mine properties in Tombstone). Shattuck believes in neither the "fairy tales" of the Right nor those of the Left (195). He wonders sagely whose "fairy tales" project fleets of airplanes saturating Germany with bombs, understanding that creative imagination is not the sole prerogative of Elizabeth and the Left, that the Right can and will respond with technology, as George Bernard Shaw's munitions magnate Undershaft knew at the turn of the century only too well. Shattuck is married to a German woman, and one of his sons has fled to Mexico to avoid the draft that might force him to fight against his mother's—his own—people. In the frightening blacklist published in the *Bisbee Review* the morning of the roundup, both Shattuck's sons are listed, "called sympathizers with the IWW and the 'Prussian engine of war'" (235). For Shattuck has refused to be railroaded into an extremist position. In the new rhetoric of us and them, that particular position of non-identity turns out to be risky. But in the world of the novel, admirable.

Bo's position of non-identity seems admirable, too. For it transcends ideological rigidity and connects the suffering victim of tragedy with the material world. Not the fertile world Tita and Pedro bequeath, but the world of shell casings—like those from the machine guns turned on strikers and their wives and children in Colorado by hired guns of the Rockefellers (87). The world of cattle-cars transporting humans packed like standing sardines and knee-deep in shit and without water to their final destination, the final solution. The world of mounted police ready to bust rallies and bust heads. But also the world of Mother Jones's cane and ready wit and indomitable spirit. The world of coppers that can barely buy bread but, amassed slowly, painstakingly, person by person, city by city, might eventually, Houston's fine novel seems to say, buy freedom from exploitation. Because you may kill individuals but you can't kill an idea born from that material reality. Not even with Harry Wheeler's guns.

Bisbee 17 seems an appropriate place to end this study because 1917 marks the end of the early Southwest in the borderlands. Like the Wild Bunch and the Wyatt Earps and the Miles Calendars and the Geronimos, the Harry Wheelers are now anachronisms, appropriate to Wild West Shows but not to the West itself. The *villistas* are defeated, the Apaches long defeated, the Winchester '73 and the Colt 45 superseded by the machine gun, the horse by the car, the car nearly by the plane. Not that there are not great mavericks in film and fiction set on this border in later years: the protagonists of *The Salt of the Earth, Lone Star,* McCarthy's trilogy spring to mind. But the Southwest as wilderness seems now conquered and in some sense diminished.

One is tempted to draw sweeping generalizations about these dozen and a half works. But I cite again Castronovo's caveat:

> Telling this story demands an ambivalent narrative, one that refuses a clear teleological narrative line in favor of a series of competing tales that compromise and undercut one another. Single stories cannot be told because stories do not exist in some sort of fixed isolation, but are instead always bordered by some

other story. In their several overlaps, they describe a culture criss-crossed by defeats that are ultimately as temporary as the victories to such an extent that perhaps the only certain thing that can be said about national-border culture is that it is experienced across spaces of continuing struggle. (216)

But perhaps my own story will interact profitably with others. The stories I have written about themselves border each other and overlap, describing a crisscrossed culture. Let it suffice to say that works like these that place their protagonists on the border do so because the artists want to portray crises of identity, ideology, *conscience* in the rich French sense of more than conscience but consciousness itself. The vast spaces, the sparseness, the harshness, the paradoxical beauty of the place alone prompt such crises without the conflicts that have raged here. Yet those conflicts have raged. They have been cultural, great clashes of alien peoples contending over the land and its immense resources.

Perhaps it is just because I love this land, am awed by it, am dwarfed by it that I am attracted to crises and conflicts situated from the swampy, eerie Big Woods of Mississippi to the parched plains of Texas and New Mexico to the unforgiving dunes of the Mojave to the cataclysmic canyons and sierras of the mountains, those "islands in the sky" as we call them in southern Arizona. The land seems to cry out for and with stories about desperate attempts to negotiate crossings from old identity to new identity, from old culture to new culture, from Old West to New West. Sometimes the movements are lateral, a feeling of solidarity between one oppressed group and another in the face of one dominant culture or another imposing its will, its supposed destiny, its hegemony on another. These works are as often about failed as successful crossings, about achieved as dashed hopes. But hopes seems a key word. Hope springs eternal. We neglect the second line: "Man never is, but always to be blest." Becoming is incomplete. It seems to need conflict, resistance to nurture it. It is, as so many of these artists imply, generational, yet *to be*—with a real possibility that we may destroy each other, the wilderness, the planet before we get there. Old Ben's paw, the scattered bones of Tiguas and Apaches, Demetrio's skeleton at the bottom of that cathedral-like canyon, Bo's pennies may just be archeological curiosities to some future intergalactic Columbuses landing on our world.

In the meantime, however, these works may help us to recognize what Fuentes calls "la frontera de nuestras diferencias con los demás, de nuestros combates con nosotros mismos" (13; "the frontier of our differences with others, of our battles with ourselves" [5]). According to Fuentes, this is the most difficult frontier to cross, because we realize we are not alone but interimplicated with others whose differences we have all too often hypostatized into radical Otherness, which we fear and, because we fear, must dominate. These works force us to confront aspects of our cultural history and identity we as Americans, perhaps North Americans, must confront: our rapacity, racism, machoism (sexism) in our dealing with this land and its peoples. They also present us with admirable acts of choice, as we continue to define ourselves for worse or for better against a backdrop that threatens void but promises the sublime, climbable peaks of possibility. If that is the mere rhetoric of desire, so be it. I for one prefer the daisy and the dance. If we cannot, like Ike McCaslin or Tomás Arroyo, restore original rights, we can at least respect human rights at the crossroads.

NOTES

INTRODUCTION

1. Montserrat Fontes, telephone conversation with author, 21 January 1999.

2. Examples of historical fiction and film that do not fit thematically, that is, as existential crossings: *Ramona,* by Helen Hunt Jackson; *Apache,* by Will Comfort; the important Chicano film *The Ballad of Gregorio Cortez;* the well-written recent novels *The Pistoleer* (i.e., John Wesley Hardin) and *The Friends of Pancho Villa,* by Mexicano/Chicano author James Carlos Blake; *Gardens of the Dunes,* by my old colleague and friend Leslie Silko. Keith Anderson, my graduate student in comparative cultural and literary studies, thinks Gregorio Cortez makes an existential decision *not* to escape into Mexico even though he has reached the Rio Grande, for he self-identifies finally not as a Mexican but as a Mexican-American and surrenders in the cabin of a fellow Mexican-American so he will get the reward. Nevertheless, faithful to the *corrido* tradition, the film is far less about Cortez's consciousness than about (raising) cultural consciousness: Cortez is a figure whose resistance moves from active to passive, as the film becomes a court melodrama. See R. Saldívar, who extrapolates from Américo Paredes's classic study of the *corrido* in general and of this *corrido* in particular the lesson, "Mexican communities on the United States side of the border will find neither aid from nor refuge in Porfirio Díaz's Mexico but must instead fend for themselves" (29); "the private sphere of interior consciousness has not yet become the concern of the balladeer; the private quality of life has not yet coalesced into a central, independent identity that is distinct from the identity of the community. Life is one and it is 'historicized' to the extent that all existential factors are not merely aspects of a personal life but are a common affair" (37).

3. See especially Michaelson and Johnson's recent collection, *Border Theory:* their introduction and the contributions of Alejandro Lugo and Russ Castronovo.

1. IKE McCASLIN'S FAILED CROSSING

1. Readers who care to see the relationship of this essay when first published to previous scholarship may do so by consulting the original. Writing at virtually the same time as I, Matthews reads *Go Down, Moses* quite similarly, that is, employing poststructuralist strategies, his more Derridean, perhaps, mine more Lacanian. Barker, my former student, has extended my and Matthews's poststructuralist readings, adding a Nietzschean twist.

2. For the importance of the word "home" and all its connotations as some-

thing devoutly to be wished, see Faulkner's "Address to the Graduating Class Pine Manor Junior College," Wellesley, Massachusetts, June 8, 1953, in *Essays, Speeches & Public Letters by William Faulkner* 135–42.

3. May 9, 1942, reprinted in Utley et al., *Bear, Man, and God* 149–64.

4. Elsewhere Faulkner uses this image of urn or vessel in ways that may elucidate his use in *Go Down, Moses:* his poem to Meta Carpenter; poem X of *A Green Bough;* Horace's vase (significantly named Narcissa) in *Flags in the Dust;* Joe Christmas's attempt to deal with his girl, Bobbie Allen's periods, and Gail Hightower's dreams of perfection in *Light in August;* the image of Lena Grove's progress in the same novel; Addie Bundren's extraordinary image for both her womb and Anse in *As I Lay Dying;* Lucas Beauchamp's image for possibility in the other major story in *Go Down, Moses,* "The Fire and the Hearth"; Faulkner's image for his attempt to make the perfect vase out of *The Sound and the Fury.* For an analysis of these images, see my "Faulkner's Grecian Urn and Ike McCaslin's Empty Legacies."

5. See Early, *The Making of Go Down, Moses* 13. See also Glissant, *Faulkner, Mississippi* 76–77 for a recent, intelligent treatment of Sam's paternity against the background of the quest for legitimacy that is at the heart of Western tragedy.

6. Page 160. It is worth noting that in "A Justice" Sam's mother was not sold (to Quentin's great-grandfather, not Ike's grandfather) until he was a grown warrior and could himself have stayed by dispensation of Ikkemotubbe (*Portable Faulkner* 28–29).

7. See Glissant passim, but especially chapters 3 and 6.

2. TRAGIC GLORY

1. For a reading of Clark's other novels, which establish another context for *A Bright Tragic Thing,* see my "Tragic Glory."

3. THE BORDER OF BECOMING

1. Pughe 379. In fairness to Pughe, whose article I admire, I should note that a couple of pages later he writes: "[T]he notion of 'progress' is just a Eurocentric obfuscation of the 'law' of the more powerful and ruthless" (381). I shall return to this Nietzschean notion later.

2. The best treatment to date of the quest for meaning amid a dark metaphysic is Bell's chapter on *Blood Meridian,* "The Metaphysics of Violence."

3. Wallach writes, "The kid's double negative and the judge's portentous reply evoke both the Augustinian double bind of western theodicy, and the ubiquitous aporia uncovered by deconstructive readings" (134). Wallach's own reading pursues more the latter than the former interpretive possibilities.

4. For the abject, see Kristeva. For grace in the abject, see Joyce, T.S. Eliot, Graham Greene, John Logan, and others. Interpreting the judge's collecting impulse in the light of Harold Bloom's theory of an American religion centered in the Emersonian self, Parrish writes, "To maim, rape, kill, is, in effect, to feel God's dirt and blood beneath his fingernails" (35).

4. BROKEN ARROW

1. Quotations directly from the film are punctuated as in the script—if they are there—but given no citation. The lack of citation, then, signals that the dialogue is the final, film dialogue.

2. The existential dimension of the film is added to the original novel, Arnold's *Blood Brother*. The entire drama of Jeffords's learning Apache and seeking out Cochise is based on an uncorroborated account given by Jeffords in 1913 to one Robert Forbes. In his definitive biography of Cochise, Sweeney doubts anything like it ever happened. Jeffords, who already knew Cochise, was once hired to find him in his Stronghold, and Jeffords was certainly a remarkably close friend of Cochise for a white man. He brought Cochise together with General Howard, was named agent to the Chiricahua Reservation, and helped Cochise stay at peace for the rest of his life.

3. Though Manchel's attack on *Broken Arrow* for its distortions of history is well taken, he himself distorts a bit by asserting that Jeffords wounds the Apache boy (96). The most important omissions and distortions are that the film indeed neglects the long war between the Apaches and Mexico, exacerbated by repeated Mexican slave raids (see Forbes, passim); the peace treaty Jeffords helped negotiate was hedged by the U.S. government from the beginning in the refusal to provide promised food and supplies to the Chiricahuas and in the attempt to remove them from their homeland after all—an attempt that was successful after the death of Cochise. The distortion of history in the portrayal of Geronimo (Manchel 100) may perhaps be excused as poetic license anachronistically beginning Geronimo's defiant resistance a decade early. On the other hand, Sweeney time and again associates Geronimo with the great war chief Juh and the resistance of the southern Chiricahuas (Nednhis) throughout the peace process.

4. This idea was also expressed in a part of the screenplay cut from the film (95).

5. See not only Sweeney but Brown, *Bury My Heart at Wounded Knee* 188–200.

6. The figure here exaggerates the actual treaty by at least a factor of ten: fifty thousand square miles would be half the state of Arizona!

7. Major omissions from the screenplay alone that reveal intentionality critical of Anglo ideology include the following: Jeffords expresses "shame" at his country (112); Teese makes fun of the white man's greed for gold (11). Duffield calls the betrayal of Cochise at Apache Pass "a cold-blooded Judas trick" (27). An entire scene of peaceful Apache village life is cut at the end of which Cochise declares, "[W]e will not be slaves on a reservation" (46–48); Cochise develops his negative image of life on the reservation in another cut: "To go on a reservation and give up our weapons and be guarded by soldiers who hate us. To give up our hunting and stand in line and beg food and clothing from the white man's agent. We will not live like that! When the last old woman is dead, we will stop fighting. Not before" (95). Cochise lashes out at the subtle conquest of Indians through whiskey: "The Americans have no more poison? Like they put in whiskey for my wife's cousin to drink?" (97). Jeffords tells Cochise that Howard "believes that all people

are children of God"; Cochise responds, "So? (sarcastically) If the white man's God knows that, His American children have not yet learned it" (98). An Apache chief during the deliberation over whether to accept Howard's peace offer exclaims, "There is only one peace I will accept. We will put all the whites on a reservation and then *we* will guard *them*" (118). Nochalo the shaman's reference to "Earth Woman," upon which the betrothed couple should kneel, is changed to simply "the earth" (129); Sonseeahray's ejaculation, "Life Giver sends us love down to us" is cut entirely (130). Jeffords's theodicean challenge at the death of Sonseeahray, "God in Heaven, no!" is changed to the simple prayerlike lament, "Oh, God in Heaven" (144).

8. Seeking a way to articulate this last insight, I encountered Armando José Prats, "His Master's Voice(over)," which reads a series of revisionist films in the light of critics Roy Harvey Pearce, Robert F. Berkhofer Jr., and (implicitly) R.W.B. Lewis and theorist Edward Said. Prats concludes brilliantly of *Broken Arrow* that Sonseeahray's "sacrifice suggests that no amount of good intentions can bring forth the participation of the Indian Other in the American Garden. Jeffords's hopes may now be fairly dashed in form, but not in substance. In the long shot at the end, he ranges the full extent of the deeded land. The Arizona that Cochise signed away— the America that the Indian 'ceded'—belongs, it seems, with the Indian's blessing, to this one white Adam. Alone (not an Indian or a trooper in sight), he claims the West, and if he no longer harbors a fervent conjugal hope as before, he at least appears within Paradise's boundaries with a clear conscience—Adam still, to the extent that he is outside 'history,' still Eve-less, yet also guiltless—and it is this last that satisfies the essential precondition of the Edenic patrimony" (26), the patrimony we—revisionists and New Agers alike—inherit. "[W]e eagerly exempt ourselves from taking part in the demise of the Indian. Ours, to be sure, is not a connivance against the Indian, but neither is it a New Age transcultural coalition of common humanity. Ours shall be the covenant only with the white hero and his ethical voiceover, and this bond constitutes our hope of participation in an Edenic future" (27). Prats mistakes only that Cochise "deeded" his land.

5. Lateral Freedom

1. The film is fictional but based on a certain amount of history: There was a war with Victorio, Mimbreño chief, who refused any reservation but Warm Springs, his native ground; Victorio raided throughout southwestern New Mexico, crossing at will into Arizona, Mexico, and Texas; although he was finally killed by Mexican soldiers in an ambush at Tres Castillos, he had been fairly ridden down by Buffalo Soldiers from the Ninth and Tenth Cavalries; the Tenth made an epic march to beat Victorio to Rattlesnake Springs in Texas, where he "suffered a decisive defeat." But Col. Benjamin Grierson, historical regimental commander, was never wounded, never relinquished command of his men, and was the genius of the Rattlesnake Springs maneuver; the general in charge of the Victorio wars was not "Pike" but John Pope (Leckie, *Buffalo Soldiers* 210–27). Maj. Eugene Carr of the Sixth Cav-

alry is also historical, and makes another appearance in *Geronimo* as the infamous commander sent to quell the shaman at Cibecue Creek.

Another historical figure is of great interest: John Horse, legendary chief of the Black Seminoles, who fought against Gen. Zachary Taylor and U.S. suzerainty in Florida and subsequently sought a home for his independent nation in Indian Territory, Mexico, and Texas. He and Seminole chief Wild Cat "envisioned a unity among all red and black people in the southwest," but they could never escape their putative identity as slaves, and sought a home in Mexico, where slavery was officially outlawed. The Black Seminoles served in the Mexican army, on one campaign routing outlaw Texas Rangers. Then after the end of the Civil War and the abolition of slavery, the U.S. Army lured the Black Seminoles back into Texas with promises of necessities and land if the men served as scouts to track rustlers and Indian raiders. Armed first with Spencers (like Todd Blair), then with Sharps, they are described thus: "As desert fighters and trackers, they were probably the finest soldiers the U.S. Army ever sent into the field." They brought their independence with them, for "[t]heir monarch [John Horse] had negotiated their hiring as a representative of a sovereign nation." It was a Quaker, Lt. John Bullis, who volunteered to lead black troops, and under him several Seminole scouts won Congressional Medals of Honor. But the U.S. government reneged on the treaty, no copy of which could be found, and they denied this brave people their promised land, despite repeated protests and petitions by John Horse. "By 1882 Bullis and his scouts had virtually pacified a terrifying no man's land" (Katz, *Black Indians* 64–88). But John Horse could not have had any part in the Tenth Cavalry's tracking Victorio, for in 1876 he was severely wounded in an ambush in Fort Clark, Texas, home of the Black Seminole settlement. After recovering from his wounds, he returned to the Black Seminole land-grant settlement in Nacimiento, Mexico. In 1882, John Horse, by then an old, bent man, traveled to Mexico City to secure that land grant in perpetuity. There he died, perhaps of pneumonia, but not, apparently, before he succeeded in his quest (see *Black Seminoles,* part 5, by Porter, whose scholarly work, published posthumously, has superseded Katz's more popular history). Not illogically in a film celebrating black history, *Buffalo Soldiers* gives this great chief a major—though anachronistic and fictionalized—role.

2. I have adapted the concept of *lateral* as opposed to *horizontal,* hierarchical from Cornel West's idea of *identity from below* in contrast to *identity from above,* as modified into an idea of moving across in Robert Burgoyne's analysis of *Glory* in *Film Nation,* chapter 1. For West's exposition of the idea, see "Matter of Life and Death."

3. Actually, Henry O. Flipper won his commission as a cavalry second lieutenant on June 14, 1877, and thus became the first black graduate of West Point. See his recently published memoirs.

6. Geronimo Framed

1. I am responding to both Tunney's review and Prats's fine article. The former sees Hill's film as "an annoying muddle," especially because of Davis's naïve voice-

over. The latter sees the voice-over, especially at the end, as denying the vanishing Geronimo (synecdoche for the American Indian) "authority even to pronounce his own definitive disappearance": "There is a strange consistency here, for the voiceover, to take up the Indian's cause, must be present from the first moment of the Indian's absence. The voiceover locates the Indian at the vanishing point, and there it also *dis*locates him, because the vanishing point betokens permanent Indian exile. As the train continues its inexorable movement, the Davis voiceover declares its own birth, the emergence of an ahistorical perspective destined to tell the Indian's story mostly for the sake of affirming its own freedom from the guilt of conquest" (24).

2. See Debo 270; Davis 194, 114, 213.

3. Historically, it was Naiche, son of Cochise, who years later articulated something of this justification to Crook (see Debo 270).

4. The incident with the "Dreamer" actually took place in 1881 at Cibecue Creek during Geronimo's first sojourn on a reservation. For economy's sake, the film employs poetic license and telescopes Cibecue and Turkey Creeks. The breakout at Turkey Creek, where Geronimo and his band were farming peacefully and successfully, took place in 1885. See Debo 127 ff, 133 ff; see also the recent, full-scale treatment by Collins.

5. See even the sympathetic Thrapp's rationale for choosing Victorio instead of Geronimo as a subject for an extended biography:

> Geronimo had often been written about—too frequently for one of his limited military talent and accomplishments. Publications about him far outranked in number his actual deeds over a lifetime. He in no way illustrated that side of the Apache character I considered sufficient for my purpose.
>
> Victorio, on the other hand, stood out as the very embodiment of Apache resistance to white aggression. (*Victorio* x).

6. Debo 264–66. The screenplay includes such a scene, 73–74, that was obviously cut. Geronimo says simply that he "feared treachery," a fear based on distrust of Crook, who, Geronimo seemed convinced, had issued orders at Turkey Creek to arrest him as a prisoner of war or kill him (*Geronimo's Story of His Life* 139). Geronimo's speech to Crook at Cañon de los Embudos is based loosely on his speech many years later to President Theodore Roosevelt, which he concludes, however, by declaring himself a fool for his statement that they would never yield (Debo 420–21).

7. Historically, Geronimo uttered these words at Cañon de Los Embudos as he apparently surrendered (Debo 262).

8. Debo insists that Gatewood did not have "Davis's liking for the Apaches" (280).

9. The scene was perhaps added just to showcase Robert Duvall as Sieber.

Sieber's presence is unhistorical (see Thrapp, *Sieber* 313). But the scene works thematically, for Sieber dies defending Chato, much to his surprise: "God damn, I never thought I'd get killed trying to help save an Apache." Sieber's death underscores the shift in evaluation of the Apaches—and the value of Chato himself, who unhistorically is given the role here of tracking down Geronimo. Chato historically had gone to Washington to appeal to the president not only for peace but for the return of his captured and enslaved wife and children. He awaited the outcome of this last Apache war at Fort Leavenworth, then joined Geronimo in Florida and Alabama (Debo 273–77, 345–46).

10. Tunney sees the comment as especially lame when juxtaposed to Geronimo's "Once I moved about like the wind."

11. This entire scene is, of course, fictional. There is nothing like it in either Geronimo's or Gatewood's accounts. Found by the two scouts, Martine and Kayitah, Geronimo requests a conference with Gatewood, in which the latter gives him Miles's terms that they are to go to Florida and await there the president's decision on their final disposition. When asked to think like an Apache and tell them what to do, Gatewood counsels trust in Miles. Interestingly, the early scene of the film in which Gatewood and Geronimo separate from Davis and the others to avoid the Tombstone posse derives from Gatewood and Geronimo's travels from Mexico to find Miles. Threatened first by Mexican and then by American troops, all of whom wanted vengeance against Geronimo, Gatewood rides alone with Geronimo and has the following conversation: "Geronimo asked me what I would do if the troops fired upon his people. I replied that I would try to stop it, but, failing that, would run away with him" (Gatewood 16).

12. Ironically, Davis concludes his narrative thus, referring to Miles's deceptions: "IN HOC SIGNO VINCES: Which in this instance might be freely translated BY THESE MEANS WE CONQUERED THEM" (237).

13. Historically inaccurate. Gatewood's son informs us that though he requested a transfer because of ill health, Gatewood was not immediately reassigned after he found Geronimo but was assigned as an aide to Miles. Then he rejoined his troop at Fort Wingate, and was sent to the Dakotas "to take part in the Sioux War of 1890–91" [was he at Wounded Knee?!]. Then he was assigned to duty in Wyoming, where he was injured fighting a post fire, died shortly thereafter at "home" (6).

7. TOMBSTONE

1. The title of the chapter is a play on Girard's famous *Violence et le sacré*. Though I think sacrifice plays a key role in *Tombstone*, Doc Holliday is hardly the Christ-like innocent scapegoat. I have employed Girard's Christian template elsewhere, but here it will not fit.

2. For a good discussion of the Cowboys' running battle with the Mexicans, culminating in massacres in Guadalupe and Skeleton Canyons shortly before the shootout behind the OK Corral, see Barra 148–57.

3. For purposes of economy and drama, the film telescopes the time sepa-

rating these two assassination attempts. The film omits mention of Wyatt's two other brothers, James and Warren, both of whom were involved in the Tombstone war, Warren as an avenging angel himself. The film also eschews detailing the Earps' many attempts to obtain justice through the system, the battle over them in the press and in the courts. See Tefertiller and Barra passim.

4. My attention was drawn to this image by my student Bethany Shepherd, who in an unpublished seminar paper writes, "In the first screen image of Doc, he is seated so that his face is framed by the crotch of a reclining naked woman on the fresco behind his card playing table; between a woman's legs is precisely where this film locates death" (20–21). Shepherd argues that Josephine becomes Doc's surrogate replacement in his homoerotic relationship with Wyatt and that the film replaces the normal effacement of the gunfighter from the domestic (as in *Shane*) with his escape into the wild freedom represented by Doc.

5. That Jarre was thinking along these lines may be inferred by his instruction that the Faust play be performed against the background of Saint-Saëns's *Danse Macabre* (21).

6. Barra has a compelling if brief reading of Doc's desire to die with his boots on in cavalier fashion as his death wish. With regard to the historical death of Johnny Ringo, according to Burrows, Ringo, though dead near Rustler's Canyon of a single gunshot to the head under strange circumstances, could not have been killed by Doc, who appeared in a Denver courthouse within forty-eight hours of Ringo's death on 12 July 1882. See Burrows, chapter 10. In fulfillment of our wishes, the great Earp historian—and trickster—Glenn Boyer provides us with corroborating narratives from both Doc and Josie that detail the secret mission of Wyatt to kill Ringo: Wyatt gets the escaping Ringo in the twilight with a rifle (*Wyatt Earp's Tombstone Vendetta* 269–74, 300–307). For Boyer's tricksterism, see "Mudslingers of the O.K. Corral." Yet in private conversation, Boyer maintains the truth of his narrative, obtained from an old-timer in Colorado. In response to Burrows's point that Doc was in a Denver courtroom too soon after Ringo's death, Boyer maintains plausibly that many a defendant is said to be present in court *in propria persona* when he is really only represented by his lawyer. For Boyer's response to his critics, who accuse him of fictionalizing history, see *Earp Curse*.

7. This story seems to have been romanticized by Jahns, passim. Myers, a more reliable biographer, gives it only the barest hint. Most recently, Tanner, who has exhaustively researched the Holliday family records in Georgia, does not give it the time of day.

8. Boyer now admits publicly that he composed these memoirs, gleaned from accounts and conversations, into a coherent voice himself. Even if they were consistently in Josie's own voice, that would not guarantee their veracity. Boyer's constructed account is only one remove from Marcus's own reconstructions from memory in both writing and discourse.

9. Conventional condemnation persists: my beloved niece and goddaughter

has nicknamed Sadie "Trash." Recent scholarship has cast doubt on whether the infamous photograph is really of Josie/Sadie (see Hutton). I think that fact, if true, would disappoint my niece—but not change her assessment of Sadie's character. I know it would disappoint me. In private conversation, Boyer defends the authenticity of the photo.

10. Liberated though she may be, Sadie does not take to the streets along with the women in the film agitating for "equal pay for equal work." Her agency is thus limited and fails to transcend the world of male bonding in the film.

8. "I'D BECOME MY OWN MOTHER"

1. On the basis of new material discovered by her and her husband, Glenn Boyer, Coleman has written a sequel to *Doc Holliday's Woman*, titled *Doc Holliday's Gone: A Western Duo,* in which she pairs the later life of Kate with that of Mrs. John Slaughter, spirited wife of the legendary sheriff who completed the cleaning up of Arizona's Cochise County after the departure of the Earps and Doc Holliday. See also Boyer, *Who Was Big Nose Kate?*

9. L'ÉTAT C'EST MOI

1. Tatum has a brilliant reading of this film amid an excellent detailing of versions of the legend for a hundred years.

2. Vidal's original teleplay, *The Death of Billy the Kid,* was produced in 1955 for Philco Playhouse and published in 1956 in *Visit to a Small Planet and Other Television Plays.*

3. Fackler, in her concluding "Author's Note" to *Billy the Kid: The Legend of El Chivato,* sees Billy as a different kind of sacrifice: "A scapegoat for the sins of his Anglo contemporaries, Billy was sacrificed because he refused to submit to the political and social order of his time. As such, he was a freedom fighter on the western frontier, and the Lincoln County war was a battle for individual rights against the machine of big business. The war was lost, and is continuing to be lost in America today" (630). Alas, Fackler's historically accurate novel has neither Drunk nor judge nor even Billy himself with the consciousness of such a perspective. Her Billy remains as shallow as that of *Young Guns.*

11. LATERAL CROSSING

1. For details about the deportation of Yaquis into slavery, consult Spicer, chapter 3.

2. For a contemporary expression of this opinion—as well as other reasons the Yaquis should be subjugated and civilized—see the letter of Dr. Manuel Balbás reproduced by Spicer (141–42) and Spicer's following commentary (142).

3. This *paredón* will reappear as a leitmotiv in *Gringo viejo.*

4. This passage provides an excellent example of Fontes's minimalist style. Such understatement restrains the narrator—be it Alejo or Fontes—from screaming at us.

5. Dark shades of Faulkner's Turl running away to be with Tennie in "Was," the opening story of *Go Down, Moses*.

6. Shades of Peaches's betrayal of Juh and Geronimo in the Sierras.

12. THE IMPOSSIBLE CROSSING

1. See Cawelti, *Six-Gun Mystique* 106–7. Cawelti's recent third edition, titled *The Six-Gun Mystique Sequel,* gives even shorter shrift to this theme in *The Wild Bunch* (104), but it is part of a fresh and important chapter on "The Post-Western."

2. Mitchell discusses the effect of both Peckinpah and Sergio Leone in the aptly titled chapter 8, "Violence Begets."

3. For a more thorough interpretation of the film in the light of Vietnam and of a failed, inadequate American theory for the use of force, see Slotkin 380–400.

14. MONSTERS FROM BELOW

1. The parenthetical citation 1.1 refers to part 1, chapter 1. My quotations are from the definitive edition in *Obras completas* 1:320–418, but I have cited them by part and chapter so that those using more readily available editions can find them more easily. Fornoff's translation is generally superb. Occasionally, I take the liberty of inserting a more literal translation in brackets when I want to call attention to some nuance, for example, etymological, that the translation does not convey— or when I simply want to call attention to the more literal meaning. Here the text reads literally "truly brave men," but Fornoff's choice to make the phrase more idiomatic in English is a good one, and I will not quibble with him over these liberties.

2. Ruffinelli points out that the interpretation of the novel as nihilist has been around since a newspaper article in 1925 (160).

15. THE FEMINIZING OF FREEDOM AND FULFILLMENT

1. Because some nuances seem to me to be lost in the Christensen translation, I have provided my own, which is often more clumsily literal in order to highlight those nuances, but I also provide page references to the English edition for the English reader's convenience. Writing conventionally in the critical, historical present, I occasionally take the liberty of paraphrasing translations from past (imperfect or preterit) tense into present.

2. I have tried to capture the connection between pushing (*empujar*) and the press etymologically latent in *impresionante*.

3. The novel is full of phallic images, especially the chile, which Tenenbaum assures us in Mexico is "slang for the male organ" (165).

4. The film offers a nice touch to the chiles at the end: Earlier, Tita would not eat the last chile because it would not be decent; at the end, in the novel, all the chiles are consumed, symbolizing the collective fertility. But in the film, there is again one last chile on the plate, and its image is juxtaposed to John Brown as he drives away alone, the only one at the wedding not to make love at the end. For he alone—among the living—is without fulfillment.

16. Mirrors, Dreams, and Memory

1. There are problems with the Peden-Fuentes translation. The relationship between the Spanish and the English versions of the novel is vexed (e.g., the English omits significant passages and rearranges chapters [18 and 19]). See Gunn and Roy. I quote from both versions, when possible, reserving as usual the right to interpolate my own translations, sometimes haltingly literal, to call attention to nuances. But as Gunn opines, "[Both] versions have authorial validity of an exceptional kind" (61).

2. This card to his niece Lora Bierce in October 1913 epitomizes the tropes of Bierce's macabre farewell: "Good-bye—if you hear of my being stood up against a Mexican stone wall and shot to rags please know that I think that a pretty good way to depart this life. It beats old age, disease, or falling down the cellar stairs. To be a Gringo in Mexico—ah, that is euthanasia!" (Bierce, *Sole Survivor* 296). For the most recent account of the problematics of reconstructing Bierce's disappearance, see Morris, *Ambrose Bierce,* chapter 12. As did reviewer Enrique Kranse in *The New Republic* in 1988 (see Gunn), Morris notes that one of the elements Fuentes has folded into his fiction is the bizarre story (from Villa's "memoirs," composed by Martín Luis Guzmán) of the assassination of the Anglo rancher in Chihuahua, William S. Benton, for insulting and trying to kill Villa over his lost ranch; Villa apparently ordered his men to exhume the hastily buried body, place it in front of an adobe wall, and riddle it with bullets as if Benson had been executed by firing squad for his attack on Villa. Carranza's blustering about international repercussions if the investigation of Benson continued seems to have stifled this bizarre conclusion to the affair—until Fuentes seized upon it for his novel (Morris 256–58, 266–67). Morris also opines, in piercing Biercian fashion, that the film version of Fuentes's novel, *Old Gringo,* starring Gregory Peck, Jimmy Smits, and Jane Fonda, "stiffed at the box office" (267). Unfortunately, the film, unlike *Como agua para chocolate,* captures virtually nothing of the novel's sophisticated profundity, ignoring its leitmotivs of mirrors, dreams, and memory.

3. Bierce's father died in 1876, his mother two years later. Concerning his being orphaned, Morris conjectures Bierce's response by quoting from Bierce's infamously diabolically satirical *Devil's Dictionary,* written later, s.v. orphan: "a living person whom death has deprived of the power of filial ingratitude" (159)—a definition that would appeal to McCarthy. Gunn discusses the relationship of this episode to Bierce's story, "The Horseman in the Sky" (66).

4. Going considerably beyond the Spanish, the English reads, "Do what you conceive to be your duty, sir" (56).

5. By choosing to translate "errante" as "ranging" Peden (and Fuentes himself) suppress the connotation of "errant" in the sense of *straying outside proper bounds.*

6. By employing the second-person singular in La Luna's speech, I attempt to convey the original's meaning that her refusal to use the more polite, more formal "Usted" is tantamount to her refusal to grant Villa rank and dignity: she knew him when.

7. The English version interpolates here the passage "not like you, like another woman I never had"—meaning his mother and making the repressed perhaps too obvious.

8. I have taken the liberty of adding quotation marks, omitted in the English version except for the last sentence, for all of what Harriet says; I have also moved that last sentence into the main body of the paragraph instead of making it a separate paragraph, as in the English.

9. For one of the best and most thorough treatments of *Gringo viejo,* see my colleague Lanin Gyurko's "Self and Double."

EPILOGUE

1. Houston uses this phrase several times. *Bisbee 17* has just been republished by the University of Arizona Press (1999).

2. For the classic history of the Bisbee Deportation and its background and aftermath, see Byrkit; for a recent analysis of the labor movement in the early Southwest, with an emphasis on race, see Mellinger.

3. None of the big three organizers—Flynn, Big Bill Haywood, Mother Jones—was actually present at the Bisbee strike. For the sake of his story, Houston has taken poetic license.

4. Houston writes his chapters in either the familiar third-person narrative or, in a daring innovation applied to the famous historical characters, in the second-person singular. Thus he does not put us directly in the heads of his characters by having them speak first-person soliloquies. But it is as if the camera is either focused over their shoulders or directly upon them.

5. Houston graciously discussed his novel with me on several occasions during 1998. Our discussion about the theory of tragedy behind Bo's relinquishment occurred on 25 and 26 August.

BIBLIOGRAPHY

Allmendinger, Blake. *Ten Most Wanted: The New Western Literature.* New York: Routledge, 1998.

Ambush. Starring Robert Taylor and Arlene Dahl. Screenplay by Marguerite Roberts. Based on a story by Luke Short. Directed by Sam Wood. MGM, 1949.

Anzaldúa, Gloria. *Borderlands/La Frontera: The New Mestiza.* San Francisco: Aunt Lute Books, 1987.

Arnold, Elliott. *Blood Brother.* New York: Duell, Sloan and Pearce, 1947.

Azuela, Mariano. *Los de abajo: Novela de la Revolución Mexicana.* In *Obras, completas.* Vol. 1. Mexico City: Fondo de Cultura Económico, 1958. 320–418.

———. *The Underdogs.* Translated by Frederick H. Fornoff. Critical Edition. Pittsburgh: University of Pittsburgh Press, 1992.

Bakhtin, Mikhail M. *Rabelais and His World.* Translated by Hélène Iswolsky. 1968. Bloomington: Indiana University Press, 1984.

The Ballad of Gregorio Cortez. Starring Edward James Olmos. Screenplay by Victor Villaseñor. Adapted by Robert M. Young. Directed by Robert M. Young. Embassy Pictures, 1982.

Barker, Stephen. *Autoaesthetics: Strategies of the Self after Nietzsche.* Atlantic Highlands, N.J.: Humanities Press, 1992.

Barra, Allen. *Inventing Wyatt Earp: His Life and Many Legends.* New York: Carroll and Graf, 1998.

Bell, Vereen M. *The Achievement of Cormac McCarthy.* Baton Rouge: Louisiana State University Press, 1988.

Bierce, Ambrose. *A Sole Survivor: Bits of Autobiography.* Edited by S.T. Joshi and David E. Schultz. Knoxville: University of Tennessee Press, 1998.

Blake, James Carlos. *The Friends of Pancho Villa: A Novel.* New York: Berkeley Books, 1996.

Blankfort, Michael [and Albert Maltz?]. "Arrow." Revised screenplay for *Broken Arrow.* 1949.

Boyer, Glenn G. *The Earp Curse.* Rodeo, N.M.: Historical Research Associates, 1999.

———. *Who Was Big Nose Kate? Wyatt Earp: Family, Friends & Foes,* 1. Rodeo, N.M.: Historical Research Associates, 1997.

———, ed. *Wyatt Earp's Tombstone Vendetta.* Honolulu: Talei Publishers, 1993.

Broken Arrow. Starring James Stewart, Jeff Chandler, and Debra Paget. Written by Albert Maltz [and Michael Blankfort?]. Directed by Delmer Daves. Twentieth Century Fox, 1950.

Brown, Dee. *Bury My Heart at Wounded Knee: An Indian History of the American West.* 1971. New York: Bantam, 1972.

Buffalo Soldiers. Starring Danny Glover and Carl Lumbly. Teleplay by Frank Military and Susan Rhinehart. Story by Jonathan Klein and Frank Military. Directed by Charles Haid. Trilogy Group/Citadel Entertainment, 1997.

Burgoyne, Robert. *Film Nation: Hollywood Looks at U.S. History.* Minneapolis: University of Minnesota Press, 1997.

Burrows, Jack. *John Ringo: The Gunfighter Who Never Was.* Tucson: University of Arizona Press, 1987.

Byrkit, James W. *Forging the Copper Collar: Arizona's Labor-Management War of 1901–1921.* Tucson: University of Arizona Press, 1982.

Canfield, J. Douglas. "Faulkner's Grecian Urn and Ike McCaslin's Empty Legacies." *Arizona Quarterly* 36 (1980): 359–84.

———. "Kit Carson, John C. Frémont, Manifest Destiny, and the Indians; or, Oliver North Abets Lawrence of Arabia." *American Indian Culture and Research Journal* 22 (1998): 137–53.

———. "Tragic Glory: L. D. Clark's Existential Vision." *Journal of the Southwest* 40 (1998): 107–26.

Castronovo, Russ. "Compromised Narratives along the Border: The Mason-Dixon Line, Resistance, and Hegemony." In Michaelson and Johnson, *Border Theory* 195–220.

Cawelti, John. *The Six-Gun Mystique.* 2nd ed. Bowling Green, Ohio: Bowling Green State University Popular Press, 1984.

———. *The Six-Gun Mystique Sequel.* Bowling Green, Ohio: Bowling Green State University Popular Press, 1999.

Clark, L.D. *A Bright Tragic Thing: A Tale of Civil War Texas.* El Paso, Tex.: Cinco Puntos, 1992.

———, ed. *Civil War Recollections of James Lemuel Clark: Including Previously Unpublished Material on the Great Hanging at Gainesville, Texas in October, 1862.* College Station: Texas A&M University Press, 1984.

Coleman, Jane Candia. *Doc Holliday's Gone: A Western Duo.* Unity, Maine: Five Star, 1999.

———. *Doc Holliday's Woman.* New York: Warner Books, 1995.

———. *I, Pearl Hart: A Western Story.* Unity, Maine: Five Star, 1998.

Collins, Charles. *Apache Nightmare: The Battle at Cibecue Creek.* Norman: University of Oklahoma Press, 1999.

Como agua para chocolate. Starring Marco Leonardi, Lumi Cavazos, and Regina Torne. Screenplay by Laura Esquivel. Directed by Alfonso Arau. Arau Films International, 1991.

Daugherty, Leo. "Gravers False and True: *Blood Meridian* as Gnostic Tragedy." *Southern Quarterly* 30, no. 4 (Summer 1992): 122–33. Special Issue on Cormac McCarthy.

Davis, Britton. *The Truth about Geronimo.* New Haven: Yale University Press, 1929.

Debo, Angie. *Geronimo: The Man, His Time, His Place.* Norman: University of Oklahoma Press, 1976.

Early, James. *The Making of Go Down, Moses.* Dallas: Southern Methodist University Press, 1972.

Earp, Josephine Sarah Marcus. *I Married Wyatt Earp: The Recollections of Josephine Sarah Marcus Earp.* Edited by Glenn G. Boyer. Tucson: University of Arizona Press, 1976.

Esquivel, Laura. *Como agua para chocolate: Novela de entregas mensuales con recetas, amores y remedios caseros.* 1989. New York: Anchor-Doubleday, 1994.

———. *Like Water for Chocolate: A Novel in Monthly Installments with Recipes, Romances and Home Remedies.* Translated by Caro Christensen and Thomas Christensen. New York: Anchor-Doubleday, 1992.

Fackler, Elizabeth. *Billy the Kid: The Legend of El Chivato.* New York: Forge–Tom Doherty Associates, 1995.

Faulkner, William. *Big Woods.* New York: Random House, 1955.

———. *Collected Stories.* 1950. New York: Vintage-Random, 1977.

———. *Essays, Speeches & Public Letters by William Faulkner.* Edited by James B. Meriwether. New York: Random House, 1965.

———. *Go Down, Moses.* 1942. New York: Vintage International–Random House, 1990.

———. *The Portable Faulkner.* Edited by Malcolm Cowley. New York: Viking, 1946.

Flipper, Henry O. *Black Frontiersman: The Memoirs of Henry O. Flipper, First Black Graduate of West Point.* Edited by Theodore D. Harris. Fort Worth: Texas Christian University Press, 1997.

Fontes, Montserrat. *Dreams of the Centaur: A Novel.* New York: Norton, 1996.

Forbes, Jack D. *Apache, Navaho, and Spaniard.* Norman: University of Oklahoma Press, 1960.

Fuentes, Carlos. *Gringo viejo.* Mexico City: Fondo de Cultura Económica, 1985.

———. *The Old Gringo.* Translated by Margaret Sayers Peden and Carlos Fuentes. 1985. New York: Noonday-Farrar, Straus, Giroux, 1997.

Gatewood, Charles B., Jr. "Lieutenant Charles B. Gatewood 6th U.S. Cavalry and The Surrender of Geronimo." In *Proceedings of the Annual Meeting and Dinner of the Order of Indian Wars of the United States. Held January Twenty-sixth, Nineteen Hundred and Twenty-nine.* N.p. Copy in Special Collections, University of Arizona Library; a handwritten note signed with the initials CBG informs, "A number of facts have been left out simply because they would be distasteful to other actors in this affair" (7). The original ms. is in the Arizona Historical Society, Gatewood Collection, Tucson.

Geronimo. *Geronimo's Story of His Life.* Taken down and edited by S.M. Barrett. New York: Duffield, 1906.

Geronimo. Starring Joseph Running Fox. Written by J.T. Young. Directed by Roger Young. Turner Pictures/Yorktown, 1993.

Geronimo: An American Legend. Starring Wes Studi, Jason Patric, Gene Hackman, Robert Duvall, Matt Damon. Screenplay by John Milius and Larry Gross. Directed by Walter Hill. Columbia Pictures, 1993.

Glissant, Edouard. *Faulkner, Mississippi.* 1996. Translated by Barbara Lewis and Thomas C. Spear. New York: Farrar, Straus and Giroux, 1999.

Gore Vidal's Billy the Kid. Starring Val Kilmer, Duncan Regehr, Wilford Brimley. Written by Gore Vidal. Directed by William A. Graham. Von Zerneck–Sertner Films, 1989.

Green, Walon, and Sam Peckinpah. "The Wild Bunch." Screenplay. October 26, 1967.

Gross, Larry [and John Milius]. "Geronimo: Revised Screenplay." January 25, 1993.

Gunn, Drewey Wayne. "A Labyrinth of Mirrors: Literary Sources of *The Old Gringo/ Gringo viejo.*" *Revista de Estudios Hispanicos* 26, no. 1 (Jan. 1992): 61–79.

Gyurko, Lanin A. "Self and Double in Fuentes' *Gringo viejo.*" *Ibero-Amerikanisches Archiv* 17, nos. 2 and 3 (1991): 175–244.

Houston, Robert. *Bisbee 17: A Novel.* New York: Pantheon Books, 1979.

Hutton, Paul. "Showdown at the Hollywood Corral: Wyatt Earp and the Movies: Fashioning an American Legend." *Montana: The Magazine of Western History* 45, no. 3 (Summer 1995): 2–31.

Jahns, Pat. *The Frontier World of Doc Holliday, Faro Dealer from Dallas to Deadwood.* New York: Hastings House, 1957.

Jarre, Kevin. "Tombstone: An Original Screenplay." 6th draft. 2 July 1993.

Katz, William Loren. *Black Indians: A Hidden Heritage.* New York: Atheneum, 1986.

Kristeva, Julia. *Powers of Horror: An Essay on Abjection.* Translated by Leon S. Roudiez. New York: Columbia University Press, 1982.

Leckie, William H. *The Buffalo Soldiers: A Narrative of the Negro Cavalry in the West.* Norman: University of Oklahoma Press, 1967.

The Left-Handed Gun. Starring Paul Newman. Screenplay by Leslie Stevens. Directed by Arthur Penn. Warner Brothers, 1958.

Lugo, Alejandro. "Reflections on Border Theory, Culture, and the Nation." In Michaelson and Johnson, *Border Theory* 43–67.

Manchel, Frank. "Cultural Confusion: *Broken Arrow.*" In *Hollywood's Indian: The Portrayal of the Native American in Film,* edited by Peter C. Rollins and John E. O'Connor. Lexington: University Press of Kentucky, 1998. 91–106.

The Mask of Zorro. Starring Anthony Hopkins and Antonio Banderas. Story by Ted Elliott, Terry Rosso, and Randall Jahnson. Directed by Martin Campbell. TriStar Pictures, 1998.

Matthews, John T. *The Play of Faulkner's Language.* Ithaca: Cornell University Press, 1982.

McCarthy, Cormac. *Blood Meridian; or, The Evening Redness in the West.* 1985. New York: Vintage International–Random House, 1992.

Mellinger, Philip J. *Race and Labor in Western Copper: The Fight for Equality, 1896–1918.* Tucson: University of Arizona Press, 1995.

Michaelson, Scott, and David E. Johnson, eds. *Border Theory: The Limits of Cultural Politics.* Minneapolis: University of Minnesota Press, 1997.

Mitchell, Lee Clark. *Westerns: Making the Man in Fiction and Film.* Chicago: University of Chicago Press, 1996.

Morrell, David. *Last Reveille.* 1977. Reprint, with an introduction by the author, New York: Warner Books, 1994.

Morris, Roy, Jr. *Ambrose Bierce: Alone in Bad Company.* 1996. New York: Oxford University Press, 1998.

"Mudslingers of the O.K. Corral." *Arizona Daily Star,* July 24, 1998, pp. 1A, 6A.

Myers, John Myers. *Doc Holliday.* Lincoln: University of Nebraska Press, 1955.

Old Gringo. Starring Gregory Peck, Jimmy Smits, and Jane Fonda. Screenplay by Aida Bortnik and Luis Puenzo. Directed by Luis Puenzo. Fonda Films Production. Columbia Pictures, 1989.

Parrish, Tim. "The Killer Wears the Halo: Cormac McCarthy, Flannery O'Connor, and the American Religion." In *Sacred Violence* 25–40.

Pat Garrett and Billy the Kid. Starring James Coburn and Kris Kristofferson. Written by Rudolph Wurlitzer. Directed by Sam Peckinpah. Director's cut. MGM, 1973, 1991.

Peters, John G. "Repudiation, Wilderness, Birthright: Reconciling Conflicting Views of Faulkner's Ike McCaslin." *ELN* 33, no. 3 (March 1996): 39–46.

Porter, Kenneth W. *The Black Seminoles: History of a Freedom-Seeking People.* Revised and edited by Alcione M. Amos and Thomas P. Senter. Gainesville: University Press of Florida, 1996.

Prats, Armando José. "His Master's Voice(over): Revisionist Ethos and Narrative Dependence from *Broken Arrow* (1950) to *Geronimo: An American Legend* (1993)." *ANQ: A Quarterly Journal of Articles, Notes, and Reviews* 9, no. 3 (Summer 1996): 15–29.

Pughe, Thomas. "Revision and Vision: Cormac McCarthy's *Blood Meridian.*" *Revue Française d'Études Américaines* 62 (1994): 371–82.

Roy, Joaquín. "Historia, biografia, cine y ficcion en *Gringo viejo.*" *Revista de Critica Literaria Latinoamericana* 17 (1991): 147–63.

Ruffinelli, Jorge. "From Unknown Work to Literary Classic." In Azuela, *Underdogs* 157–65.

Sacred Violence: A Reader's Companion to Corman McCarthy. El Paso: Texas Western Press, 1995.

Saldívar, José David. *Border Matters: Remapping American Cultural Studies.* Berkeley: University of California Press, 1997.

Saldívar, Ramón. *Chicano Narrative: The Dialectics of Difference.* Madison: University of Wisconsin Press, 1990.

Sepich, John Emil. "A 'bloody dark pastryman': Cormac McCarthy's Recipe for Gunpowder and Historical Fiction in *Blood Meridian.*" *Mississippi Quarterly* 46 (1993): 547–63.

Sewell, Richard B. *The Vision of Tragedy.* New Haven: Yale University Press, 1959.

Shaviro, Steven. "'The Very Life of the Darkness': A Reading of *Blood Meridian.*" *Southern Quarterly* 30, no. 4 (Summer 1992): 111–21. Special Issue on Cormac McCarthy.

Shepherd, Bethany. "Bordering on Death: Gunfighting Lives in George Stevens' *Shane* and George Cosmatos' *Tombstone.*" Term paper for J. Douglas Canfield's course in Literature of the Southwest, University of Arizona, fall 1997.

Slotkin, Richard. *Gunfighter Nation: The Myth of the Frontier in Twentieth-Century America.* New York: Atheneum, 1992.

Sonnichsen, C.L. "From Savage to Saint: A New Image for Geronimo." In *Geronimo and the End of the Apache Wars: Commemorating the Centennial of the Surrender of Naiche and Geronimo, September 4, 1886.* Specially bound ed. of the *Journal of Arizona History* 27, no. 1 (Spring 1986). Tucson: Arizona Historical Society, 1987. 5–34.

Spicer, Edward H. *The Yaquis: A Cultural History.* Tucson: University of Arizona Press, 1980.

Sweeney, Edwin R. *Cochise: Chiricahua Apache Chief.* Norman: University of Oklahoma Press, 1991.

Tanner, Karen Holliday. *Doc Holliday: A Family Portrait.* Norman: University of Oklahoma Press, 1998.

Tatum, Stephen. *Inventing Billy the Kid: Visions of the Outlaw in America, 1881–1981.* 1982. Tucson: University of Arizona Press, 1997.

Tefertiller, Casey. *Wyatt Earp: The Life behind the Legend.* New York: John Wiley & Sons, 1997.

Tenenbaum, Barbara A. "Why Tita Didn't Marry the Doctor, or Mexican History in *Like Water for Chocolate.*" In Donald Fithian Stevens, ed., *Based on a True Story: Latin American History at the Movies,* Wilmington, Del.: SR Books, 1997. 157–72.

Thrapp, Dan L. *Al Sieber, Chief of Scouts.* 1964. 11th printing. Foreword by Donald E. Worcester. Norman: University of Oklahoma Press, 1995.

———. *Victorio and the Mimbres Apaches.* 1974. 3rd printing. Norman: University of Oklahoma Press, 1991.

Tombstone. Starring Val Kilmer and Kurt Russell. Screenplay by Kevin Jarre. Directed by George P. Cosmatos. Cinergi Productions, 1993.

Tompkins, Jane. *West of Everything: The Inner Life of Westerns.* New York: Oxford University Press, 1992.

Tunney, Tom. Review of *Geronimo: An American Legend. Sight and Sound* 11 (1994): 47.

Utley, Francis Lee, Lynn Z. Bloom, and Arthur F. Kinney, eds. *Bear, Man, and God: Seven Approaches to William Faulkner's The Bear.* 1st ed. New York: Random House, 1964.

Utley, Robert. *Billy the Kid: A Short and Violent Life.* Lincoln: University of Nebraska Press, 1989.

Vidal, Gore. *The Death of Billy the Kid.* In *Visit to a Small Planet and Other Television Plays.* Boston: Little, Brown, 1956. 173–216

Wallach, Rick. "Judge Holden, *Blood Meridian*'s Evil Archon." In *Sacred Violence* 125–36.

Waters, Frank. *The Earp Brothers of Tombstone.* Lincoln: University of Nebraska Press, 1960.

West, Cornel. "A Matter of Life and Death." *October* 61 (Summer 1992): 20–23.

The Wild Bunch. Starring William Holden, Ernest Borgnine, and Robert Ryan. Written by Walon Green and Sam Peckinpah. Directed by Sam Peckinpah. Director's cut. Warner Brothers, 1969, 1995.

INDEX

Note: References to extended treatments are in boldfaced type. Only characters (historical or fictional) referred to outside the chapters where the works in which they appear are discussed have been indexed. Such fictional characters are identified by the titles of those works.